PRAISE FOR *HOW TO TELL WHEN WE WILL DIE*

"This is a book for the moment and for the ages. It's questing, pissed, propulsive, funny, generous, pervy, and original—full of love and pain in all their entwined glory. Hedva lays waste to *solidarity* and *care* as buzzwords and returns them to us enlivened with all the blood and paradox they deserve. I will be thinking in the wake of this important collection for a long time, no doubt alongside so many grateful others."

—MAGGIE NELSON,
author of *The Argonauts*

"Hedva, a committed reader of queer and female artists, creates, in reaction to their influences, a new construction of themselves: a nonbinary and Asian disabled intellectual, as a lens through which to see the world. By centering their experiences into a cohered perspective, they make a contribution on the fronts of fragility and rage, justice and systems, desire and limitation that expands preexisting frameworks for conceptualizing human experience."

—SARAH SCHULMAN,
author of *Let the Record Show:
A Political History of ACT UP
New York, 1987–1993*

"Monstrous good. How did [Hedva] write the most metal kink crip book about death, survival, crip viscera, and reality ever that we need right now? This book is for grown-up runaways who stay feral and awake in theafterfuture we inhabit, people who desire and are rare delights, anyone with a body or a mind of any kind, the crips who GET IT and NEED IT, and everyone else who does too. It's exactly what we need right now and goes so beyond the 101 that it blew my brain out of my ears. As we live into the disabled future and claim our crip crone crowns, this book is delicious required reading."

—LEAH LAKSHMI PIEPZNA-SAMARASINHA,
author of *The Future Is Disabled*

"A tremendous work of thought and feeling, packed with profound insight and illuminated throughout with a radical vulnerability that transmutes before your eyes into phenomenal power."

—MICHELLE TEA,
PEN-award winning author of
*Against Memoir: Complaints,
Confessions & Criticisms*

"This transcendent collection operates like a kaleidoscope of memoir, manifesto, cultural criticism, even found object, and how Hedva tackles and untangles every aspect of their identity made me feel like just maybe the people I am rooting for most will win in the end!"

—POROCHISTA KHAKPOUR,
author of *Sick: A Memoir*

"A book that will rearrange you . . . Granular and kaleidoscopic in its relentless search for embodied truth, this book twists and turns in pain and ecstasy, shifting form to make room for revelation."

—MATTILDA BERNSTEIN SYCAMORE,
author of *Touching the Art*

How to Tell When We Will Die

On Pain, Disability, and Doom

JOHANNA HEDVA

HILLMAN GRAD BOOKS
A zando IMPRINT
◆ NEW YORK ◆

Hillman Grad Books is an imprint of Zando.
zandoprojects.com

First Edition: September 2024

Design by Neuwirth & Associates
Cover design by Sarah Schneider

The publisher does not have control over and is not responsible for author or other third-party websites (or their content).

Library of Congress Control Number: 2024937284

978-1-63893-116-4 (Hardcover)
978-1-63893-117-1 (ebook)

10 9 8 7 6 5 4 3 2 1
Manufactured in the United States of America

For Johannes,
without whom I wouldn't.

Contents

Being born ruined my health.

CLARICE LISPECTOR

◆

Yes, yes, of course, this is gonna hurt.

NINE INCH NAILS

How to Tell
When We Will Die

In order to live, we tell ourselves stories that do not include illness. Our heroes die on the battlefield, not from chronic pain. Diarrhea never makes its way into myth. Tragedies are devoid of menstrual cramps. Irritable bowel syndrome is, oddly, absent from the suspense genre. Suffering is purposeful, glorious, noble, deserved, punitive—Ajax falls on his sword, Juliet drinks the poison, Jane Eyre is undone by fire, Prometheus pays for his transgression with his liver. It is not caused by the terrestrial inconveniences of co-pays, misdiagnoses, long lines at the pharmacy, the vanishing of time in waiting rooms, or symptoms that demand supineness while the hours crawl on.

In the stories we tell ourselves, the stuff of life is the stuff of decision, action, determination, and grit, not the times when we had to cancel plans because pain furred around us in a cloud, when we clutched the side of the bed from nausea, when we hinged ourselves in half because our bodies were oozing gunk. We tell ourselves that our personalities are defined by our brilliance, curiosity, orneriness, and passion, not our panic, brain fog, or fatigue. We speak of strengths and weaknesses—it's how we categorize everything—and we never get creative with these. We count among our strengths our strength, and among our weaknesses, our weakness, and the only radicality we can yield to this binary is to invert it, to count what is usually considered weak as maybe some other kind of strength.

If we give up because of an illness, injury, or disability, we keep it secret, ashamed. If we cannot do something because our bodies won't let us, like walk to the mailbox or pick up a grocery bag—if we simply are not able to—we hang our heads humiliated. When we need help, we tell ourselves it's because we have shamefully lost our independence, and we pray this is temporary. If we feel that we need too much for too long, we vow to pay it back, motivation heated with guilt, for we must not be permanently marked by our insolvency. This is just a blip, a rough spot, bad luck. *Don't worry*, we tell ourselves. *We'll get back to normal soon.*

When it dawns on some of us that we will always need, that we have no choice but to be permanently marked by our insolvency, the first response is to hate ourselves. And why wouldn't we? After all, this version of ourselves, as it exists in the stories we tell, is needy, weak, too much to deal with, and unable to do anything worthwhile. It's usually a villain, driven to evil *because* of our disability or illness. We are the Joker slipping through the cracks of society to be lost to diabolical lunacy. We are the Phantom of the Opera, born disfigured, a symbol of the subhuman. As nothing else does, we animate the horror genre as the deformed, the monstrous, the worst thing that could possibly be imagined. The first horror movie ever, 1917's *The Black Stork*, tells the eugenics-motivated story of a disabled baby being murdered in order to keep society safe from the nightmare the baby augurs. If not outright evil, we are the abject character with little dimensionality or depth, a nagging burden or an unflinching stoic suffering in silence. We are Joan Crawford, pathetic in a wheelchair in *What Ever Happened to Baby Jane?* We are Hilary Swank demanding to be euthanized in *Million Dollar Baby* after becoming paralyzed. At best, we get to be bafflingly mystical, like *Rain Man*'s Raymond Babbitt, or a vehicle to tell a redemption arc, like Lieutenant Dan in *Forrest Gump*. When we are granted any accomplishments, they have been flattened by the insidious super-cripple myth ("They never let their illness get the better of them! Look at how much they achieved despite it all!"), and often these are biopics—*The Theory of Everything, Stronger, Breathe*—our few chances at representation allowed only when we can be depicted as simple vectors of success.

In the stories we tell ourselves, a sick or disabled person's condition does not expand and traverse its voltaic, crackling, multivalent world, but collapses under its own limit. What I want to know is: What happens when the stories we tell ourselves in order to live are forced to include illness and disability and all the many words that are attendant to them—sick, sickly, poorly, crippled, lame, incapacitated, diseased, broken, blighted, ailing, afflicted, infected, infirm, indisposed, incapable, limited, restricted, confined, invalid, bedridden, bedbound, wheelchair-bound, immobilized, weak, impaired, damaged, paralyzed, mutilated, debilitated, harmed, maimed, ailing, declining, down, downcast, cast down, weighed down, washed out, frail, feeble, unfit, out of action, impaired, in pain, incurable, anguished, agonized, aching, rotten, run down, dejected, despondent, destitute, disadvantaged, daunted, deteriorating, reduced, lowered, leveled, queasy, seedy, doomy, crummy, morose, blue, valetudinarian, unbalanced, disturbed, deranged, demented, contaminated, under the weather, out of whack, out of sorts, off-color, green about the gills, sick as a dog, in a bad way, like death warmed up, laid up, laid low, unwell, wrecked? How do we write stories that use these words in ways that unfurl, rather than foreclose, their nuance? How exactly does deterioration feel different than dejection? Where is the line between unfit and incapacitated, and who lives there? What about the surreptitious mercies, little lights of insight and vision, dark wisdoms and darker jokes, that are also in attendance? What happens to our stories when a subject long confined to the narrowest of tropes breaks in and takes over, screaming its bloody head off as it also whispers, groaning as it pontificates, speaking cogently at the same time that it riddles?

Sometimes, for the purposes of economy, I myself will use only the words "illness" or "disability" instead of listing all the many other words above. The reason I chose the word "disability" rather than "illness" for the subtitle of this book is to put this condition, often feared as the worst conceivable outcome, up front and in the foreground, to not let it lurk on the periphery as a distant possibility that happens only to the unlucky. Do note that whenever I write only "illness" or "disability," I could brandish that list of words, expand it, add dozens more words, follow their forking paths, tunnel into a particular word's specificities, and let this take up pages and pages. The question becomes, then: Why, in the face of such a kaleidoscopic list of words, which promise so many possible meanings and stories from them, have we insisted, in everything from our myths to our laws to our TV shows, that illness and disability are not universal facts of life that teem with some of the most vivid, varied, and important experiences we will ever have, but are shameful measures of our own individual failure, to be hidden away and denied?

It's not a rhetorical question. I want to know whom and what it serves to tell ourselves that illness or disability mean but one or two things. To be alive on this earth is to live in the abundance of the body's peculiarities, and to have a body is to be determined by that body's ceaseless needs, and bodies, even at their best, even if they aspire to nothing else, are so delicate and dependent that they can't get by alone. I want to reckon with the twinned facts that our bodies are fragile and in need of constant care and support, but that we have built our world as if the opposite were true. Why have we told ourselves stories that begrudge and outright renounce our inevitable incapacities, declines, and succumbences when such stories are lies? Who benefits—who *profits*—from these lies? What exactly is supported, even strengthened, under the regime of the singular story that tells illness as the temporary aberration to a fantastical norm of wellness; that asserts we are sovereign individuals dependent on no one, and we should pity and fear those whose needs topple that sovereignty; the story that tells us care is only required sometimes, and that those who are defined by it, either because they need it or practice it, are less valuable, less human? What does it do when we force disability into the background of our stories, as something either bad or bad but useful if it can be overcome, when it *could* be treated like love, war, coming of age, family, identity, et al.—a major subject that is strange, rich, powerful, and necessary to telling the story of life?

What about stories that are enlivened, vivified, not *despite* illness and disability but *because* of them?

The definition of "the body" that I like the most is that it's *anything that needs support*. It's a human body that needs food, rest, sleep, shelter, care, other humans. It's a social body that needs to be propelled and maintained by a collective's aims, the tension of many convergences and disagreements coalescing into a whole. It's a body of water that needs a solid ground on which to rest and surge.

I like to truncate this definition, to make the body, especially the human kind, simply a thing *that needs*.

Because what else would support be—but needed?

I started writing about the ways in which bodies are shot through with need because my own became disabled through an injury and the onset of multiple chronic illnesses over a decade that spanned my twenties and thirties, which I now live in the wake of (or is it a beginning?). I was finishing my bachelor's degree at UCLA, then went on to the MFA program at CalArts—not a great time to become disabled, but is there any? I am a queer and gender non-binary second-generation Korean American writer, artist, and musician who comes from a long line of mechanics, nurses, maids, and fortune tellers, which means that I have no money, and neither does my family. Which means the meager health insurance for poor people that I was eligible for in California was insignificant in the face of all the ways my body needed care. I had good insurance through school, so I stayed to get a second master's so my health care wouldn't be interrupted—a decision that means I now have, with interest that nearly doubled the amount I took out, over $250,000 in student debt. I will never be able to pay this amount back in my lifetime.

Becoming disabled, for me, was an education in many things, but sometimes I think it was elementally about relearning how to understand dependency, and how disability makes it impossible to ignore that we are ontologically dependent, knotted into each other and everything. It was an education in how time and debt are entangled, with how disability troubles capitalism's unholy marriage of time and money, putting a person again and again into the condition of financial and bodily insolvency, where there is never enough time and nothing can be paid back. It was learning how to count, hold, wait for, and let go of different kinds of time—and the word "time" could here be replaced with "debts," and the meaning wouldn't change.

During those years of becoming disabled—when illness and all its words broke in and took over—time got slow and sedulous and, although full of labor, it was "unproductive" in the capitalist sense, which is to say, it became crip. (Similar to "queer," "crip" is an intentional reclamation of the slur "cripple" that proposes a politics of empowerment that agitates against that which is considered deviant about disability.) I spent countless hours going from clinic to clinic, trying to get a diagnosis, a referral to a specialist, the indicated treatment, an authority to take me seriously, a scrap of empathy. At the pharmacy I was informed that the medication I needed to stay alive cost $800 a month, which was more than I made in a month. I waited on hold with the insurance company for afternoons, to be told that there was no specialist in my network within two hundred miles of where I lived. I spent ten years waiting in emergency rooms to be seen, waiting in bathrooms while the pain passed, waiting in bed for my symptoms to ease, and I waited in the waiting rooms of doctors, specialists of all kinds, psychiatrists, psychologists, acupuncturists, physical therapists, occupational therapists, somatic therapists, Reiki practitioners, psychics, witches, tarot readers, shamans. I felt like a gold prospector, swirling dirty water in a tin pan, looking for any glint of light. I waited for answers, legitimation, a cure.

This waiting complected into another experience. I was not only slumped into a Godotian scene, solitary in my illnesses and expectant for what would not come—I was also ricocheting through judgments of what that meant. By medical doctors baffled by my symptoms and dismissive of their validity; by social workers and bosses and other cogs in the wheels of capitalism who demanded the continuity of my labor while simultaneously denigrating me to the category of worthless because my body disrupted my labor's continuity; by institutions who swept in to finesse my condition into something that could be rendered into an art-historical and cultural product; by friends, family, lovers, and enemies who didn't believe it could be as bad as I said it was: I was now read, told, as a thing resplendent with pathology, simply because I had a body that needed more than it was supposed to need. Who decided this, who exactly was the arbiter of what a body was supposed and not supposed to do, need, and be, decided a status that was not in fact produced by my internal condition. No, this was the accumulation of a thousand tiny and not-so-tiny external events, tones of speaking, methods institutional and otherwise of disregard and dismissal, mechanisms built to dole out the story of pathology to a thing like me.

As a sick person, I watched as the perceptions of others amassed and clustered onto me, like a little pile of arrows that got aimed, shot, and stuck. If one arrow was tweaked, they all started to move, and it hurt, the pain went deep. After a while, I couldn't tell where the pain came from—if it originated from somewhere inside me or was caused by something outside me that had gone in too far. I knew that this was how ideologies of oppression work: they seep into you, get into your cells, hunker down and dig in and make a home out of you. I also knew that, no matter where it came from, the hurt was real, it sounded like my own voice, and it lived in me now. It was a story being told about me that I started to tell about myself.

I began writing what would become "Sick Woman Theory" on December 18, 2014, in a flare, lying in bed. Over the next year, the essay was rejected by over a dozen publications, helmed by some of the biggest names in feminism, before finding a home in *Mask* magazine, which was ad-free, online, run by a volunteer group of anti-capitalists in their twenties, and now defunct. I was paid eighty-one dollars, the highest amount *Mask* paid its writers. Because there were no ads, no one made any money as that essay went on to become one of *Mask*'s most viewed, with hundreds of thousands of clicks. It has since been translated by fans into a dozen languages, making its way through covens, hackerspaces, queer hair salons, and crip collectives around the world. It is included in anthologies published by prestigious presses (one of which was edited by a person who'd originally rejected it) and quoted, cited, and taught widely. It is on the syllabus in classes in a range of departments at universities, from ethics classes in medical schools (although with the anti-capitalist bits redacted, I guess to spare the aspiring doctors a confrontation with too much "politics") to courses in religious studies, design, literature, and feminist theory (where I'm told it is one of the texts that stirs students most vehemently to *become* anti-capitalists).

This response stunned me—I'd felt so alone in my condition when it descended upon me, and that first year of rejections confirmed the dread I'd felt that my experience of illness was one that would be nearly impossible to mitigate with a sense of connection, community, or anyone else who might be going through it too. But, now, here was evidence of how urgently these issues were felt not by a few, but by many. I should have known this would be true when, in late 2015, I was to read a working draft of "Sick Woman Theory" to a public audience at a feminist space in Los Angeles. It had just been accepted at *Mask* magazine, so I wanted to try out the ideas with a small group of friends and colleagues to get it ready for publication. The space announced the event on Facebook, and within a few days, more than five hundred people had RSVP'd. We were shocked. The feminist space could hold about thirty, so we scrambled to move the event to a venue with a much bigger capacity. My surprise continued when the ninety-minute video of the talk that we put on Vimeo rose to over one hundred thousand views in a few months.

Over the years, what began for me as a kind of desperate fury at what being sick and disabled meant has galvanized into a politics, which is to say that a shock of nascent but critical consciousness guided me toward a community that cared. I reached for them, and they found me. I call them my crip fam. They are the only group to whom I've felt I ever belonged, even though we are scattered around the world, our friendships marked by asynchrony, virtual communication, distance; for there is always the negotiation of our own limits and flares with each other's, and this is always also a negotiation with the ways ableism keeps us apart. We email, leave long voice notes, send a lot of memes. We order each other groceries, books, medical supplies. Once, while at a crip friend's house on the night they had a dinner party, I couldn't leave the bed on the second floor because I was in a flare. The crips who could climbed the stairs and got into bed with me, and we FaceTimed the crips who are wheelchair users who were on the first floor. That was the best dinner party I've ever been to, and I never made it to the table.

In crip community, interdependence, support, and mutual aid are held closer than anything else, but we also understand and know in our bones that to be crip and political about it, one must keep one's fury and surrender in equal balance. To be crip and political about it is to redefine what being dependent means, how we understand our autonomy at all—which means it requires an unflinching look at how we are so much more fragile and reliant than we think we are, or might like to be, and how bodies are so much more bizarre and defective than might at times be bearable, and how much fucking suffering we must endure, and how close we are to death, because society has put us there, and because our bodies can sometimes feel like they put us there too. All the ways we cannot do something, all the ways we won't be able to do something—what sort of political dreams can come from this as a starting place?

We are not alive because of our stories, but it is true to say that, in telling them, they birth and rebirth us, and who doesn't need to be reborn from time to time? When I began this book, I thought I was trying to tell the story of how I became disabled. I reached for language to hold an experience that had taken over my life, and I reached wretchedly, unstoppably, because I needed that mess to be held by something other than my own body. It was so heavy to carry around. Pulling it out, word by word, sentence by sentence, putting it into a form other than my own flesh, did something to metabolize it. It's not that it pulled me out of the hole I was in, but it made the hole something other than only a hole. Finding this sense of capaciousness felt like an actual miracle—that it's the capacity for transformation, for meaning to change, that gives, yields, produces, indeed *means* the most. So, as I watched my story do a thaumaturgic shapeshift during the decade of writing this book, I realized I was reaching, not for the one story of illness or disability, but for how this can be more than one story.

In that reaching, I chased illness on the pages of others, looking for accounts, records, documents so that I might build a constellation, a little cosmos, in which I could situate myself and the language I had caught. I didn't find many, which struck me as odd since illness is something we are all guaranteed to live through, and disabled is what we are all going to become; and what I did find all had a similar ring to it. Rather than the motley list of words pulling the page in many directions, only a few appeared, making a couple well-worn ruts. Pain was blinding, anxiety crippling, every disabled person feels they are a burden, et al. These were slotted into service of narratives whose arcs—instead of heaving through the multiple peaks and valleys which I knew were true about being disabled—went down to one low place, then forced an ending that skewed upward into triumph. How unnerving to listen for a symphony of myriad sounds and instead hear back the same one or two notes.

You know when you can see a writer's prejudices, biases, unsavory opinions creeping onto the page without that writer's knowledge? It's like noticing a drunk person spill something on their shirt before they notice it themselves. Once I started looking for stories about illness, I noticed it—the stains of ableism spreading over the shirtfront—and could tell when the writer didn't. It seemed to me that when I read stories about illness, there were a lot of gaps and holes and leaps and huge elephants in tiny rooms that were unaccounted for. I don't want or need writers or artists to be good, pure, ethically uncompromised. They can have gaps and holes and leaps; I do not need their apologies, penance, or punishment. What I *do* want is writers and artists unafraid to be honest in accounting for when their beliefs take them to somewhere they didn't deliberately aim for, when their actions are determined by ideological beliefs they have absorbed uncritically and now express without notice. If they cannot give me the *why* of these lacunae, I at least want the *how*. "How did you arrive at that thought?" I kept asking.

There are many definitions of ableism, and I'd encourage you to look them all up, especially the ones written by disabled people. One of my favorites is by Talila A. Lewis, who updates it every year as a working definition so it changes as the world and Talila's thinking does. Here's the 2022 definition:

able·ism /ˈābəˌlizəm/ noun: A system of assigning value to people's bodies and minds based on societally constructed ideas of normalcy, productivity, desirability, intelligence, excellence, and fitness. These constructed ideas are deeply rooted in eugenics, anti-Blackness, misogyny, colonialism, imperialism, and capitalism. This systemic oppression leads to people and society determining people's value based on their culture, age, language, appearance, religion, birth or living place, "health/ wellness," and/or their ability to satisfactorily re/produce, "excel," and "behave." You do not have to be disabled to experience ableism.

If you remember one thing from that definition, I'd like it to be the last sentence.

Over the last decade, we have seen large-scale reckonings with the ideologies of oppression and domination that are named above. In the face of these, the movements of Black Lives Matter and #MeToo have arisen; the fight for queer and trans people to have basic respect, freedom, and rights has arrived in the mainstream. Globally, there have been uprisings against the corporate and imperial exploitation that powers climate change; and revolts against fascist and authoritarian regimes have fomented in the streets on six continents. There was even a women's march that took place on a ship off the coast of Antarctica.

But we have yet to see the vastation of ableism at the same scale. Of course, disability justice activists have been and are still out here, and we will continue to be. But our work has not yet gotten into the world's water supply. The public understanding of terms like "disability" is still the medical model, that it is a body impaired and malfunctioning that requires course-correction. Notions of how to treat disabled people are often washed in infantilization, if not outright eugenics. When reckonings with ableism have entered the mainstream, they are usually superficial—a little sizzle about words, say, a celebrity using, intentionally or not, a slur and then apologizing for it.

I am waiting. I am getting impatient.

I return to the same question over and over: What does ableism give us that we can't let go of? Why do we keep it so close, stick to its well-worn ruts?

Let me venture a guess:

The word "ability" that is codified in the term "ableism" rests atop the condition of *dis*ability, and the most important part of the word "disability" is precisely the *dis*: the *not*, the *lack*, the *apart from*. Disability describes a condition that is both more othered from and profoundly closer to one's body than any other political condition that I can think of. It is a radical encounter with the needs of that body and therefore the ways in which that body's autonomy is limited and its dependency decided—and this dependency, this ontology of need, is what yokes it into a matrix of power: how it has, or does not have, power, and what sort of material conditions that determines. Is this body empowered to decide its own fate? Does this body have the power to guarantee its own survival, support, resources, thriving? With disability, the answer to these questions is often *no*. This is what makes disability political—because the political is foremost about power: who has power, who does not, why, and what can be done about it. As a crip friend once said, in reply to someone using the euphemism "differently abled," which the disabled community sees as a prevarication in service to ableism, "Yo, it's the *dis* part that makes it political."

There are so many ways one can enter the category of disability: It can be a condition one is born into. It can be an injury caused by an accident. It can be the creep and seep of a long illness. It need not be an illness or disease at all (and some who see themselves as disabled but not sick might object to my conflating the two syntactically and synonymously throughout this book, which is a fair critique, to which I'd reply with the probably insufficient acknowledgment again at how profuse this category is). It can be a diagnosis not agreed with. It can be a disease or injury recovered from, that still requires monitoring, adjustments, medications, treatment. It can be a realization far into adult life about a condition, diagnosed or not, that has been there for decades. It can be all of these things. A teeming list.

And yet, I am in agreement with those in the disabled community who would portend that, no matter how it arrives, disability *will* arrive for everyone, sooner or later. In a way, this vastly disparate category is the most universal condition of all—the horizon of it is just closer to some than others. It is always there, and the question is not *if* but *when* it will arrive for you. This is not the same as any other political identity. Not everyone on this planet will one day become queer or not white or a woman or colonized, but they will become disabled.

Despite its myriad differences and sweeping totality, however one enters this category, once there, a disabled person is fundamentally, materially different than an abled person. There is no way around this. When one is disabled, when one becomes attached to that long list of words, this is a markedly real difference from one who is not (yet) those things. Being lame is felt every time you try to move. Being sick is an obvious diversion from not having to contend with pain, fever, snot, vomiting, headache. Being mentally ill cuts to the quick of one's facility for any given day. Not being able to climb stairs, or open a door, or carry something, or process language defines one's entire life. No matter what form of disability arrives for you, it *will* bring struggle, suffering, incapacity, limit, and pain. It will make basic tasks like trying to survive on this planet seem impossible, *be* impossible. Sometimes your daily to-do list must include things like "cook" and "shower," and sometimes you won't be able to check them off as done. As conditions, illness and disability measure what cannot be done now—and as direction, telos, prophecy, they divine what, one day, we won't ever be able to do again.

This is why we need ableism. Ableism protects us from the most brutal truth: that our bodies will disobey us, malfunction, deteriorate, need help, be too expensive, decline until they finally stop moving, and die. Ableism is what lets us believe that this doesn't have to be true, or at least, that we can forestall it, keep it at bay, and that this is based entirely upon our own will. Ableism and its fantasies allow us to operate as if our abilities, our bodies, are always at our command, under our control, and that they will function when and how and for as long as we want them to, as we need them to. Of course, we'd prefer to believe that rather than the opposite.

How, then, to ask people to execrate ableism as an ideology of harm, discrimination, and oppression when it is the very thing that insulates us from the fact of our own impending limits and mortality? How to demand society divest from the consolation, no matter how deceitful and delusory, in which ableism swaths us? What will it take to spur people on a massive scale to tear down the system of ableism when doing so will leave no cushion between us and the actuality of all the ways we *will* suffer, we *will* be in pain, we *will* be unable to do what we want, and eventually, inevitably, we *will* die? How do we build a politic that stares into the face of our own end and finds a way to continue?

It's an unendurable task.

The only way I can think to do this is to say, "Let's do it together."

I once tried to describe the different genres of heavy metal to a friend. There are so many kinds: hair, glam, black, sludge, speed—and they each have specific qualities, forms, concerns, and rhythms.

I found myself describing my two favorite kinds: "Death is fast, and doom is slow."

Of course, this is not only true about metal.

On August 8, 2012, I held my maternal grandmother's swollen, dark-purple hand in a hospital in Pasadena as she died. I was lying next to her in the bed, my head on her shoulder. She'd been unconscious for about a day, she'd been in the hospital for months. She was eighty-eight years old. I was twenty-seven. As her breathing shredded, I watched the readings from the machines she was connected to lessen and drop, the numbers getting lower, the meters twitching in smaller amounts, they would never go back up. Her last breath was the most shredded of all. It happened so fast, that final moment of life, even though we'd all been expecting it for months. I remember that it seemed she turned gray immediately after she died, but that can't be true, it must have been my brain imposing a kind of meaning on what it was looking at, helping me process the incomprehensibility that someone I'd known my entire life would no longer be here. When the hospital staff came into the room to start doing the bureaucracy of death, I went outside and walked slowly around the block. It was afternoon, and I squinted into the August Los Angeles sun. I remember that I was wearing a linen dress the color of the sky, but I don't remember if I cried on the walk. I had been crying for days and would cry for years, but on the walk I could see only the colors of the cement, the beige stucco of the hospital building, the sun-bleached shrubs, and how my dress blended into the sky. Maybe it's that tears don't have a color, which is why I cannot see them in this memory.

On April 30, 2018, my mother died. She had been sixty-three for less than two months; I would turn thirty-four in five days. We had not seen each other in seven years, and spoken only sporadically since 2002, which was the year when, at eighteen years old, I had drawn a boundary that said I could not have a relationship with her until she got sober and clean. She never got sober or clean. So I did not have a relationship with her. (Of course, there was a relationship still happening, it was just not the one that either of us wanted.) For my entire life, I had anticipated her death—every day, coming home from school, I'd prepare myself to find her lifeless body; I'd prepare myself to find it strung up, emptied out, by her own hand, because she'd often threaten this very thing—but that did not make the actual death feel less incomprehensible. My mother is some of the most elemental experiences I've ever felt in my body—she was a fist hitting my face, she was the smell of crack, she seemed to never stop crying, she taught me how to read the sky, the ocean, my heart—so how exactly did it make sense that her own body would no longer exist?

I want to say something here about how my grandmother had a chronic illness for her adult life, that I inherited; and how my mother, in addition to being physically disabled and neurodivergent, also had several chronic illnesses that she carried in her body, the effects of which she passed on to me. I want to say that my grandmother used a wheelchair in her last years, and my mother used a cane ever since I was a young child, and that I have used both of these since; they are part of my inheritance. I held one's hand as she died, and although I'd let go of the other's hand long before, we still held on to each other in many ways.

It has occurred to me that maybe I've become so ferocious in my disability activism because it retroactively rescues my mother. The story of her suffering as it was told by my family was the dominant, rutted one of ableism that said she was faking it, wanting attention, psycho, too much, weak. As an adult, I searched for another story. I set about interviewing family members, reading her diaries after her death. I became a kind of detective trying to understand why she had been so sad, so troubled, why she could never let go of her addiction. In that process, I learned that, in her early twenties, my mother had been in an abusive relationship with a man who broke into her house and set fire to her bed while she slept in it. I learned that he forced her down and injected her against her will with a dirty needle, which gave her hepatitis. I came to believe, based on the accounts of how and when her behavior changed, and when she started using drugs, that she'd been sexually assaulted or molested, maybe repeatedly, as a teenager, and whenever I suggest this to my father or my mother's sister, they scoff in disbelief. "She was just spoiled," they say. I want to shout, "She drank herself to death alone in a dirty room on a broken mattress because she was *spoiled*?" I learned that when she met my father, she was living in a cheap motel room with a man, perhaps the one who'd abused her, and I can see this room in my mind, the stained carpet, the drugs on the bed. I learned that she'd had a miscarriage around the time she met my father, and some night after coming home from the doctor, while on the toilet, she watched the dead twin that had been somehow overlooked slip out of her in a clot of tissue and a sea of blood.

I was not holding my paternal Korean grandmother's hand when she died at age ninety-four on October 10, 2023. I was thirty-nine. She'd just been moved to a care home for people with Alzheimer's. The staff had had to trim her nails because she kept attacking them. They called her a "troublemaker." She was four feet ten inches tall. Two years before she died, at age ninety-two, she was still pouring concrete in her garden by herself. Whenever I'd visit, she'd pinch my soft bicep, then make me grip her own arm so I could feel her muscles. "I'm strong, you see," she'd say. "I'll break your arm." She'd come to America at age twenty-eight and worked as a janitor in a hospital for thirty-three years, never once taking a day off. In the weeks leading up to her death, my father had moved her and her oldest son (his brother, my uncle, who also had Alzheimer's), to an Airbnb because the house where they both lived was infested with a Dickensian number of rats. The state had condemned the building to be bulldozed to the ground. My dad said he'd shot nine rats with a BB gun and didn't make a dent. There were hundreds swarming over the carpet and sofa and the silk cushions embroidered with cranes present in every Korean household.

At the Airbnb, my grandmother became confused and enraged because she could no longer see her beloved chickens, which my father had left in the backyard of her house. In an attempt to see them, Grandma broke into a car that she thought was hers so she could drive herself home, which led to her being arrested. She'd been arrested a week before, when my father wasn't in town, but we don't know the details as to why, they get hazy in the telling.

We learned that you cannot 5150 someone in California for dementia; and there is a difference between "suicidality" and "homicidality" in terms of how a person's danger is measured and whether this will land them in the hospital or jail. We couldn't get Grandma into a hospital because she didn't want to kill herself—unapologetically, she wanted to kill her sons. She threatened to murder my father in his sleep. He took several videos of her viciously clanging knives from the kitchen against themselves, speaking in Korean with such fury that she spits. When she does speak English, she says, "Who do you think you are?" When I was growing up, my father told stories about how she regularly beat him with a baseball bat. "The hardest I've ever been hit was by my mom," he'd say. My father was hit by plenty of men—his older brother, his various stepfathers, and his mother's boyfriends—and this fact always made his assertion that his mom hit hardest all the more stunning.

When she died, I was packing my suitcase to get on a flight to California to see her. I got the news, sank into my suitcase, and sobbed. I missed her by a few days. Soon after, I had a session with my Korean shaman to try to communicate with her, to tell her I was sorry I didn't get to her in time, and to let her know I was committed to honoring her life and legacy. The shaman only got a few seconds into the ceremony before she stopped and said, "Whoa. Is this her personality? She's like a tank!"

We laughed.

"Yes," I said. "That's her."

As Alzheimer's eroded her mind, it cut her down to the quick of herself. She became always angry, stubborn, and busy, wouldn't sit down or be still. She did not want to be told what to do by anyone. If a person attempted to curtail her independence, murdering them was the first option she reached for. *Who do you think you are?*

My father, as the caretaker of his mother and brother, thought the best course of action was to not do anything until it got worse. He let them stay in their home and hired a nurse to stop by a few times a week. How did the house become infested with rats? Because if you wait for something to become worse, it will.

Death is fast. Doom is slow.

I want to say something about the ableism behind the idea that disability is "a fate worse than death." But, since disability and illness are the most universal facts of life, aren't they the *only* fates?

When I was nine years old, I took a handful of sleeping pills and lay down on the couch to die. As much as it was a choice, it was not a choice. My story begins in places, conditions, with people that I did not consent to, and yet they are mine. There is my mother, her mother, my father, his mother, they are my ghosts, my agon. There I was. On that night, what I wanted and what I did not want from my life crumpled into something too onerous for me to keep carrying, so doing whatever it took to get rid of that felt necessary, inevitable. I did not yet comprehend the immensity of what life might offer me, and I could not find a way to keep moving for the weight of what I comprehended of it so far. I understood that life made me feel the question "Why me?" in equal extremes—that my life was extraordinary, a miracle of random chance and luck, and that it was the most elemental burden, to be thrown here without choice.

My parents and younger sibling were asleep, it was the early hours of the morning, one or two or three. The sleeping pills were over the counter and would not kill me, but I didn't know that. I swallowed them and closed my eyes. Our couch had holes which were themselves covered with frayed towels that had holes. It was holes covering up holes, and in the shadows everything was the dirty color of greasy white. When I started to lose consciousness, I felt the sharp fact that this would be the last time I'd have consciousness at all. I sat up, the consequence of the pills smoldering in my stomach, and I panicked. I ran to the bathroom and looked at myself in the mirror. I looked at my open mouth, my terrified eyes. I don't know what I thought, what I felt, what was decided or not decided in that moment. Maybe I thought, *Fuck it*. Maybe I thought, *I've made a terrible mistake*. I was a child. I try not to think of this memory often. Maybe so I can keep living, it is not part of the story I tend to tell about myself. But here I am telling it.

Nothing that happened next was spiritual, nothing got me close to anything with grace. There was only the expectation, and then the arrival, of total darkness. It was linear, causal. Something that happened after, because of, something that happened before. Dying was so mundane, it wasn't even pathetic—it was just bathetic, a sad little thud. Consciousness was given and taken, and one day it would never be given back, and that is what I thought as I lost mine. But then I woke up the next day, groggy, headached, and I didn't tell anyone what I'd done, I just got dressed and went to school. Life went on. One day it wouldn't. But for now, something happened, and then more things happened.

With this event, I became marked by the knowledge that death won't be romantic, it won't be grand, it's a small thing that's always close by, very close, in fact, at any given moment you can reach out and hold it, if you want to you can, without even reaching very far, go ahead, it's right there, so close, what's stopping you?, exactly what, if anything, is stopping you?

This knowledge has followed me every day of my life since, but perhaps it's inaccurate to say it follows me, as though it were behind me, like a little animal I keep on a leash. Because it's also in front of me, around, above, below. It's a kind of atmosphere, a climate. It's total in its ubiquity, but I can also forget about it sometimes.

Like the weather that is getting worse.

I start with Didion and her famous line—"We tell ourselves stories in order to live"—sort of antagonistically. Because whenever I think of that sentence, I want to know: Who is the *we*? Whose stories are being told? What sort of life is being lived? And from here, I want to know who gets to tell the story of their own death? Whose stories, whose deaths, are not their own to tell?

What about those of us whose lives are described not as lives at all, but as fates worse than death?

It's been suggested by people who knew her that Joan Didion wrote to find out what she thought. In the hagiographical wake of her death, this has now become a favorite way to talk about writing as such: rather than writing to express yourself, writing is the act of finding something out about yourself that you didn't already know. I like that idea, it has a nice ring to it, allowing for an unknown that can only be known through writing. It foregrounds an interiority that must be reached into and trusted, not for what it telegraphs on the surface but for what mysteries might be waiting in its depths. It rewards the reaching into the dark with a kind of bright light of clarity at the end.

But it is not why I write. I write to find out what is *possible* to think, meaning it's the changing of the thought that I chase, that miraculous capacity that can expand. Once I have a phrase, a sentence, a paragraph down on the page, what thrills me is to watch what happens to the thought if it's written in questions versus statements, this word rather than that word, a different syntax, vocabulary, punctuation. I want to know what thinking *can do*—what it makes, destroys, negotiates, protects, transgresses against; how it can be knife, fist, kiss, well, map, key.

Perhaps I want this, to watch something change, because this is how my body feels. Something I was told was one thing but was in fact many. Something that keeps branching into unknowability. Something that broke open, and in that breaking—oh, what I became.

"Tell" is the most important word in the title of this book. You tell a story, as you tell the future, as you tell time, as you tell me your name.

We have invented many languages—from ancient Greek and Hangeul to mathematics and quantum mechanics—with which to make meaning from what it feels like to carry ourselves and each other through life. Divination is one of them, and I see it as a desire to know what might be possible in the future, and this is why it feels so inconceivable. The future does not exist. Not yet. We cannot tell it, which is to say we cannot know it. And yet we must live as if we can. I have arrived at a working definition of the future that sees it as a shimmering cast off by the past and the present. Our materiality seems to shimmer the most, pointing toward terminuses determined by physical laws of gravity, action and reaction, motion. The question divination asks is: Can we deviate from that which is determined? It is a question of fate versus free will.

The book you hold in your hands is a record of how I've tried to hold fate in my hands, turn its pages, read it, divine meaning from the shimmering cast off by its raw material. It is a coming to terms with how fate and will are not antipodal, as is usually believed. I have found that more often they are superimposed on top of each other, converging and constituting each other. This book then has been an act, in equal measure, of reading and authorship, both of reading the stories of others as much as I have been trying to author my own, and the inverse of this: reading my own story as if it were authored by someone else. I have tried to find my way to stories that have long been denied—the ones that we have worried, if told, might *not* help us live. I have found that telling them has produced more life, not less.

Because I wrote this book as a disabled person, I have also wanted to know what thinking can do when it coexists with the incoherence of a day soaked in pain, the grind of a life negotiating poverty, bargaining for time, the desolation of being broken down by the medical-industrial complex, if thinking can happen at all after going up flights of stairs because an elevator is broken and all energy is lost for the day.

It's taken more than ten years to write, and it is not a document that shows the path toward one complete thought, a question asked at the outset and answered by the end. It asks more questions than it answers. It's not what I thought but what I have found thinking can do, all the contradictions, lucubrations, ways in which my mind changed. It sprints and peregrinates, drops me off at the wrong bus stop, stands still, goes backward. It gets lost. It stays lost. It doesn't return home because home was never a place of shelter. Who built *that* house?

Most of all, this book is an archive of the different languages I've reached into to tell the many stories that orbit around the subjects of illness, disability, ableism, and care, which ultimately took me into questions of pain, fate, doom, and death. This all took me down the paths of twelve-inch cocks, psychotic women, ghosts, Susan Sontag, transness, fighting, witchcraft, and BDSM. In these journeys, I met memorable, irascible, wonderful characters: The Freak, The Goblin, a priestess, a queen. My languages are shaped and shape-shifted by these paths, the reasons and contexts for which I turned to them, and life was noisy, so expect a cacophony. Sometimes I wrote to survive, because it was the only thing that made sense to do when all other purpose had been evacuated from my days. In the wake of my mother's death, for instance, I wrote down notes of inane details—the way the room smelled, what was on the walls, something to hold onto in the senselessness of grief—and they appear here unchanged from how I first put them into my notebook. Other parts needed two years of work, then two years of trying to forget, then another four, five, six years of revision before I understood what they could be. Sometimes I wrote *not* to understand but to complicate and flummox; sometimes I wrote into what scared me the most; sometimes I had fun. Sometimes I use the language of astrology—for I have found it to be one of the most robust and supple languages we've invented to articulate what is difficult in life*—and sometimes all I wanted to do was write about sex and violence and ambition, the ways my skin gets hot.

For many years I was uneasy about this book going into the world as mine because the normative aesthetics of care and illness are just not my vibe. I'm a goth kink queen, a faggy big-cock power-top who plays doom metal—it's a different sort of mood board. Care is so domesticated, maternalized, tied up with notions of nurturing and selflessness. But to be disabled and require care is to deal constantly with the nastiest of body horrors: diarrhea as if from a broken spigot, skin slit into slices, so much pus, unstoppable bleeding, clots of it like black ash, not to mention the sublime-like horror of being spalled by pain, of encountering one's mortal limit, the place where one stops and can go no further. This book is somewhat swayed by Susan Sontag's famous notion that illness is the night side of life, but one of its central aims is to not linger too long in only one kind of vague but glamorous gloom. There are as many kinds of light as there are darknesses. I want to find and hold and tell you about as many as I can.

I bring doom into the conversation to show that it is a place to begin, not to end. Once I started thinking of doom as liberatory, I felt free from the dread it constitutes when it looms in the future. How many of us have already met our doom and then had to get out of bed and go on? How many groups of people have had their worlds end, keep ending, and still they found ways to cook for each other? How privileged are you if you first require hope in order to act? What about those where hope was a luxury they couldn't afford, and still they wrote books, they made music, they sang? They keep singing.

----

* And to those who would say they don't "believe in" astrology, I would reply, Do you not believe in all the languages you don't know how to speak? Do you not believe in calculus, Guaraní, C++?

I wrote this book during a time when it felt like the world became more brutal than we can take, but somehow we are still supposed to take it. I sold the book during the global health crisis and mass disabling event of the COVID-19 pandemic. While finishing the edits, I had COVID, the bitter taste of Paxlovid in my mouth as the weather outside my window grew more chaotic, flash thunderstorms that broke open into the brightest sun, and then the sky darkened in thirty seconds and all the windows needed to be closed again. The news was beset with atrocities alongside algorithmically determined ads for skin care. I scrolled from news of the genocide in Palestine to memes about being a millennial. AI sent me alerts that my bank account was below its limit. Writing was my companion in this reality, accompaniment for what feels unbearable but must nevertheless be borne, and my wish in finally putting the writing into the world is not to claim it as mine but to offer it as companion to whomever might need it.

More and more of us feel the urgency of forging new paradigms around health, support, and bodies both physical and social, and are actively seeking a path to social and political transformation—or at least some recognition of the fact that staying alive in late capitalism is fucking hard. This book is for the ones who find themselves anywhere in that sentence. It is a book of the breaks (throughs and downs), the smells and leaks and gasps and scabs, the storms and structures, fates and gods, that rend and bend us. It is a book about how our needs are our very ontology, which means it is a book about pain, and this means it's also about care. It is about the words we reach for to carry us, the stories we tell to keep ourselves and each other not only alive but reborn. It is written in languages that collide will and fate, that raw material we make and remake, how we hold it, make use of it, all the paths where that takes us as we drag our delicate little centers of gravity around this Earth.

The trick of the title is that we can't tell how we will die—and that we're already doing it all the time. What might be possible, then, to say, to know, to make, to mean, to do in the space of that paradoxical story?

Another way to say that is, the body is the page upon which we write our lives.

So, let's reach for that page, that story, the entire thing, including the ways it will end, together. Let's tell the whole story, then all the possible versions.

Let's watch, look here: how it can change.

My editor asks:

"Why does it need to be painful?"

My partner asks:

"Why do you fight so much?"

My audience asks:

"But where is hope in the darkness
of your work?"

My ancestors ask:

"Why do you make your hands claw
around the lie of your solitude?"

My government asks:

"Why won't you let us use your
body to feed the worms?"

I ask:

"What can I write down?"

Sick Woman Theory

1.

In late 2014, I was sick with a chronic condition that can get bad enough to render me, for anywhere from days to weeks to months at a time, unable to walk, drive, do my job, sometimes speak or understand language, take a bath without assistance, and leave the bed. This particular flare coincided with the Black Lives Matter protests, which I would have attended unremittingly had I been able to. At the time, I lived one block away from MacArthur Park in Los Angeles, a predominantly Latinx neighborhood and one colloquially understood to be the place where many immigrants begin their American lives. The park is not surprisingly one of the most active places of protest in the city.

I listened to the sounds of the marches as they drifted up to my window. Attached to the bed, I raised my Sick Woman fist, in solidarity.

Solidarity is a slippery thing. It's hard to feel in isolation. In bed, in pain, I started to think about the kind of solidarity in which I could participate as someone stuck at home, alone. I started to think about what modes of protest are afforded to sick and disabled people at all.

I thought of the many others who were not at the protest either, who could not go because it was in some way inaccessible to them, all the other invisible bodies, with their fists up, tucked away, out of sight. It seemed to me that many would be the people for whom Black Lives Matter is especially in service. I thought of how they might not be able to be present for the marches because they had to go to work, or because they lived under the threat of being fired from their job if they marched, or because they were literally incarcerated. They might not be able to go to the march because of the threat of violence and police brutality that exists at any protest. They might not be able to go because their bodies were this peculiar convergence of hyper-visible and invisible, marked and unmarked, which instantiated a dangerous vulnerability around them. They might not be able to go because of their own illness or disability, or because they were caring for someone with an illness or disability. They were many, and we were different from each other in key ways, but what was true for all of us was that we were not there.

If we take Hannah Arendt's definition of the political—which is still one of the most dominant in mainstream discourse—as being any action that is performed in public, we must contend with the implications of what, of whom, that excludes. If being present in public is what is required to be political, then whole swathes of the population can be deemed *a*political simply because they are not physically able to get their bodies into the street.

In my graduate program, Arendt was a kind of god, and so I was trained to think that her definition of the political was radically liberating. Of course, I can see that it was, in its time (the late 1950s). In one fell swoop she got rid of a political defined by the need for infrastructures of law, voting, elections, and the reliance on individuals who've accumulated the power to affect policy; she got rid of the need for policy at all. Until then, all of these had been required for an action to be considered political and visible as such. No, Arendt said, just get your body into the street, and *bam*—political.

There are two failures here though. The first is her reliance on a "public"—which requires a private, a binary between visible and invisible space. This means that whatever takes place in private is not political. So, you can beat your spouse in private and it doesn't matter, for instance. You can send private emails containing racial slurs, but since they weren't "meant for the public," you are not racist. Arendt was worried that if everything can be considered political, then nothing will be, which is why she divided the space into one that is political and one that is not. But for the sake of this anxiety, she chose to sacrifice whole groups of people, to continue to banish them to invisibility and political irrelevance. She chose to keep them out of the political sphere.

I'm not the first to take Arendt to task for this. The failure of Arendt's notion of the political was exposed in the civil rights activism and feminism of the 1960s and '70s. The slogan of the time, "The personal is political," can also be read as saying, "The private is political." Because, of course, everything you do in private is political: how long your showers are, if you have access to hot water for a shower at all, if you clean the shower afterward or if you pay someone else to clean it, and so on.

There is yet another problem with Arendt's formulation, which persists in today's discourse about public space. As Judith Butler put it in a 2015 lecture, "Vulnerability and Resistance," Arendt failed to account for who is allowed into public space, which means she failed to account for who's in charge of public space. Public space is never free from infrastructures of power, control, and surveillance; in fact, it is built by them. As Butler says, there is always one thing true about a public demonstration: the police are already there, or they are coming. This resonates with frightening force when considering the context of Black Lives Matter. The inevitability of violence inflicted on Black lives *at* a demonstration—particularly a demonstration that ignited around insisting that Black lives should not be subjected to such violence—ensures that a lot of people won't, because they can't, show up. Couple this with the multiple forms of inaccessibility of public space, then couple that with people's physical and mental illnesses and disabilities that require more rather than less access and support, and we must contend with the fact that many whom these protests are for are not able to participate in them, which means they are not able to be visible as political subjects.

There was a Tumblr post that came across my dash, during those weeks in 2014 of protest, that said something to the effect of: *Shout out to all the disabled people, sick people, people with PTSD, anxiety, etc. who can't protest in the streets with us tonight. Your voices are heard and valued, and with us.* Heart. Reblog.

Since I wrote that last paragraph about the 2014 protests, there have been countless uprisings around the world. During the weeks in 2022 that I was preparing a revised version of this text to be published online, Russia invaded Ukraine. While the manuscript was in its final edits for the book to go into production, Israel was perpetrating genocide on Palestine; a week before my deadline, Aaron Bushnell self-immolated in protest. In the years that come after this, perhaps for a second edition, or an anniversary edition, I assume I will be writing while yet another atrocity happens, following the ways in which people are organizing resistance to it. I assume I will be equal parts furious and exhausted, despairing and determined to act. I'll watch videos recorded with shaky phones from the street, I'll share links and doomscroll, then need to log off, fatigued and weeping as the images of war, oppression, and genocide proliferate on my screen. Like a lot of others, I have participated in the uprisings of the twenty-first century primarily through social media. Liking, sharing, reposting; donating to mutual aid, GoFundMes, charities. This makes me think of the surveillance embedded in the internet, a force we know is there but can't see, and how digital space has both expanded public space and narrowed it, making this distinction between private and public even more occluded and confusing. I think of how COVID-19 put our lives, but not our bodies, into digital space in an unprecedented way. I think of how bodies are real, that they have gravity and needs, and are fucking expensive—that this fact forms the world, as much a problem as a poetic.

When I think of this, I feel heavy with my own body and what it looks like, how it carries its Korean Americanness in skin and bone that pass as white, and what this means about where I can and can't take it, about how visible it is and is not. I am heavy with the violence that's been inflicted on it and on those who look similar. Then it feels heavier when I think of those who don't look like me, what violence comes to them and why. The weight increases when I consider what my and other sick and disabled bodies would need to attend these protests, what kinds of support, and how such supports are not there. I think of all the nuances of violence, the many ways it is oriented toward specific groups and why, but then I think of the totality of it, and this feels heaviest of all.

So, as I have participated in protests over the years while unable to march, hold up a sign, shout a slogan, or be visible in any traditional capacity as a political being, the central question of Sick Woman Theory has been formed and honed: How do you throw a brick through the window of a bank if you can't get out of bed?

2.

I have chronic illness. For those who don't know what chronic illness means, the word "chronic" comes from the Greek "chronos," χρόνος, which means "time" (think of "chronology"). In certain contexts, it can mean "a lifetime." So, a chronic illness is an illness that lasts a lifetime. In other words, it does not get better. There is no cure.

And there is the weight, the texture, the assonance of time. Yes, that means you feel it every day. On very rare occasions, I get caught in a moment, as if something's plucked me out of the world, where I realize that I haven't thought about my illnesses for a few minutes, maybe a few precious hours. These moments of oblivion are the closest thing to blessedness that I know. When you have chronic illness, life is reduced to a relentless rationing of energy. It costs you to do anything—to cook for yourself, to get dressed, to answer an email. For those without chronic illness, you can spend and spend without consequence: the cost is not a problem. For those of us with limited funds, we have to ration, we have a limited supply, we often run out before lunch.

Sometimes a question shoots through me: Are there people who don't have to think about their bodies? It makes me wonder what conditions, what supports, have conspired in the world to make this true for them. Why is it not true for someone like me? For so many others?

Ann Cvetkovich writes: "What if depression, in the Americas, at least, could be traced to histories of colonialism, genocide, slavery, legal exclusion, and everyday segregation and isolation that haunt all of our lives, rather than to be biochemical imbalances?" I'd like to change the word "depression" here to all mental illnesses. Cvetkovich continues: "Most medical literature tends to presume a white and middle-class subject for whom feeling bad is frequently a mystery because it doesn't fit a life in which privilege and comfort make things seem fine on the surface." In other words, "wellness," as it is talked about and sold in America today, is a white and wealthy idea.

Let me quote Starhawk, in the preface to the new edition of her 1982 book *Dreaming the Dark*: "Psychologists have constructed a myth—that somewhere there exists some state of health which is the norm, meaning that most people presumably are in that state, and those who are anxious, depressed, neurotic, distressed, or generally unhappy are deviant." I'd here supplant the word "psychologists" with "white supremacy," "doctors," "your boss," "neoliberalism," "heteronormativity," and "America."

For those living outside of America, the reach of this American imperialist ideology becomes a horizon of doom. Dr. Samah Jabr, the head of the Mental Health Unit within the Palestinian Ministry of Health, has noted that PTSD altogether is a Western concept: "PTSD better describes the experiences of an American soldier who goes to Iraq to bomb and goes back to the safety of the United States. He's having nightmares and fears related to the battlefield and his fears are imaginary. Whereas for a Palestinian in Gaza whose home was bombarded, the threat of having another bombardment is a very real one. It's not imaginary . . . There is no 'post' because the trauma is repetitive and ongoing and continuous."

I think of this in regards to the recursion of trauma. Parul Sehgal in "The Case against the Trauma Plot" wrote: "The expanded definition has allowed many more people to receive care but has also stretched the concept so far . . . [that] people could conceivably have a unique set of symptoms and the same diagnosis. The ambiguity is moral as well as medical: a soldier who commits war crimes can share the diagnosis with his victims." This takes me to the fact that trauma in soldiers in World War I was often not diagnosed as such because it was seen as a humiliating diagnosis for a man, something that weakened him, lowered him to the position historically occupied by women.

There has been a slew of writing in recent years about how "female" pain is treated—or rather, not treated as seriously as men's pain in emergency rooms and clinics by doctors, specialists, insurance companies, families, husbands, friends, and the culture at large. In a 2015 article in *The Atlantic*, called "How Doctors Take Women's Pain Less Seriously," a husband writes about the experience of his wife Rachel's long wait in the ER before receiving the medical attention her condition warranted (which was an ovarian torsion, where an ovarian cyst grows so large it falls, twisting the fallopian tube). "Nationwide, men wait an average of forty-nine minutes before receiving an analgesic for acute abdominal pain. Women wait an average of sixty-five minutes for the same thing. Rachel waited somewhere between ninety minutes and two hours," he writes. At the end of the ordeal, Rachel had waited nearly fifteen hours before going into the surgery she should have received upon arrival. The article concludes with her physical scars healing, but that "she's still grappling with the psychic toll—what she calls 'the trauma of not being seen.'"

What the article does not mention is race, which leads me to believe that the writer and his wife are white. Whiteness is what allows for such oblivious neutrality; it is the premise of blankness, the presumption of the universal. (Studies have shown that white people will listen to other white people when talking about race far more openly than they will to a person of color. As someone who is white-passing, let me address white people directly: look at my white-looking face and listen up.)

The trauma of not being seen. Again, who is allowed into the public sphere? Who is allowed to be visible? I don't mean to diminish Rachel's horrible experience—I myself once had to wait ten hours in an ER to be diagnosed with a burst ovarian cyst, so I get it—I only wish to point out the presumptions upon which her horror relies: that vulnerability should be seen and supported, and that we should all receive care quickly and in a way that "respects the autonomy of the patient," as the Four Principles of Biomedical Ethics puts it. Of course, these presumptions are what any person with a body should have. But we must ask the question of which bodies are allowed to enjoy such assumptions. In whom does society substantiate such beliefs? And in whom does society enforce the opposite?

Compare Rachel's experience at the hands of the medical establishment with that of Kam Brock's. In September 2014, Brock, a thirty-two-year-old Black woman, born in Jamaica and living in New York City, was driving her BMW when she was pulled over by the police. They accused her of driving under the influence of marijuana, and though her behavior and their search of her car yielded nothing to support this, they nevertheless impounded her car. According to a lawsuit brought against the City of New York and Harlem Hospital by Brock, when Brock appeared the next day to retrieve her car, she was arrested by the police for behaving in a way that she calls "emotional" and involuntarily hospitalized in the Harlem Hospital psych ward. (As someone who has also been involuntarily hospitalized for behaving "too" emotionally, this story makes a rip of recognition through my brain.) The doctors thought she was "delusional" and suffering from bipolar disorder because she claimed that Obama followed her on Twitter—which was true, but the medical staff failed to confirm it. She was then held for eight days, forcibly injected with sedatives, made to ingest psychiatric medication and attend group therapy, and stripped. The medical records of the hospital—obtained by her lawyers—bear this out: the "master treatment plan" for Brock's stay reads, "Objective: Patient will verbalize the importance of education for employment and will state that Obama is not following her on Twitter." It notes her "inability to test reality." Upon her release, she was given a bill for $13,637.10.

The question of why the hospital's doctors thought Brock "delusional" because of her Obama-follow claim is easily answered:

because, according to this society, a young Black woman can't possibly be that important—and for her to insist that she is, must mean she's "sick."

How many people are rendered "sick" in this way? How many times has the autonomy of a person been stripped from them in the name of "care"? Why does it happen so differently to a person like Rachel than to Kam Brock? When both are made into Sick Women, but this determines radically different outcomes, how do we understand the Sick Woman? Should she exist at all? Why does she?

3.

Before I can speak of the "Sick Woman" in all of her many guises, including the ways in which you might read me or others as one, regardless of whether we claim her or not, I must first speak as an individual and address you from my particular location.

I am antagonistic to the notion that the Western medical-insurance-industrial complex understands me in my entirety, though they seem to think they do. They have attached many words to me over the years, and though some of these have provided articulation that was useful—after all, no matter how much we are working to change the world, we must still find ways of coping with the reality at hand—first I want to suggest some other ways of understanding my "illness."

Perhaps it can all be explained by the fact that my Sun is in the sixth house of labor, work, and health; and my Moon's in Cancer in the eighth house, the house of death; and my Mars, Saturn, and Pluto are all retrograde in the twelfth house, the house of illness, suffering, misery, bane, and toil. Or, that my father's mother left South Korea during the war, pregnant by an American soldier who left her not long after, and she then spent the next thirty years in

America working double shifts as a janitor in a hospital, not once taking a day off. Or, that my mother spent her life suffering from undiagnosed mental illness and was probably neurodivergent, both of which were actively denied by her family, conditions then exasperated by a forty-year-long drug and alcohol addiction, sexual trauma, and hepatitis from a dirty needle, as she made her way in and out of jails, squats, and homelessness. Or, that I was physically and emotionally abused as a child, raised in an environment of poverty, addiction, and violence, where sometimes there wasn't enough to eat. Perhaps it's because I'm poor—according to the IRS, in 2014, when I started writing this text, my adjusted gross income was $5,730 (a result of not being well enough to work full time)—which meant that for years my "primary care doctor," as offered by the health insurance I was eligible for in the state of California, was a group of physician's assistants and nurses in a clinic on the second floor of a strip mall, and that I relied on food stamps to eat. Perhaps it's because I'm queer and gender non-binary, first coming out to my parents at age fourteen, finally leaving home at age sixteen with the last black eye I was willing to receive from my mother's wasted hand. Perhaps it can be encapsulated in that mutable word "trauma." Perhaps my dead need me too much. Perhaps I've never gotten over anything. Perhaps I've had some bad luck.

Or perhaps this is not something that should be scaled down to my own individual experience. Perhaps right now I'm not only writing about personal issues but structural ones. Perhaps the more accurate way to account for myself is to say that I am alive on this planet and imbricated into its social, political, economic, and historical systems—that my individuality is determined far more than I might like by institutions of domination and the ideologies that feed them.

Where the distinction can be made between a condition that is debilitating rather than simply different from the normative has to do with when such conditions keep me from participating fully in my life, work, relationships, and society—when my flares keep me from protesting, yes, but also from having the energy to cook dinner for my partner and myself, or to write, or see a friend, or dance, or go to work, to make enough money to pay rent. Participation in the stuff of life is always a negotiation with how I want to participate on my own terms and how my participation is dictated by terms over which I have no control. This is true for anyone contending with an illness, disorder, disease, or disability—and this is exactly why such experiences are never only about one's individual body or mind but always an indicator of how we are enmeshed in forces beyond our own skin that nevertheless determine our experience within it.

It's important that I also share the Western medical terminology that's been attached to me. Whether I like it or not, it can provide a common vocabulary: "This is the oppressor's language," Adrienne Rich wrote in 1971, "yet I need it to talk to you." Of course, I fucking hate that in order for my testimony to be validated as true, I have to legitimate myself in this way. Yet, I also understand that my specific embodiment is an important thing to attach to my words.

Let me offer another language too. In the Native American Cree language, the possessive noun and verb of a sentence are structured differently than in English. In Cree, one does not say, "I am sick." Instead, one says, "The sickness has come to me." This feels like a more productive and accurate understanding of illness because it respects both the self and the illness as separate entities that can interact with and encounter each other, rather than one subsuming the other.

So, here is what has come to me:

Endometriosis, which is a disease of the uterus where the uterine lining grows where it shouldn't—in the pelvic area mostly, but also anywhere, the legs, abdomen, even the head. It causes chronic pain; gastrointestinal chaos; epic bleeding; in some cases, cancer; and means that I have miscarried, can't have children, and have a surgery or two to look forward to. It means that every month, those rogue uterine cells that have implanted themselves throughout my body "obey their nature and bleed," to quote fellow endo warrior Hilary Mantel. This causes cysts, which eventually burst, leaving behind bundles of dead tissue like the debris of little bombs. Yeah, the pain is annihilating. And for someone with a shitload of gender dysphoria, who does not identify as a woman, having a uterus at all, let alone such an abject one, has been a mindfuck. When I explained the disease to a person who didn't know about it, she exclaimed: "So your whole body is a uterus!" That's one way of looking at it, yes. (Imagine what the ancient Greek doctors—the fathers of the theory of the "wandering womb," in which the uterus was said to roam the body in search of fertilization, supposedly the cause of madness or "hysteria"—would say about that.) I try to keep close something someone else once said to me when I told them how confusing this disease has been as a person who does not identify as a woman: "Well, you shouldn't identify as a uterus either." (But can a dysfunctional body part ever not be pathologized, pathologizing?)

Complex PTSD, bipolar disorder, panic disorder, and depersonalization/derealization disorder have also come to me. I know that I inherited some, and that some were caused by the sort of childhood I had, but no matter from where or why they came to me, they have come, they are here. Over the last few years, as research and scholarship develop, I've found a place in the Autistic and Neurodivergent community, and I have started to identify as neurodivergent, because many of my "symptoms" are not symptoms at all, but simply the way my mind works, and here we are again in that multiplicity that is disability. There is disagreement that mental illnesses count as disabilities in the same way that physical ones do; and some might want a stronger delineation between mental illnesses and neurodivergence, a distinction between a sickness and a condition. I have ruminated on these questions for years as well. I have found that I prefer to let the category of disability be unruly, overflowing, crawling with variety rather than the opposite, forcing it to follow rules, building hard limits, insisting on its immutability. What body or mind would fit in such a carceral space? There are many ways we recognize, and even celebrate, bodies and minds functioning well—what would happen if we allowed for such capaciousness when we consider the plethora of all our possible deviations?

What the deviating conditions of my mind mean is that I notice too many details, have a preternaturally good memory for esoteric trivia, can obsess the house down, and will hyper-focus on a topic or task at the expense of others, like eating or sleeping—and sometimes these traits help me to excel in work, relationships, and society, and sometimes they do not. They can mean that I live between this world and another one, one created by my own brain that has ceased to be contained by a discrete concept of "self." They can mean that I have access to empyreal emotions, flights of thought, dreamscapes, to the feeling that my mind has been obliterated into stars, to the sensation that I have become nothingness, as well as to extraordinary ecstasies, raptures, sorrows, and despair. When they become obstacles to my participation in society, indeed become crises in that participation, I have been hospitalized, voluntarily and involuntarily, and these have been called "episodes," "meltdowns," "shutdowns," "breakdowns," and "collapses," and, sure, all of that sounds right. These mental-health visitors and their friends have motivated attempts at suicide (all of them while dissociated) more than a dozen times, the first when I was nine years old. I'm certain they will be guests in my house again. They cloak me with a constant fear about what might happen if I have an episode in public—though, because I pass as white, at least I know I will not be shot by the police.

It has meant that I have odysseyed through the psycho-pharmacopia trying to find the right meds, lost, waylaid, ship-wrecked. One of the medications I was prescribed once nearly killed me—it produces a rare side effect where one's skin falls off—and another cost $800 a month, and I could only take it because my doctor slipped me free samples. It took me seven years to find the right medication—in kind, dosage, and combination—and everyone I know who's struggled with mental health has had a similar odyssey. Such sagas are often hilarious in their contradictions—or, at least, it feels better to find ways to laugh at them. If I want to be able to hold a job, for instance, I must take a medication daily that can cause short-term memory loss and drooling, among other sexy side effects. It also steals my consciousness every night for a minimum of ten hours, so I can never wake up before noon, making me even more unemployable—so, the meds I need to be able to work make me unable to work.

When I was thirty, I herniated a disc in my back while doing the stupidest activity— carrying one end of a couch up the stairs because the elevator was broken on moving day. This means that I have sciatica pain that emanates from my lower back down the outside of my left leg, and if it were a voice, it would have an impressive range, from low humming to a screaming high C. When I am not in the mood to deal with ableism, I hold up this injury, rather than the illnesses listed so far, to explain why I'm in pain or walk with a cane, why I am so tired, because it's the most tangible, respectable, the one people approve of, because it has an obvious, accidental cause.

As a child, I had a severe reaction to chicken pox—the blisters covered my entire body with barely a millimeter in between them and did not abate for weeks—and as an adult, I am plagued by chronic shingles, which appear on my lower back and have appeared so often that they have gone into the hip bone and damaged the nerves. This means that my flares can take me out for weeks, months, at a time

because shingles are a reliable part of them, bringing flu-like symptoms, scorching nerve pain, the inability to walk without a limp or
to walk at all. In 2016, a neurologist diagnosed me with "100 percent
fibromyalgia" as a "place to start." More than one year before that,
my doctor had referred me to see a neurologist, rheumatologist, and
immunologist so I could begin testing for MS and other autoimmune
diseases that some of my symptoms pointed to. My insurance never
approved these referrals, nor could it find a specialist within two
hundred miles who was covered by my plan. The neurologist who
diagnosed my fibromyalgia agreed to see me out-of-network,
cash-only, as a favor to my psychiatrist who was his friend.

Sometimes I fit into the symptoms of fibromyalgia—there are
places on my body that shriek in pain when touched gently, and my
joints are always mutinying—and sometimes I don't. This is true
for all of the diagnoses I have listed above. At some point, the need
to obtain the "correct" diagnosis dissipated in me, as my diagnoses were changed over the years as new research and terminology
arrived, and as I managed to access the combination of medications
and treatments that have worked, and as I got tired. As I said, I need
them to define and categorize me—submitting to them affords me
meds and therapies at the same time that it yokes me to the medical-
industrial complex—and this is the conundrum all sick and disabled
people live with. To be pathologized is to be allowed to survive.

In June 2016, I moved to Berlin with my partner, who is a German
citizen, basically so I could have better health care. My life changed.
Now we have affordable rent, pensions, and I can just go to the doctor when I need to. My German health insurance has no deductible,
no co-pay, and it comes to me from a state program made specifically
for freelance artists. Sometimes I need a prescription that is not covered by my insurance, and it costs a whopping fifteen euros. When I
come back to LA every year (where I live during the winter), my
friends marvel at how healthy I seem, how strong. I miss LA every

day, feel bereft that I don't live here year round, but I also know it's not possible. America is an unlivable place for nearly all of its citizens, but especially the disabled. Very, very few people have the privilege I have, which made living in America a choice.

I remember that I had an appointment with my new German doctor on November 9, 2016, the day after the US election. I arrived as if shell-shocked by the news of Trump winning. I sat in the waiting room and stared at the wall. When she called me in, the first thing she asked was how I was doing with the news. Then she told me, "If you ever need anything, if you start to feel bad when you think of him and you need to talk, you can always come here. No appointment necessary." It was the first time in my adult life that I thought a doctor's office might be a place of care.

I will not say that, since I've moved away from America, I am now cured or healed or any other ableist conclusion to this narrative, because none of that is true. I still have chronic illnesses and chronic pain that I need to manage every day, and I still have flares that level me for months. What I will say is that living in a society that supports my body and its needs has proven almost inexplicably different from living in one that did the opposite. But the difference is not immeasurable—it is the difference between my being able to live or not.

4.

The early instigation for this project of a "Sick Woman Theory," and how it found its name, arrived from a few sources. I was moved to write mostly because I felt swarmed with ideas, and the language attendant to them, that I disagreed with and wanted more critique around. Like any good instigator, they sparked my fury and made me want to fight. The primary idea was how illness, disability, and

vulnerability *feminize*—e.g., render "weaker" and "more fragile"—
any person regardless of gender who requires, or is defined by, care.
That disability and femininity are co-constructed, and why—what
and whom this benefits—got stuck in my throat. It did not intuitively
make sense to me to say that the sick are weak because being sick is
fucking metal. It has nothing to do with weakness and everything to
do with blood, shit, agony, vomit, pus, pain, and death. What narrative does it serve, then, to denigrate the sick to the sphere historically
occupied by women? The one kept out of the public sphere? The one
not legible as political?

Another instigator was my desire to create a response to Audrey
Wollen's "Sad Girl Theory," which proposes a way of redefining historically feminized pathologies into modes of political protest for
girls. Critical of Sad Girl Theory's centering of whiteness, beauty,
heteronormativity, and middle-class resources, I started to think
through the question of what happens to the Sad Girl who is poor,
queer, and not white, when—*if*—she grows up. Although I understand the impulse behind pretty girls taking selfies in hospital gowns
in their doctors' offices, I can't help but wince at them. I think about
how I waited a year to see a specialist and never did because my
insurance wouldn't cover it. I think about how lucky these pretty
white Sad Girls are to be able to afford to go to the doctor at all.

While reading Kate Zambreno's *Heroines* at the time, I felt an
itch to fuck with the concept of heroism that gets leveraged by white
feminism. I loved the premise of Zambreno's book—a reclaiming
of the wives and mistresses of twentieth-century art and literature
who'd been institutionalized and/or pathologized as crazy and hysterical for what was essentially their talent—but as I made my way
through chapter upon chapter of Zambreno's writing about white
women through the lens of a normatively patriarchal heroism, I
felt my excitement be replaced by a familiar scowling. The cover

of Zambreno's book features a collage of people like Simone de Beauvoir, Jane Bowles, Sylvia Plath—and Nina Simone is front and center, the only person who is not white. I kept waiting for the chapter on Nina, and when it didn't come, I closed the book, simmering with rage. I wanted to propose a figure with traditionally antiheroic qualities—namely illness, idleness, and inaction—as capable of being the symbol of a grand theory, but I also wanted to recuperate such a heroine from the white supremacy and cis-heteronormative patriarchy that normally attends her. I wanted to dig into the apparatus that differentiates between the "sick woman" of the white upper class, and the "sickening women" of the non-white working class, a notion expressed in Deirdre English and Barbara Ehrenreich's 1973 book *Complaints and Disorders: The Sexual Politics of Sickness.* I wanted to follow how this has accelerated, especially under the logic of eugenics wrought by COVID-19, which saw lives categorized as disposable, based on their class, race, gender, and disability.

Not all the instigations came from things that stoked my fury. If Sick Woman Theory has a guardian godmother, it is Audre Lorde. Her writing on erotics is as formative to this text as her writing on her own cancer. What so impresses me about Lorde is how she lets herself fall open, with curiosity and questions as much as in pain and despair, but never abandons her body. Rather, she insists on its aliveness, what it needs and wants, how it hurts and how it pleasures. I love her most for how she insisted on survival for herself and those who were never meant to survive.

With these instigators and godmothers, Sick Woman Theory was born as a manifesto for those who were never meant to survive, for those who must live in a reality that is unbearable but which nevertheless must be borne. It is for those who are faced with an untenable amount of vulnerability and fragility every day, who have to fight for their experiences to be not only politically valued, but first made visible as such. It's for my fellow sick and crip crew. You know who you are, even if you've not been attached to a diagnosis. One of the aims of Sick Woman Theory is to resist the notion that one needs to be legitimated by an institution, so that they can try to fix you according to their terms. You don't need to be fixed, my queens—it's the world that needs the fixing.

I offer this as a call to arms and a testimony of recognition. I hope that my thoughts can provide articulation and resonance, a rallying cry, a mirror as much as a door, tools of survival and resilience, a bed in which to rest.

For those of you who are not chronically ill or disabled, Sick Woman Theory asks you to stretch your empathy this way. To face us, to listen, to see. I ask you not to turn away from the guarantee that you, inevitably, will join us.

5.

Sick Woman Theory is an insistence that most modes of political protest are internalized, lived, embodied, and often invisible. Sick Woman Theory redefines existence in a body as something that is primarily and always vulnerable, following from Judith Butler's work on precarity and resistance. Because Butler's premise insists that a body is defined by its vulnerability, not temporarily affected by it, the implication is that it is continuously reliant on infrastructures of support in order to endure, and so we need to reshape the world around this fact. Sick Woman Theory maintains that the body and mind are sensitive and reactive to regimes of oppression— particularly our current regime of neoliberal, white-supremacist, imperial-capitalist, cis-heteropatriarchy. Sick Woman Theory argues that all our bodies and minds carry the historical trauma of oppression, and that, although they manifest in each of us differently, these differences ought not to be erased or flattened into any totalizing condition. Sick Woman Theory claims that it is the world itself that is making and keeping us sick.

To take the term "woman" as the subject-position of this work is a strategic, all-encompassing embrace and dedication to the particular. Though the identity of "woman" has erased and excluded many (especially women of color and trans/non-binary/gender-fluid people), I choose to use it because it still represents the un-cared-for, the secondary, the oppressed, the non-, the un-, the less-than. The problematics of this term will always require critique, and I hope that Sick Woman Theory can help undo those problematics in its own way. I loved Andrea Long Chu's thesis in *Females*, that everyone is female and everyone hates it. I'm inspired to use the word "woman" because it can still be radical to be a woman in the twenty-first century. I use it to honor a dear friend of mine who came out as gender-fluid in her mid-thirties. For her, what mattered the most was to be able to call herself a "woman," to use the pronouns "she/her." She didn't want surgery or hormones; she loved her body and her big dick and didn't want to change any of it—she only wanted the word. That the word itself can be an empowerment, a transgression, an insurgency, a problem, an honor, is the spirit in which Sick Woman Theory is named.

The Sick Woman is an identity and body that can belong to anyone denied the privileged existence—or the cruelly optimistic promise of such an existence—of the white, straight, healthy, neurotypical, upper- and middle-class, cis- and able-bodied man who makes his home in a wealthy country, has never not had health insurance, and whose importance to society is everywhere recognized and made explicit by that society; whose importance and care dominates that society, at the expense of everyone else.

The Sick Woman is anyone who does not have this guarantee of care.

The Sick Woman is the person upon which care that is in fact a tool of eugenics—care that masks control, surveillance, and domination—is inflicted.

The Sick Woman is told that, to this society, her survival does not matter.

The Sick Woman is the person whose suffering, rather than instigating support, is the very thing that pathologizes her.

The Sick Woman is all of the "dangerous" and "in danger," "badly behaved," "crazy," "incurable," "traumatized," "disordered," "diseased," "chronic," "uninsurable," "wretched," "undesirable," and altogether "dysfunctional" bodies belonging to women, Black and Indigenous people and people of color, poor, ill, neuroatypical, disabled, queer, trans, and gender-fluid people, who have been historically pathologized, hospitalized, institutionalized, brutalized, rendered "unmanageable," and therefore made culturally illegitimate and politically invisible.

The Sick Woman is the elderly or already sick person that society fed to COVID first.

The Sick Woman is a Black trans woman having panic attacks while using a public restroom, in fear of the violence awaiting her.

The Sick Woman is the child of parents whose Indigenous histories have been erased, who carries in their body the trauma of generations of colonization and violence.

The Sick Woman is an unhoused person, especially one with any kind of disease and no access to treatment, whose only access to mental-health care is a seventy-two-hour hold in the county hospital.

The Sick Woman is a mentally ill Black woman whose family called the police for help because she was suffering an episode, and who was murdered in police custody. Her name is Tanisha Anderson.

The Sick Woman is a fifty-year-old gay man who was raped as a teenager and has remained silent and shamed, believing that men can't be raped.

The Sick Woman is a disabled person who couldn't go to the lecture on disability rights because it was held in a venue without accessibility.

The Sick Woman is a white woman with chronic illness rooted in sexual trauma who must take painkillers in order to get out of bed.

The Sick Woman is a straight man with depression who's been medicated (managed) since early adolescence and now struggles to work the sixty hours per week that his job demands.

The Sick Woman is a trans man whose transness and masculinity are called delusional, diseased, dangerous.

The Sick Woman is the queer person, the gender-nonconforming person, whose gender and identity are seen as pathologies and problems.

The Sick Woman is someone with a chronic illness whose family and friends tell them they should exercise more.

The Sick Woman is a queer woman of color whose activism, intellect, rage, and depression are seen by white society as unlikable attributes of her personality.

The Sick Woman has been in therapy for years with a therapist who tunnels into her every childhood trauma but has not once brought up capitalism as a cause of her suffering.

The Sick Woman is a Black man killed in police custody, and officially said to have severed his own spine. His name is Freddie Gray.

The Sick Woman is a veteran suffering from PTSD on the months-long waiting list to see a doctor at the VA.

The Sick Woman has been purposefully maimed by her colonizer's military, her population kept in a state of debility so as to be easier to control.

The Sick Woman is a single mother, emigrated without papers to the "land of the free," shuffling between three jobs in order to feed her family, and finding it harder and harder to breathe.

The Sick Woman is the refugee.

The Sick Woman is the abused child.

The Sick Woman is the neuroatypical person whom medicine is trying to "cure."

The Sick Woman is the starving.

The Sick Woman is the dying.

And, crucially, the Sick Woman is whom capitalism needs to perpetuate itself.

Why?

Because to stay alive, capitalism cannot be responsible for our care—its logic of exploitation requires that some of us die. For capitalism to support care would be the end of capitalism.

"Sickness" as we speak of it today is a capitalist construct, as is its perceived binary opposite, "wellness." Under capitalism, the "well" person is the person well enough to go to work. The "sick" person is the one who is not well enough to work.

What is so destructive about this conception of wellness as the default, as the standard mode of existence, is that it invents illness as temporary. When being sick is an abhorrence to the norm, it allows us to conceive of care and support in the same way.

Care and support, in this configuration, are only required sometimes. When sickness is temporary, care and support are not normal.

Here's an exercise: Go to the mirror, look yourself in the face, and say out loud, "To take care of you is not normal. I can only do it temporarily."

Saying this to yourself will merely be an echo of what the world repeats all the time.

What would happen if we decided to say the opposite?

6.

The most anti-capitalist protest is to care for another and to care for yourself. To take on the historically feminized and therefore invisible practice of nursing, nurturing, caring. To take seriously each other's vulnerability and fragility and precarity, and to support it, honor it, empower it. To protect each other, to enact and practice a community of support. A radical kinship, an interdependent sociality, a politics of care.

Because, once we are all ill and confined to the bed, sharing our stories of what helps, what we need, how we cope, what makes it feel better, bearing witness to each other's tales of trauma, prioritizing the parts of our bodies that are sick, pained, expensive, sensitive, difficult, deviant, and fantastic, and there is no one left to go to work, perhaps then, finally, capitalism will screech to its much-needed, long overdue, and motherfucking glorious halt.

The Blast Radius
of Disability

"The blast radius of disability" is a phrase that will make demolishing, bone-deep sense if you're in it already. Unless born with a disability, you are like many to whom it happens because of an injury, illness, or diagnosis. In these cases, there is a clear before and after, your life sliced into two parts—what you used to be like, and what you are now—and disability functions narratively in this story as the dramatic pivot. There is before the blast. There is after. And now there is you in that devouring cloud that won't stop eating everything.

First, it eats the body part that hurts the most; maybe this is more than one part. Then it eats the other parts of you trying to hold this new pain. Then it swallows your whole body and, with it, your sense of who you are. The pith of yourself which feels most purely your own now no longer belongs to you. How unfathomable, your body's recalcitrance against yourself. How churlish of it, of your doggish mind, that they refuse to do what you want them to do. How exactly does this happen—your own capacity severed, as if by a cruel and precise blade, from your will? How can you hope to live at this place, the site where you exploded into what can never be recovered, from now on?

Around this time, searching for language that might rescue you with some utterance of recognition, you might start using the word "disabled" to describe yourself. But you likely do not. You are in the wreckage, debris up to your knees, you don't know who you are. How can this inexplicability be something you will recognize, be recognized by? You've lost people—where did they go? The blast radius is chewing into your loved ones, your partners, friends, family. You start asking for help, trying to explain your new self and all of its embarrassing needs. *I need help, I need someone to carry this for me, open this, move this, I need, need, need.* Many of your sentences now begin with "I can't." Many of them must be built as the question that begins, "Can you?" Maybe you don't ask yet. Or, if you do, you apologize every time, try to make yourself small. You feel you are a terrible burden. You try to suffer the right way, be a good cripple, be the respectable kind of sick person. Your guilt and shame are worse than the disability itself. You hide it whenever you can, you try to pass, perform healthy, capable, abled. As if you could hide something as boundless as the explosion of disability. As if this thing destroying the world as you once knew it could be controlled simply because you wish it so.

Soon, the blast radius of disability bites into your colleagues at work, your boss, your clients. Maybe you tell them you're sick, but you keep it vague. Maybe you tell them, and yourself, that this won't last much longer. You send emails that mention your condition, possibly even ask for support, adjustments that would help you do the work. Above all, you ask for more time.

Perhaps now you start calling yourself disabled. Perhaps you Google words and terms you'd never thought about before. Perhaps you feel unseated, contaminated, when you consider attaching those words to yourself. Maybe you start trying to connect with other disabled people, liking their social media posts, scrolling through their hashtags, reading their work, looking at their art. Perhaps you learn that in the disabled community, some of us like to add "temporarily" to the category of the "abled," for they are simply those for whom the blast has not happened yet. Perhaps you notice that those not yet in their own blast radiuses look at you as if you're no longer human—and then there are those smiling at you, waving at you, through their own debris.

Hopefully, without having to wait too long, you learn about ableism. Hopefully you come to understand that it is the thing that makes disability so much worse, as difficult as that is, because it is the ideology, infesting you as it has infested us all, that has built the world to make us believe there is a way bodies and minds ought to function, and anything that deviates from that invented category of normalcy should be punished, devalued, mocked, dismissed. Perhaps you understand that you now deviate from the category of the normal, the correct, the good, the valuable; and perhaps, for a time, because of this, you believe you deserve to be punished, mocked, and dismissed, that you have lost your value. Perhaps you come to see that this declaration of value is formed by systems that suck, but despite knowing that, some part of you still carries its standards against your own spine and chastises yourself for not measuring up.

Perhaps, from here, you reach for support, and like a kind of rescue, you find it. Perhaps you start advocating, agitating, dreaming political dreams together with others. Perhaps you start thinking, acting, living in solidarity with a community that welcomes you.

Or maybe you don't.

Maybe you are disabled but don't call yourself that. Maybe you use the words "cripple" or "crip" as slurs, "lame" as a word to describe something shitty. Maybe you are trying to love yourself, but it's so hard. Maybe you are in too much pain, too exhausted. Maybe you hate yourself, hate your obstreperous body, your difficult brain. Maybe you disagree with your diagnosis, dispute the pathology assigned to you, don't want to talk about it as something true in your life. Maybe you were at the heart of the blast, but now you've been granted a reprieve, moved as if by grace just beyond its horizon, and you pray with all your might that it won't ever get you again. Maybe if it does, you will feel you've failed, the purest, starkest disappointment you've ever known. Maybe you are undeniably in the blast without hope of ever leaving it, and—but—so—you are too unsupported, discriminated against, and oppressed to be resilient. Maybe when you hear someone praise the value of resilience, you want to smash something—you still sting from all the times trying to be resilient leveled you. Maybe you need to take it day by day, hour by hour. Maybe your hours and days are dominated by pain, fear, dread, and doom. Maybe you want to give up. Maybe you've tried to give up, maybe you will try again. Maybe you feel too broken to ever be repaired. Maybe you *are* too broken to ever be repaired.

Maybe all of that pain, fear, anger, hatred, dread, and doom exists in you alongside your resilience, activism, joy, compassion, courage, and perseverance. Maybe you want to give up and you still keep going. Maybe your self-loathing is riven by moments when you are certain you deserve to exist. Maybe you are deformed and gorgeous, lazy and doing everything you can, malingering and crawling, crutching, dragging, scooting yourself forward, and you need to rest.

Maybe the blast radius of disability destroys everything and also makes new worlds. Maybe these are worlds of paradox: both a radical limitation of what you used to be able to do and an explosion of the horizon around what you thought would ever be possible.

When I was newly disabled, freshly detonated in the blast radius, the good fortune of my life is that other disabled people reached through their mushroom clouds into mine. They'd been disabled longer than I, some from birth. They were artists, thinkers, workers, activists, visionaries, geniuses; they were kind, they were furious, they were good cooks, they took care of animals and their friends, and they taught me all they could. One thing I noticed that they did very well, which I did not yet know how to do, was recognize ableism while it was happening. They could detect it, as if they had X-ray vision, when it swam through my interior and made me punish myself for not living up to an ableist standard. They could elucidate it, like experts in their field, when it occurred in the external world, pointing it out when it appeared in conversations between us, or in larger arenas—social media, culture, movies, politics, urban planning, legislation. As I have continued to live in the blast radius of disability, I have become better at detecting ableism, as if I'm gaining fluency in a language.

This is the same process for coming to critical consciousness about any oppressive ideology—I went through it when I started to learn to speak the languages of abolition, anti-racism, feminism, queer and trans liberation, decolonization, and anti-capitalism. The analogy of learning a language fits: these are no one's mother tongues. In fact they are forbidden languages, and many must persist fugitively. They will always require effort, translation, we'll be clumsy when we speak them, make mistakes, some of us will have to practice in whispers.

It should give us pause to notice that illness and disability—the most universal facts of life—are languages very few of us know how to speak, and, more than that, they are languages we are taught we should not speak in public, and if we do, we must use the language of ableism to do so. Why would this be true?

I love this quote from the scholar Amalle Dublon, writing about my work in 2020, a few months into COVID:

> The thing about illness and uprisings is that they both show up as surprises when they're not. Illness, debility, disability, a pronounced dependency, are the most inevitable, the least surprising, the most commonly held experiences for every living being. Why do they appear so untimely? In one way, the answer is obvious: it's just ableism that makes us turn away from this thing we share. But it's also interesting to think about the form of this surprise, what it is to be jolted by what was there, is always there, all along.

Disability as a surprise, something amazing, not only a decimating eruption. My *Chambers* dictionary defines *surprise* as "the emotion caused by anything sudden or contrary to expectation," and I wonder why something like illness would be contrary to our expectations.

When it first happens, you are swarmed with questions about how and why it could possibly happen. You ask, "Why me? Did I bring it on myself? What did I do to deserve this?" Inconsolably, you want to know how to get back to normal. Cutting the story of your life in half—before you got sick, after you got sick—feels good because it feels causal, chronological, breadcrumbs in the forest that haven't yet been carried away by the birds, you just have to follow them to get back to where you were before. Defining yourself in binaries feels good—binaries are easy to use, after all; quick, simple relief from what is messy—so you understand yourself as having been once healthy/happy/strong/independent, and now you're the opposite. Point A to Point B: a story that goes in one direction.

But the longer you are in the blast radius, the longer you linger in its lucubratory after, the more you start to notice that the totality of it does not move in a straight line. Questions, ambiguity, creep in.

Was there really such a simple plot? Point A to Point B? Healthy to sick? Whole to broken? You will look behind you, expecting that causality to be clearly marked, but it will be evasive, tricky, even gone. Rather than a straight line, there will be a constellation, many points, distant and far. Did Point A even exist? What about all the moments you've been sick, in pain, incapacitated, debilitated before? How to fit those into a linear storyline that moves in only one direction? What about all the movement, the changeability, how you've gone into pain then come out of it, then gone into a new, different kind? How to include all the places of experience within your body that you've discovered, orbited, and to which you've returned?

If there is a Point A, it is you, at the center, and the fact of your disability moves outward in all directions, 360 degrees. Which means it is not a chronological force—or, rather, it is not only that. Time goes haywire in the blast radius of disability. It slows down, stands still, folds back on itself, branches. It is cyclical time, haunted time. It is time shot through with memory, flashbacks, nostalgia, daydreams, nightmares, reassessments of the past, hopes and fears for the future, speculations of what happened, what might still happen. Think of bullet time in *The Matrix*, a 360-degree encircling sweep. In the blast radius of disability, a body like Neo's twists and flails in slow motion, time bent to a crawl while it is also expanded into a cosmos. Bullet time in cinema visualizes, as Dublon writes, "the fantasy of watching lines of contingency become necessity." The way this feels in the blast radius of disability is akin to that swirl of slowness that becomes its own universe, the everything-ness of ourselves pierced by the everything-ness of our environment.

One of the reasons disability is so devastating to capitalism is because the main thing it devastates is chronological, quantitative time. The ableism that capitalism feeds on requires and enforces chronological time, enshrining quantity over quality, dictating eight valuable hours per day, forty hours per week. Time that never deviates from its rote linearity can be flattened into one kind, counted and priced, bought and sold. Time without quality can work ceaselessly, for day is no different than night, winter no different than summer, time soaked through with the need to rest, mourn, care, breathe, no different than time driven by labor and profit. Capitalism loves this kind of time because it needs it in order to work.

Disability, however, operates according to "crip time," a foundational term in the language of disability justice. Alison Kafer describes crip time as the kind of time that "requires reimagining our notions of what can and should happen in time, or recognizing how expectations of 'how long things take' are based on very particular minds and bodies. . . . Rather than bend disabled bodies and minds to meet the clock, crip time bends the clock to meet disabled bodies and minds."

When I'm in the hospital, in flares, or sick in bed, I tend to read math and physics books because it gives me solace to think of a cosmos beyond my own fallible, human one. Because I'm morbid, I also tend to read biographies of creative people who eventually suicided, and there are many from the fields of science and math who fit this category; for they are as creative, dreamy, eccentric, and outlandish as the freakiest artists, writers, and musicians. I often think of Ludwig Boltzmann, the Austrian physicist who first articulated the equation for entropy, what became the second law of thermodynamics: that entropy is a physical constant in any system, determining that heat will cool, disorder will increase. This means that there is an inescapability to time, that it moves in one direction, something physicists call "time's arrow." If a glass falls from a table and breaks on the floor, we cannot reverse this, we cannot go backward from it. Boltzmann eventually killed himself, suffering from what has been retroactively suggested to be bipolar disorder. This is a death hard to disentangle from the life's achievement. That the man who first gave mathematical language to the law that everything in the universe will inexorably move toward disorder could not bear the inexorability of his life's arrow is a fact that visits me on dark days.

I also think of Georg Cantor, the Swiss mathematician who invented set theory, saw that there are different *sizes* of infinity, which means that there are many different infinities. He saw the infinity of whole numbers, where you can add one to any number no matter how big. And he saw the infinity between those numbers, where you can divide by any number no matter how big. He saw that you can fit these inside each other, and make these sets themselves infinite—the large and small infinities, each infinity infinite. How to even comprehend this? Cantor also suicided.

I am not going to say here that you should move heaven, earth, and the underworld to find a way to only ever be happy about the different infinities of your disability, the inevitable entropy of your chronic illness, all the determined terminuses of how your painful, malfunctioning body and mind won't obey you. I am not going to tell you that these conditions can be overcome if you just believe in yourself. There will be no narrative arc that swoops upward at the end. I am not in the business of selling triumph.

What I will suggest is that, when you can, maybe be curious about why your disability makes you hate yourself. Think about why this is different than your symptoms. Where does that impulse come from? Who, what, taught you to do that? What purpose does it serve?

If I am in business, maybe it's the one where I peddle instruments that might help you see vast distances, the large-scale organizations to systems and their patterns, the different sizes of infinities. And once you start seeing them, may I suggest that finding ways to move your perspective around, to find new vantage points, more ways of perceiving, like the camera that surrounds Neo, might help remind you that a blast radius, as much as it is caused by a devastating explosion, is also a powerful repositioning of matter that grows, which means it makes more volume, more space that such matter can occupy, rather than less.

The blast radius of disability lasts a long, long, long time. Some of us who've lived in it awhile would say it lasts forever. Some would point out that if all of us are living in our own blast radiuses that unceasingly keep expanding, won't it be true that at some point the whole world will be eaten by this?

There is a term for when a planet's orbit takes it close enough to the sun that we can no longer see the planet—"*cazimi*." The word "*cazimi*" is a Latin transliteration of the Arabic term "*kaṣmīmī*," which means "as if in the heart." Some myths explain this in narratives that have the sun eating that planet.

In the blast radius of disability, are you the planet? Which sun ate you? Whose heart are you close to now? Whose heart are you inside of?

In Defense of De-Persons

"We must now collectively undertake a rewriting of knowledge as we know it."

SYLVIA WYNTER

I want to make a defense of "de-persons." Because—according to the institutions of the medical-industrial complex—I am one.

I have been diagnosed with several conditions that mean that, at various times, my body, self, environment, and the world do not feel real; i.e., they do not feel as though they belong to me. It's that I am outside of them, detached, hovering above, it is all unfamiliar, strange, and I cannot lay claim to anything. This is described in the clinical symptoms termed "depersonalization" and "derealization." The former characterizes a feeling that I am disconnected from my own thoughts, feelings, or body, while the latter describes this same sense of disconnection in relationship to other people, objects, and surroundings outside of myself. The official language of the diagnostic criteria in the *Diagnostic and Statistical Manual of Mental Disorders* (DSM) is surprisingly poetic: that you "feel like a robot," or that "your head is wrapped in cotton," or that "you're living in a movie or a dream," that the "people you care about . . . [are] separated by a glass wall." Depersonalization is about an internal dislocation, while derealization is an estrangement from the external, but both describe a state where things do not feel to be under one's control, which means they do not feel "real."

Note the logical leap here from a clinical perspective: that what cannot be controlled ceases to be real. So, is controlling reality what determines that it is real?

A defense of de-persons asks about this relationship between control and reality, but it locates the crux of the question, not at the site where these might converge within an individual, as if that place were a neutral, ahistorical ground each of us stands on. A defense of de-persons worms its inquiry into the soil. Who works that land? Who owns it? Who has claimed it as their own despite who else might be standing there?

I am not a representative for a specific kind of experience; I am *presentative* of it. That is, I'm doing it right now, in front of you and myself. I am a proponent of aporia: thinking with holes in it, thinking that contradicts itself, that circles back, that reveals the knotting and fraying and reweaving of an argument so that it contains all of its digressions, dead ends, detours, so that you can see them, and so that I won't forget how I got here. It's a way of marking movement, where I've been, where I aim to go. It marks my address, both the place at which I live, and from where I speak to you. My address is from the position of a de-person, which means it's an affirmation of messiness, a testimony of and to disorder, an honoring of incompleteness.

A defense of a de-person could be said to be an embodiment of incompleteness, a demonstration of wayward thinking, a performance of *un*-comprehension, a refusal of mastery at all.

To define something is the act of fixing it, limiting it, establishing the boundary around it. It's from the Latin "*definire*": "to set boundaries to." It draws a line, determining what's enclosed within this boundary and what is not, orienting an inside and outside.

To claim is to insist on the truth of something—a statement, a monetary value, a piece of land, a right, an ownership. Claim comes from the Latin "*clamare*," which means "to cry out." How gorgeous, that urgency, that desperation, the many reasons one might be compelled to cry out, to insist on their truth.

There are many ways a thing can be defined or claimed, but I'm most concerned with the question of whether this happens *to* a thing or is initiated by itself. Does it have a self? Does it *own* a self?

My diagnoses come from doctors who follow the guidelines of the American Psychiatric Association (APA), which bases its conclusions on the *DSM*. This means that the APA and the *DSM* are the institutions that have had the most influence in my life in terms of how my personhood has been perceived, constructed, consolidated, policed, and immured by the medical-industrial complex, which means that my personhood as such has been defined—claimed, controlled—and had its reality made by them.

There are many ways to talk about "personhood," and many of them are discourses about what *isn't* personhood, *who does not qualify* to be part of that category, and why. If I'm going to wander around personhood, I've got to reckon with universality, because universality is the foundation for how we construct "persons" at all. It's the bedrock beneath the boundaries that are inscribed, the claims that are made.

Sara Ahmed explains it: "The universal is a structure not an event. It is how those who are assembled are assembled. It is how an assembly becomes a universe . . . The universal is the promise of inclusion . . . Universalism is how some of us can enter the room. It is how that entry is narrated as magical; as progress."

I am guilty of hoping for such magic. I've played the game of universalism, as we all have; it's the main game in town, has claimed all the soil we stand on.

But this is me trying to get out.

In December 2015, I had a dissociative panic attack for the first time in three years without my medication on hand. It was in the Copenhagen aquarium called Den Blå Planet, which has been designed to make one feel as though underwater. Stupid of me to forget my meds, especially because for twenty years I'd had the recurring nightmare of being underwater in an ocean of black water, but I'd not needed them for so long, maybe I thought I was cured. One enters Den Blå Planet as though being submerged into a sea cave. Inside, there is dim blue light. Silhouetted shadows of fish, sharks, and whales are projected onto the ceiling. One can peer up at them circling overhead. The lapping, sloshing sounds of water stream from hidden speakers, but they are mostly drowned out by the voices of children running around, darting like little fishes.

In the bathroom, where I waited for the attack to pass, the only thoughts in my brain were *thing, thing, thing*. There was blue—blue paint on the wall of the stall?—which equaled "thing." Each time the door slammed, it was with such ferocity that "my" body felt ripped—into two things, three, many. The sound of the hand dryer, even more forceful and splitting—*thing, thing, thing*.

Language breaks down (I cannot speak or understand what is being spoken to me during these states) but not because it never existed, or because it is nothing, or because it seems inadequate in a postmodern way, but because it *uncreates*. As Simone Weil puts it, decreation is "to make something created pass into the uncreated."

Something that had been created—something that had created *me*—has passed into its twinned shadow state. No longer is the first-person intact; the "I" dissolves, and all the boundaries around everything that have hitherto contained them are drained of their solidity.

A few years before this, I'd finally sought treatment for these episodes. They'd been happening to me since I was a child. I'd launch myself out of the room, the house, or crouch in a corner, hide in the bathtub, tears flowing like the waters of Lourdes, unhooked from my body and agency while I thrashed against the parts of me I could no longer move, and hours would pass until someone found me or I became locatable to myself again. After getting diagnosed with depersonalization/derealization disorder, the therapist I was assigned to see, in what was one of the best strokes of luck I've ever been granted, shrugged away the pathology I was now attached to and offered another approach. She said, "In another time, in another culture, you'd simply be considered a mystic."

I wonder what happened to that time, that culture. Where did they go? What purpose has it served to remove them from the here and now?

Self-possession and self-mastery are the most legible and preferred forms of selfhood within a society built upon the ideology of possession. What the *DSM* and APA configure, and warn against, as a "loss of self-control" can be read as a refusal of the mastery and wholeness that most of our society is built on, what Fred Moten and Stefano Harney have called "the object/ive of enlightenment self-control." That one cannot possess one's own self, it follows, precipitates the necessity of a society that can do it for you. In turn, this instantiates the construct of a self in ownership of itself as what is the most—the only—acceptable kind of person.

The concept of the "person" that has been defined and claimed by universality is one that promises self-determined completeness, wholeness, and power. In other words, that which can be both mastered and *the* master.

This makes me think of the many books I've read on healing trauma, all of them written by white doctors, that inevitably tell me that I have to regain a sense of "self-mastery" if I want to live a "productive" life. In the bestseller *The Body Keeps the Score*, Dr. Van der Kolk asks, and then attempts to answer, the question: "How can people gain control over the residues of past trauma and return to being masters of their own ship?"

Did no one stop and think about using the word "master" in the same sentence as "ship"?

Many of the conditions in the *DSM* are characterized as disorders, not diseases, and it's important to note the clinical difference between the two. It comes down to what's called "etiology," which is the cause for something. If the etiology is known, it's a disease. If no one has a clue, it's a disorder. So, embroidered into their own system of classification is the APA's acknowledgment of both the failure and recursion of its system. They've built in a kind of disclaimer for how they will recognize and validate your experience, and it is based entirely upon their own rules of what they deem recognizable. It has nothing to do with how you might recognize, or feel validated within, or define, your own experience.

The clincher for all disorders and diseases, in terms of psychiatry— that is, when you go from being "well" to "ill"—is when symptoms "impair the individual's ability to function normally." When the normative stops performing is when psychiatry intervenes. But nowhere in the *DSM* is a definition of "normal"—and you'd really think there would be, since so much in its 991 pages seems to rely upon it and what it is not.

In terms of depersonalization/derealization disorder, the DSM-5 has a little moment where it locates itself within the United States and its imperial horizon with the following passage about "Culture-Related Diagnostic Issues": "Volitionally induced experiences of depersonalization/derealization can be a part of meditative practices that are prevalent in many religions and cultures and should not be diagnosed as a disorder. However, there are individuals who initially induce these states intentionally but over time lose control over them and may develop a fear and aversion for related practices."

Then, the following is offered as a "risk and prognostic factor": "There is a clear association between the disorder and childhood interpersonal traumas in a substantial portion of individuals. . . . In particular, emotional abuse and emotional neglect have been most strongly and consistently associated with the disorder."

Aside from emotional abuse and neglect experienced in childhood, the DSM has little to say beyond this passage on symptoms that can be correlated to a cause; that is, *why* someone might experience such feelings. The extent that they allow trauma to reach is only interpersonal—never intergenerational, institutional, societal, political—yet it seems to me that the list of reasons why someone might feel that themself or their world is not real is far more explicable by phenomena that go beyond the interpersonal.

I think of the residents of Flint who had no control over whether they were in possession of the most basic resource needed for their life to be sustained—water fit to drink. I think of Joyce Curnell, a fifty-year-old Black woman who died in a Charleston County jail because she was not given any water, despite repeatedly asking for it. The article about the lawsuit filed on behalf of her family describes her spending the last twenty-seven hours of her life in jail, where she became too sick to eat or call for help. "She vomited all night and couldn't make it to a bathroom, so jailers gave her a trash bag." Instead of possession of her life, the police gave her a trash bag.

It seems to me that it would feel wholly unreal to live in a society that does not secure water fit for you to drink, that lets you die in a prison cell holding a trash bag full of your own vomit.

As we saw in the clause about "volitionally induced experiences," the main problem arises when *control is lost*. However, the agency of the individual person is the primary measure for what kind of control is at stake: the *DSM* and APA are only concerned with *self*-control—not the loss of control, freedom, or agency as it can be affected, granted, rescinded, and mitigated by the state.

When we confront the implications of these examples, we can see the state as a mechanism that *creates* depersonalization and derealization. It detaches one from their surroundings, puts the people they care about on the other side of a wall, makes the world a movie or a dream—this cannot possibly be happening, this cannot be real. It is a device that simultaneously produces and perpetuates de-personhood while negating the possibility of self-control.

So, is this a disorder (cause unknown) or a disease (cause known)?

I'd like to ask the APA: What about depersonalization when the state has made you that way, has removed your agency from yourself, has taken over control of how you are identified, claimed, and thus legitimized? What about derealization when the state has detached your environment from you, dispossessed you of your land, or turned your surroundings into something unbearable, something that cannot possibly be real?

"The self-determined thing cannot be so if it emerges *in a relationship*," Denise Ferreira da Silva writes, emphasis mine, and she has proposed to call those who've been determined by such relation-ality "no-bodies." Neve Mazique-Bianco has called them "invisible theorists." I've called them "Sick Women." Moten and Harney have traced a territory where they reside called "the undercommons" and named a co-present condition for some in that territory as, simply, "blackness."

My main question here is: For those who are *not*, for those who have emerged *in relationship to* rather than via self-determination, for those who are particular and sometimes nowhere rather than uni-versal, for those in the undercommons, for us "invisible theorists" and for us "no-bodies," how does the *affirmation* of *de-person-ness* offer a new form of political agency?

In capitalism, the primary purpose of one's life—both ideologically and materially—is to accumulate value. This is done through one's labor but of course relies upon the exploitation of the labor of others and various resources of all kinds. As Silvia Federici has argued, such exploitation requires an *accumulation of differences*, beyond Marx's "primitive accumulation" of natural and labor resources, to justify itself: self/other, white/black, male/female, society/nature, us/them, life/death.

Within such a system, the person who is unable to labor *because of their difference from the normatively ableist well* is considered not only useless because they cannot work to accumulate value, but they also stand in direct opposition to two important tenets of capi-talist ideology. The first is the premise that capitalist technology can take command of the body. As Carolyn Lazard has written:

> Capitalism objectifies the body. It views the body as an exploit-able resource and attempts to render it indestructible and

unstoppable with the aid of technology.... And yet as advanced capitalism has deemed the physical body an obsolete, outdated tool, the body still remains. It continues to fail under capitalist conditions and gets pathologized as illness. The body is another inconvenience that must be enhanced and optimized.

The second tenet the de-person antagonizes is the *promise* that neoliberalism can reduce everything, including the decision to survive, down to personal choice, a matter of willpower, and a problem the market can solve.

In neoliberalism, "wellness" is a prevarication; it usually stands in for "life," but life in terms of wealth, race, gender, power, and, primarily, *ability*. Wellness in this context is paradoxically both an innate moral virtue and an individual's own responsibility to maintain.

In the fall of 2015, I was a research fellow in a project called *at land's edge*, under the mentorship of Fred Moten. I'd sent him an early draft of "Sick Woman Theory," and we met twice for coffee while I was working on this essay. In that wonderfully generous way that Fred has at destabilizing the presumptions you don't know yourself to be making, he gently suggested that "Sick Woman Theory" had set up another cruel optimism of a humanism, making a discrete category of the "Sick Woman" to consolidate individuals under a new kind of universal subject. At the café, when he said that, my stomach dropped because I knew he was right. Over the years, I've noticed how often I have wanted the universal to consolidate my individuality, when what makes more sense is to simply be okay without it.

In our meeting, Fred pointed out that the etymological root for the words "privilege" and "private" is the same. It's from the Latin *"privus,"* which means "individual." That an individual can have privilege is also the extent to which such an individual can be private.

Fred said, "Privilege is a radical *incapacity* for sociality."

The affirmation of de-person-ness that I'm proposing is not so much a refusal of individualism, of discreteness, of personhood as such, but rather an affirmation of *in*discreteness, of a tremendous indiscretion. De-governable, de-master-able, de-possessed, de-owned, de-owning, de-private, de-privileged, de-individual.

The political manifestation of this, I think, is a radical sociality. Rather than one universal throne in a room with all of us scratching at the door to be let in, there could be a bunch of chairs strewn all over the place for everyone to sit in.

Which will certainly be a big fucking mess.

Fred also said something that I've done my best to live by: "Work is simply the document of a practice. And the document should never be more important than the practice."

Let's try it?

I once had a therapist who practiced zazen meditation. She was in her sixties or seventies, wore all black, round glasses, and had shaved her white hair to her scalp. She wrote poetry. She took no shit. She told me that one day I could hope to watch my emotions flow by me like a river. I'd be the stone in the river, and they'd sluice by: there goes joy, there goes sorrow, it would all flow. It sounded great at the time—to not be so tossed, to stay rooted even while getting wet.

But can this analogy scale up to include other people's emotions to which I bear witness, participate, hold? What about watching someone having a panic attack on the bus? What about what I watch others feel in videos on the internet—their wars, their celebrations? Should we be like the water? Should we sink into the deep together or stay on the surface so as to spread out? What possible stone could there be for us? What I mean is, can it be political?

Get Well Soon

The language of illness is a language of platitudes. Get well soon. Hoping for a quick recovery. Sending love. Take care in this tough time. Adjectives become few: *quick, tough*. The same verbs are used over and over: *get, send, take, hope*.

The language of revolutions is also one of platitudes. Ain't no power like the power of the people 'cause the power of the people won't stop, say what. The people united will never be divided. No, no, we won't go. No matter what they are asking for, protesters chant the same chants, their signs shout the slogans of before.

When we are desperate for change, as we are both in illness and insurrection, our language drains of complexity, becomes honed to its barest essentials. We feel we cannot waste time with adjectives or similes or hypotaxis. No, we have a message to get across, and it's crucial and immediate; we can't afford to risk its meaning getting lost in too many words. As illness and revolution persist, though, the language made in them and about them deepens, lets in more nuance, absorbed in the acutely human experience of encountering one's limits at the site of the world's end. Are these my own limits, or are they the limits of the world?

As they share a quality of language, illness and revolution both exist in similar kinds of time, the kind that feels crushingly present. The time is now, and it is long. However, the temporality in each can feel quite different, at first.

In illness, time slows down so extremely as to become still and unbearably heavy. For the sick person, or someone caring for the sick, time freezes, hardening around the body, locking everything into this new center of gravity, bracing in the blast radius. All that can be done is to wait. The future gets further and further away, and the present moment—the one soaked in illness—becomes huge and cruel. In illness, the now feels like punishment.

In revolution, when it's still young and fervent, time churns around the fact that the time is now. No longer will we do what we've done in the past, from today forward, we will! And it doesn't matter what comes next, its function is the same. The promise of and hope for change, the zeal for a new tomorrow—these innovate the now, and the now becomes a joyous defiance of what has felt most locked in and limited about the future.

At some point, though, the revolutionary now shifts toward the now of illness, wedged into what Arendt called "between past and future," never-ending, waiting for change to come, waiting, still, waiting. Conversely, as many chronically ill and disabled people know, the now of illness soon radicalizes, reveals its subversive power, and produces a politic.

We tend to place illness and revolution opposite each other on the spectrum of action: illness is on the end of inaction, passivity, and surrender, while revolution is on the end of movement, surging and agitating. But maybe this spectrum is more like an ouroboros: one end feeding the other, transforming into, because of, made of the same stuff as the other.

Many thought the revolution, when it came, would look like how it's looked before: a protest in the streets, some good looting and riots, a coup, a mutiny. The world has been anticipating the fury that's been building up, in everyone and everything, about everyone and everything, and we've ached for it to boil over and erupt.

Now might be a good time to rethink what a revolution can look like. Perhaps it doesn't look like a march of angry, abled bodies in the streets. Perhaps it looks something more like the world standing still because all the bodies in it are exhausted—because care has to be prioritized before it's too late.

Those of us for whom sickness is an everyday reality have long known about its revolutionary potential. We've known that a revolution can look like a horizontal body in a bed, unable to go to work. We've known that it might look like hundreds of thousands of bodies in bed, forcing the exploitative machinery of the world to a stop, separating life's value from capitalist productivity. We've known that a revolution can look like the labor of a single nurse keeping the patients in her ward alive, or the labor of a single friend helping you buy groceries. We've known that it can look like the labor of nursing and care expanded exponentially, all of us reaching out to everyone we know, everyone we know reaching out to theirs. We've known that a revolution can look like a community pitching in five dollars per person for someone's medical treatment—we've wondered when that community would notice just how revolutionary the act of communal care is.

In just a few weeks, COVID-19 changed the world into something unrecognizable. The interminable now of illness bore down upon us, and we watched the world's ableism rise to meet it. The world's ableism has always been a thing; it just got much closer to those who normally don't feel it.

What we watched happen with COVID-19—and are still watching—is what happens when care insists on itself, when the care of others becomes mandatory, when it takes up space and money and labor and energy. See how hard it is to do? How impossible to sustain as the priority? The world isn't built to give care freely and abundantly. It tried, but look how alien a concept it was, how hard it was to make happen. For some of us, life with chronic illnesses and disability had already trained us to cope with isolation, constraint, boredom, and fear of what would happen if we went outside our homes, so lockdown didn't feel that much different on a day-to-day level. It felt like the world had slowed down to crip time, the kind of time we live in always. In some ways, I liked that this pace had arrived for everyone else. I noticed that people were gentler with each other, the pressure was lower to respond to emails or be productive at all, and everyone seemed to understand and acutely feel that life is very hard, how so many of us are struggling just to get by. I liked how everyone asked how everyone was doing and understood that the answer would probably be grim. I liked that there was suddenly space in public to say you were tired, sad, suffering, sick, confused, broke, and to demand that society make room, make support, for that. But this dream of collective care and anti-ableist living floundered quickly, and things went back to "normal" while people still died of COVID by the thousands. We returned to the ways in which we separate ourselves from those who are sick, debilitated, dying—rather than insist on staying connected, interdependent, united with, and for, each other.

The reason why care is revolutionary, and specifically revolutionary for everyone and not only a few, is precisely because of this requirement of interconnectedness. Revolutionary care will take all of us—it will take all of us operating on the principle that if only some of us are well, none of us are—which demands that we live, not for the myth of the individual's autonomy, but as though we are all interconnected. Which we are. In care, we know our limits because they are the places where we meet each other. My limit is where you meet me, yours is where I find you, and, at this meeting place, we are linked, made of the same stuff, transforming into one because of the other.

Care so often feels as though it has to be given to you by someone else, and this can also seem how revolution feels. We wait for the change to be given to us by those in control, and we hope for those in power to come to their senses. So many activists know that as power can be taken, it can be taken back. As care can be given, we can also take it. I've always found succor in the fact that the words "caregiver" and "caretaker" mean the same thing. We take care, we give care, and it can be contagious, it can spread. It shows us that the limit of the world is always a place to be exploded, pushed against, transformed. Meet me there, at the end, where there is give and take, and let's follow each other into the next beginning.

Notes on Activism
(aka Notes on Failure)

The thing about activism is that it's hard. It's exhausting. It's frustrating. It burns you out. Any activist can tell you this but, for various reasons, among those of us committed to activism, it's not much talked about in public. We try to place the emphasis elsewhere, on more impressive accomplishments, exalted goals. We should be offering instigation to join the cause, sparks to light the flame, calling people in with the incandescent persuasion of our ethical force, not all the ways the fire often dims, sputters out. At the monthly meetup with our collective, we're not supposed to spend too much time talking about how, say, the organizers got in an argument because one of them said something problematic, or the website broke so no one could donate, or only four people came to the last workshop, or there's disagreement about how to spend the grant money, etc. One ought not, seems to be the unspoken rule, give too much space to this—the messy reality of how activism works—not least because it will scare off those who have not yet joined us, give them even more reason to sit on the sidelines, hands clean, resting in the purity of their neutrality.

The other reason is because it reminds us how the world actually is, not how we would like it to be. It demonstrates how the spark to light the flame of our conviction is hard to keep lit because so much of activism can feel like the opposite of action: it's a lot of little labors that are invisible but necessary; it's so many obstacles and a fuck ton of waiting; it's things not working out the way we'd hoped; and it's coming to terms with why our attempts failed. If you're in it long enough, it's coming to terms with the fact that we may always fail. It's persisting in the face of this and still choosing to try again. And this, for those of us who've been doing the work for a while, is a difficult truth to bear because it emphasizes how much more work there is to do. When you're trying to make the world not only a better place but an entirely new one, being depleted, discouraged, and dismayed seems wrong. Where does fatigue fit into insurrection?

It might not be good to air our dirty laundry like this, because it draws attention away from what is important and will keep our numbers from expanding. There are so many reasons why people won't join the cause—won't sign the petition, won't like or share or repost or even read the information, won't participate in the boycott, won't go to the march, won't go to the meeting, won't donate, won't call their representatives, won't get into a discussion with those they disagree with, won't carry a sign, won't read a book, won't watch a video, won't change their mind, won't change their behavior, won't change how they speak, won't say something, won't do something— maybe I shouldn't be giving them more.

To those on the outside, activism looks insufferably self-serious, self-righteous, and is always prone to hypocrisy. So, you tweet about Black Lives Matter, but you buy your anti-racism books from Amazon? So, you preach about the climate catastrophe, but you flew on an airplane to go on vacation? So, you are pro-Palestine, but you have not boycotted any of the corporations that support Israel?

Are these standards useful?

In my opinion it's better to risk hypocrisy, to try and fail, try and make mistakes, try again, than not to. What is gained, proved, accomplished by the not-trying? What happens by doing nothing?

When it comes to measuring the success of activism, I've learned that the more exhausted you are, the more successful your activism has probably been. This is because, at its heart, activism is about trying to do something that's never been done before—and the most important part of that sentence is the word "trying." Exhaustion is how you know that you tried, that you gave it all you had.

Insurrection and fatigue are often seen as opposites that we oscillate between, rather than parallel states running alongside each other, and there seems to be a sort of valuation about which collects, requires, and produces more care. There is the urge to distinguish between taking care of others versus taking care of oneself, as if the essence of activism flows more easily into one but dries up when we tip toward the other. Because of burnout, many withdraw from activism to rest and recharge, and this is often understood to be a time when they are no longer helping or contributing to the cause. This produces the question of who, in any collective movement, is more important to attend to: oneself or others. I'm not sure how useful this framing is either. I'm not arguing that there is no difference between self and other, nor that the times when we coil into ourselves in exhaustion ought to be seen as a kind of productive participation. Rather I wonder what is implied when we understand insurrection as only ever being animated by robustness, excluding all the other activities, feelings, and states it produces. I want to—I must—make room for what I know to be true of activism: that it is abundant with, propelled by, and forged through the ways in which it fails, far more often than its successes.

Failure has become a thing that successful people in successful fields like to talk about. In those fields, which champion success as capitalism defines it, failure is positioned as valuable because it teaches you something and pushes you to be "better." To be fair, on the left, there is a romanticization of failure as a mode of queer resistance, a currency of refusal that turns away from the hegemonic insistence on success, striving, productivity. These are all right for some, I guess, but I prefer the idea of failure being neither good nor bad, just a fact of life, what comes after what is done. There is exhaustion and failure in this work because those are there when you try to do anything.

Activism is about radically redoing how we do things, and have done them for generations, so, duh, obviously it will fail far more than otherwise, because no one has ever done this before. Yes, we are building on the work that came before, and thank god it's there to support us—thank god!—but not only is what we're trying to do new, but it agitates against a world that doesn't want to change. We want to destroy and remake structures in direct opposition to us. Why would those in power, who benefit from the systems that protect them, want to change? Why would they want to lose this fight?

Let me suggest something that might sound catastrophically pessimistic: If capitalism in all its nefarious guises is our opponent, then yo, we are absolutely, 100 percent, *going to lose*. This opponent is bigger than us, faster, stronger, meaner, and he fights dirty. *And* he has rigged the entire game!

Yo. We are absolutely, 100 percent, *going to lose*.

Now, knowing that, what happens if we do not forfeit but still get in the ring? What happens if we know we're gonna lose the fight but we do not give up? Our strategy will change. We will train differently, develop specific skills, cultivate necessary tricks. We will brace our-selves; we will know we are outmatched, in the wrong weight class; we will expect to be frustrated, overwhelmed, crushed. We will learn and adapt. We will do what we can while we can, how we can; and we will not surrender.

I like thinking that activism *will always fail*, because it means that the decision to take action, to act as though what we do matters, even in the face of certain defeat, is its own purpose. It's not going to get you paid or bring you victory or prepare you for some next success. It's not going to demonstrate your purity, your moral superiority. It's not about what you say, dream, or hope for. It's about what we can do, right here, right now, for each other. It's about starting where you are, not where you wish you were. It is important because what we do and how we do it is important. It's the difference between giving up and not giving up.

This is not nothing. In fact, this might be everything.

Letter to a
Young Doctor

DEAR ERICA,

You wrote me asking if I can think of a way, any way, that healing might happen within the current institution of the medical-industrial complex and its attendant oppressions, of which you are currently a student, set to begin your residency this year. The importance of finding a way is urgent, you wrote, because you will soon be seeing patients who come to you to be healed, in hospitals, ERs, clinics, and you'll give them treatments that will decide their lives. You feel uncertain if your chosen path as a doctor, at this moment in history, can also be a path of healing.

You wrote: "I am someone who will soon be a physician attempting to care for people, and yet I find that I still don't know what healing means."

I could graft myself onto that same sentence, but from a different position: "I am someone who will be the recipient of attempts at care from institutions and practitioners of healing, and yet I find that none of us really know what healing means."

It meant a lot to me that you used the word "attempting."

You are younger than I—twenty-seven, you said. You are the first-generation American child of immigrants and, you pointed out, we share Korean heritage, particularly a grandmother who fled Korea during the war. Although you didn't explicitly state it, I understand the kind of family pressure that probably existed in your life around choosing the right career. Becoming a doctor has a special meaning to immigrant families; it is considered the noblest profession and perhaps the greatest signifier of success in America, although it remains a symbolic promise that comes true only for a few. It reminds me of how, every time I visited my Korean grandmother as a child, she urged me either to marry a rich man or become a doctor. She'd also shake her head severely—no—when I'd ask her if, one day, we might visit her homeland together. As if I were asking her to return to a haunted house.

You asked me a lot of questions in your letter, and they all felt like questions I ask myself. They seem to be variations of asking, "What are we going to do?" which I think is the same as asking, "How can we heal?" I've come to understand that the conflation of these two questions is crucial not only to finding a way toward healing but also toward how political resistance might work, toward justice. Keeping this fact—that healing and justice might be the same—always present in your thoughts is a way, one way, I can think of that might answer your questions.

For some of us, there is a relationship between healing and justice because what oppresses us has also made us suffer trauma and its accompanying symptoms. Oppression, domination, and violence live first and foremost in our bodies. As much as they are ideological systems, their effect is always material; they deal in matter—flesh, bones, blood. They pierce tissue with bullets, crack necks with boots, make stomachs chew on their own acid out of hunger, imprison bodies in small lightless rooms. They flood brains and nervous systems with adrenaline and fear. On the less dramatic side, they work insidiously: they instantiate and re-instantiate memories of unhelpful doctors, social and government workers, and police who are not figures of help or safety but of violence and terror. They invalidate and dismiss experiences of pain and suffering, especially those experiences that they've directly caused. They deny access to medications and therapies, they frighten and alienate with categories that pathologize and discriminate, they construct a world whose very premise insists that suffering, illness, and disability are abnormal and wrong, and that banishes those who experience such stuff.

So, the process of healing is a way of reimagining a political future for the social body as much as it is about finding ways to care for and survive in our individual bodies. And, it should go without saying, bodies are fragile things. That's what makes them different from ideologies—they are bound to matter, they are flesh that can be touched, held, scarred, that can dance and laugh, that will decay, that will remember.

I received your letter months ago and have not been sure how to respond, although I've thought about it every day. I finally started writing a response from a German hospital, during January and February, where I was for three weeks, in the psych ward for depression. It was the longest winter of my life, and it made my life feel so little, even though my life often feels little. For most of my hospitalization, I was unsure that I would survive, and so responding to you felt serious and fateful, something I must take care of if I wasn't going to make it.

This letter, then, is a document of emergency. I wrote it thinking it was one of my last attempts at communication, and in many ways I was trying to communicate to myself as much as I was to you and the questions you asked. If I could articulate something about healing to you, maybe it would articulate healing for me. I wrote it by hand on pieces of printer paper that the nurses gave me from their station. I'd walk down the hallway in my pajamas and knock on the glass. I had to wait for them to unlock the door, then I'd make the gesture of writing by hand because I didn't know the German words. When my partner visited me, I'd ask him to take photos of the pieces of paper I'd written on, in case I couldn't one day take them out of the hospital myself.

It strikes me that I chose to write to you—a stranger—while I was hospitalized when I was speaking and interacting with doctors and nurses multiple times a day about these same questions. Instead of walking down the hallway, tapping on the glass, and trying to have a discussion about the relationship between trauma and justice with the people who are trained professionals in the field of medical care, I directed my voice in your direction—you, whom I've never met, may never meet, who felt very far away across a distance that was dark and unfamiliar. I think it reveals how vast the distance feels between patient and doctor. For patients, it often feels like trying to connect with a stranger with whom you have no chance of actually connecting. Many chronically ill and disabled people face this dilemma. We are forced into long-term relationships that are devoid of the things—trust, intimacy, reciprocity—that a long-term relationship needs to work.

The distance is huge, obscured, and unbreachable, but there's a special terror in it because the distance is often right in front of you, between your face and your doctor's as you sit in the small examination room together. It distorts the exchange of two bodies in close proximity, making a little void that yawns open. It can feel like you're speaking a language that your doctor not only can't understand, but one they care not to hear.

The doctor who admitted me when I arrived at the ER was summoned just for me because he was the only one who spoke fluent English in the psych ward. Because of his generic youthful and

German handsomeness, I nicknamed him Yay-Crew (in German, the *j* is pronounced like a *y*, like my first name). Yay-Crew challenged my stereotype of the uptight German psychiatric doctor because he'd say things like "for sure." Once he cautioned me against a medication because it might "fuck up" my liver. I wanted to trust him, even to like him. We seemed to be of the same age. He laughed, once or twice, at my attempts at a joke. I sometimes imagined that I might run into him outside the hospital (if I was ever released), at an art opening or at the movies, where we could meet on shared ground. "You like this director?" "Yes, I'm a fan! You too?" I don't know if imagining that we might have similar social groups or interests helped me or hurt me, because it was all fantasy. I catch myself wondering about sending him this letter, or my other essays on illness, but then I feel a swift rinse of shame, as if I've been cast as the spurned ex holding on to a false hope. I admonish myself, *But why would he want to know how you're doing? He doesn't care about you.*

I noticed that, when discussing my treatment, he'd state it like this: "What is important for me is that you are stabilized." "What is important for me is that you don't have too many adverse side effects." Always what was important for him. I wondered if he learned this technique in medical school. Are you, Erica, being taught to talk to your patients this way too? He rarely asked me what was important for me; if he did ask questions, it was the perfunctory, "And how are we today?" The vague, elusive, imagined "we" of that sentence felt like a large void that yawned open between us. Nonetheless I tried to insert myself into the conversation. "But how much will it cost?" "But I don't want to do that." It was a struggle of making myself not only have a presence, of making myself be seen and heard and understood, but of persuading him that mine was an important presence, one that mattered, one that he had to consider as much as I had to consider his.

A note I wrote down in the hospital: "What am I doing here? Malingering, lingering." Being chronically ill often feels like all I really have, which is to say all that I own, is radically temporary—a lump of painful, decaying, remembering matter whose existence is composed of different strategies for lingering.

I wonder about the idea of getting better—better for what? To be crying on the kitchen floor again? To be hit by the total absence of my mother's body from this world? To be exhausted by work? To feel the climate catastrophe detonate another day? To read another name of a person murdered by the police?

In our last meeting, on the day I was released, he told me, "You've made a tremendous accomplishment."

It made me laugh. "My tremendous accomplishment is that I didn't kill myself?" I said.

Yay-Crew made a gesture then, a little bow of the head, an opening of the hands in my direction, that I've tried to interpret but I still can't say exactly what it meant. It felt a bit parental: *Go forth now, my child. I trust that you will be okay.* He told me that I could always come back. As if his hospital were a home.

You might wonder what place an emotion like trust has in the science of medicine, but if you take anything from this, I want it to be that trust is the most important thing a doctor and her patient can share, because trust is what keeps people from falling apart, and it's what puts broken ones back together, and in the cases where the brokenness is all there is, trust can offer a small encouragement that the brokenness is bearable—that it can eventually, hopefully, ideally be reframed as not "brokenness" at all, but simply as the different parts that are there to work with. It's the only force I can think of that might alleviate the vast distance between us, as well as the vast distances between the many parts of myself, not because it will diminish the distance, but because it will honor it. It will acknowledge that it's here.

One of the problems with healing in this fucked-up dynamic is that it's presumed that you, the doctor, have knowledge that the patient doesn't, so for the patient to get better, to be cured, or to heal, they must submit themselves to Doctor's Orders. In other words, I'm supposed to give my trust to you—but not because you've demonstrated any action that would earn my trust, specifically, or because we've gone through the stages of intimacy and equal exchange together. It's that you represent a discipline that is supposed to be deserving of trust; I'm supposed to trust you simply because you are a doctor.

What if, instead, the presumption went both ways: that the patient was also a specialist, like you, in possession of knowledge, a vision of a world we'd like to build, and so by collaborating as equals, utilizing each person's skills, we might together build a world that contains multiple parts, a world that is not only one part—your part?

Erica, it was weird to get your letter for many reasons, but the primary one is that it shocked me to be seen in a position of authority to answer your questions. I realized that I've never been treated this way, as someone who might be an authority, by a medical professional. It made me ask myself what kind of knowledge I have about healing that you, trained and educated in the field of medicine, do not. What would I have to teach you? You mentioned that you'd read my essays, so I think I know why I came across as an authority on what healing might mean. The voice I've been able to construct in these essays is empowered in its sickness and vindicated by its tragedy, and although such a voice has been useful, for me and my readers, it's a voice constructed nonetheless, something I built from shards and scraps, all the many pieces that are here.

I'm out of the hospital for now and, though it feels like the emergency has been paused, I know it will return. In a follow-up appointment, a nurse expressed his shock at my certainty.

"You are so sure?" he said.

"Yes, aren't you?" I said.

He was silent for a moment, and then said, "Yes, but normally patients aren't so professional about it."

When I tell this story to abled people, or other stories I have about my inextricable and lifelong relationship with doctors, hospitals, therapists, medications, and the medical-industrial complex, they have a hard time understanding my certainty that such things are not only inevitable in my life but main players. They balk at the fact that I will have to take medication until I die. They say, "But don't you think you're giving your illness too much space?" That I would be certain I'll return to the hospital seems to betray everything they presume is true about hospitals, which I gather is the presumption that hospitals are a rare and bizarre interruption of "normal" life. That the routine appointments that take up my time—in-home care when needed, twice-a-week physical therapy, weekly psychotherapy, biweekly meetings with my social worker, monthly checkups with my general practitioner, etc.—are as woven into my daily life as work, sleep, and having tea with a friend.

In honest, neutral terms, without tragic drama or empowering vindication, I understand that no matter where I sit or sleep in this life, I will be doing it in the house of illness. Everything about living in this house is difficult, but there's a pernicious difficulty in trying to communicate these experiences to a world so structured by ableism. Sometimes it feels like the most unbearable part of it all—it's not so much that articulating the experiences is difficult, although it surely is, but that few really know how to hear and understand them from a non-ableist perspective.

As much as a writer has to learn to write, they must also learn how to be read. Over the years, I have noticed that when my essays on illness and disability are read, there is often something between my reader and I that neither of us consciously put there. There are preconceived notions, stereotypes, habits of thought, stigmas, and assumptions that are not on the page but somewhere in the air between us. This is the problem a writer faces when their subject has been wrapped in an ideology that is still unconscious in society's mind.

Working with my editors on the various essays in this book revealed to me that, even with the best intentions of trying to support stories like mine, ableism often gets in the way. None of my editors over the years were being malicious or intending any bad. They wanted, and tried, to support me as best as they knew how. With this text to you, for example, one of the editorial notes that came back was that I reimagine the letter's position once I was out of the hospital, implying it might be a healthier, more clear-sighted position. There was the fantastical expectation that I have a "true" or "real" self, and those sick, mad, crip selves are not really me. Another essay in this book, which needed to be cut for length when it appeared in a magazine, came back with all mentions of race taken out. The editor was a white woman, and when I pointed out that she'd removed all the times I brought up race, she told me she hadn't noticed. Should I laugh or scream or shrug at this?

Remember how ideologies work: as much as they settle into your bones, they also slyly structure your world. Ableism makes it normal to insist, violently and subtly, that everyone has the unlimited capacity to work and produce according to the standards of the systems in power. It makes it normal to think of disability as something that one "suffers from" and can "overcome" or "transcend," of chronic illness as something one needs to be "strong" about, of bouts of illness as disruptions of "normal" life. Every time I write the word "normal," I stare at it stupefied—what exactly is *that*? We've all been conditioned to expect that such perspectives are the norm, so much so that we don't even think about it when we perpetuate them ourselves. It's taken me years to understand how often I've had, and still have, ableist expectations about myself—even in the hospital, I pushed myself to meet the deadline for this essay, and I did. I finished writing this book while in a months-long flare, lower back dotted with shingles, joints screaming, unable to walk; every day I would wake up and power through as many pages as I could, handfuls of ibuprofen, then go lie down on the couch and stare at the ceiling.

Maybe I don't have to explain to you, Erica, how being alive in my body is to be alive always in a hospital—since you, a young doctor, and I, a professional patient, live and work under the same roof of this house of illness. Do you think of your hospital as a home only for me? Maybe you already see that the self I am in the hospital is a no-less-normal part of the self I am in the other places of my life. Maybe you already understand that your profession ought to aim for honoring the many parts and the distances between them, and the possibility that such distances might never diminish. Maybe you already know that all of us, always, live in this house of illness, but sometimes some of us can pretend we don't.

I'm learning to figure the self admitted to hospitals with psychosis or acute physical symptoms, the self who is dissociated, the self in chronic pain, the self unstoppably bleeding, the self who is medicated, as being no less than the self who is working here at my desk, the self who is publishing essays, the self who is laughing and dancing.

Let me ask you to learn this too.

On an afternoon about halfway through my stay in the bin, I had a panic attack and, because none of the nurses on Station 12 spoke English, there was a search for Yay-Crew. Intercoms through the building buzzed for him (alas, by his real name) while I flapped my hands and couldn't breathe in a room of ineffectual but concerned nurses. Some time, painful, dissociating, passed before he arrived. In

American psych wards they restrain you during attacks like these, so
I flinched when his frame appeared in the door, but Yay-Crew instead
started talking to me in a gentle, steady voice. He asked me if something had happened to trigger the attack. Once language returned, I
managed to explain that I'd become confused because I couldn't
remember how Van Gogh had committed suicide (a story I know
well, so forgetting it alarmed me), and Yay-Crew responded by telling me he'd recently seen an exhibition of Van Gogh, and was surprised at how small the canvases are, just this big, and how yellow
and vibrant the suns and flowers. He swept his hands through the air.
I followed the sound of his voice and tried to find the yellows he
described. I asked him if he was an optimist, saying he must be in
order to be an emergency-room psychiatrist, and he said, simply,
with no power in his eyes, only tiredness and sincerity, "Yes. I am."

As he would later congratulate me on my tremendous accomplishment of surviving, he then congratulated me on pulling myself
out of the panic attack by listening to him. It was then that I trusted
him: not because of his congratulations, but because he had spoken
to me in an equal exchange, and he'd listened to me and heard me,
and perhaps we'd even had a conversation. I realize only now while I
write these words that it was because he had trusted me to be my
own authority, to author the scene as a collaborator with him.

If I ever find myself sitting across from you, in an ER or a clinic
or in your private practice while you observe my presenting symptoms, categorize what you see according to your encyclopedic
knowledge, mentally summarize my problems into diagnoses and
possible etiologies and treatments, and speak to me of your "plan of
attack" or how we're going to "beat this thing," I hope that you
might also speak to me of flowers and suns and the color yellow, and
the world just this big, and of your optimism and my many pieces
that are all somehow here, lingering, remembering, and I hope you

might ask me to imagine with you some ways we might start putting things together, again, or for the first time, or that we can let them stay in pieces, just honor that they are here, that you are here, and so am I.

Yours,

JOHANNA HEDVA

I got the blood of my mind

all over everything.

Soft Blues

"The past does not influence me; I influence it."

WILLEM DE KOONING

◆

"Know amazedly how often one takes his madness into his own hands and keeps it."

LORINE NIEDECKER

◆

"No names have been changed to protect the innocent. They're all fucking guilty."

LYDIA LUNCH

Photograph #1: Soft blues, the dress and the sheets are the same color. The color, the shape of the skin is milky, as though it's spilling out of the unzipped zipper. A daub of black hair obscures the head and face, which have been pushed into the pillow. The walls are a sad beige. Wavering thin black lines make blobby shapes in and out and around the freckles on the skin of the back. They've been doodled with a swooning hand. Probably drunk.

I am face down on the bed. He has drawn on my back. I've bundled my face and arms and hands beneath my weight, prone, making the skin of my back open to attack. I've asked him to take a photo. This is an apt representation of our entire relationship.

Photograph #2: The bottom of a white toilet and white cabinets take up the top half of the frame; the bottom half is a span of terra-cotta-tiled floor, warm, reddish brown, the color of earth. A scattered mess of dark hair, in clumps and threads, some black, some brown, is strewn across the tiles. It resembles the fallen organs of a belly sliced open.

I cut all my hair off in the bathroom. Then I cut his. I'd suggested he do it; I'd just cut mine, and my resolve made purpose and meaning as if I'd begun for us a new resplendent world. He photographed it. This is a better representation of our entire relationship.

Photograph #3 (deleted): Dark red shadows surround a blurred, pale form. The view is from above, looking down on the form, which appears to have its torso below its ass, legs opened out and sideways like a crab. Down the middle of the ass is a gash-like slice of bright red. The white skin of the back blends in with the cum so we don't see it, but we know it's there. A daub of black hair obscures the head and face, which have been pushed into the rug on the floor.

I am face down on the floor. He has drawn on my back with some-thing other than ink, it will easily wash away. I've asked him to take a photo by telling him it's what I want, but once I see the photo I wonder who I am, if this person is really me, and did that person really want what she said, what she thought, she did? Is she even a she? This is not a representation of our relationship—this *is* our entire relationship.

The best thing I got from my relationship with Z was his description of Alvarado Street in Los Angeles being like a river, how the traffic just swims down it.

The second best thing I got was that I was finally disabused of the idea that De Kooning was a genius. Z, a straight cis white boy painter from Texas, without one lick of irony or self-awareness at how ironic it made him look, worshipped De Kooning, idolized and wanted to be him, studied him with righteous devotion, hunted every scrap of biographical anecdote; *De Kooning did it like this, De Kooning said this,* repeating quotes like the rosary, which was all a big yearning, a hope that, in small ways that were accumulating, through will and determination but also osmosis, by soaking himself in the sticky wet of De Kooning's everything, Z was comporting himself more and more toward De Kooning and would one day walk in the shadow that would also be the light of the master.

It's the kind of behavior that straight cis white boys are born into, the kind propelled by something that commingles faith and delusion, faith in themselves and their god-given right to be front and center and always on top, and the ability to ignore completely the possibil-ity that everything they believe to be true about themselves is a delusion. True, it's a delusion that the whole world believes in, but doesn't that fact only corroborate its being a lie?

For the purposes of this essay, I'm going to need a working definition of "the world." But there are so many! There's the world of Plato's Cave, and, crucially, the world outside it. There's Wittgenstein's "world [that] is all that is the case." There are Leibniz's multiple worlds, though for him this one is the best of all possible because (I'm paraphrasing) god is nice. There's Schopenhauer's world as representation, which is what we perceive, and then the world as will, which is beyond perception, and we must not forget that Schopenhauer also said, "Women are directly adapted to act as the nurses and educators of our early childhood, for the simple reason that they themselves are childish, foolish, and short-sighted." Lol.

I'm partial to Heidegger's world into which we are thrown, the abrupt and incomprehensible thrown-ness of existence, *Dasein*, because I feel hella thrown.

What's weird is that "the world" and "reality" are not the same, though their delineation from each other is interdependent: there can be many realities in the world but perhaps not many worlds in reality.

Until that summer, I had not yet learned this.

At that point, my definition of "the world" was that it's the thing that holds you.

Until it doesn't.

The German word "Malerschwein" literally means "painter pig," but it is figuratively used to describe an archetypal male artist: chauvinistic;

lauded; insecure and emotionally irresponsible; egomaniacal but allowed, even urged, to be that way; misogynistic in his art and life, despite the fact that both of those things could not have happened without the wives, mothers, sisters, and girlfriends who serve him in the capacity of collaborators, advocates, patrons, managers, curators, editors, critics, teachers, therapists, caregivers, mentors, librarians, accountants, assistants, cooks, maids, muses, typists, secretaries, publicists, laundresses, and nurses. No matter his medium, the *Malerschwein* is a genius of a singular kind, a trailblazer who, in a divinely directed quest à la Moses, ventures to the wild frontier of his craft, spelunks depths that he presumes—and which the world substantiates back to him—have never before been excavated, or if they have, not sufficiently so, not yet by a Genius, for we need a Genius who will show us revolutionary, seminal (from "semen") ways to understand ourselves and how to live and be.

The *Malerschwein* is always Great, with a capital G. And he always changes the World, with a capital W.

The goddamn canon is made of *Malerschwein*. Just Google "genius" and have a nice scroll through the history of civilization.

During that summer, I worked as a studio assistant to an opera set designer, who gave me the De Kooning biography to read. "You should know about him," he told me, and loaned me his copy, saying, "But I want this back." This is an apt representation of patriarchy in practice.

When I returned it to him, he did not ask me what I thought but said, "It's great, right? He was great, right?" though not said as questions. This is a better representation of patriarchy in practice.

While I was working for this man, I had a miscarriage, with complications, a biblical forty days of bleeding, which ignited a grief in me so brutal that it almost blinked me out of existence. A small hole dilated to inhale the entire universe, and everything that had been explicable before was now negated, totally, radically, and I was left in a pool of tears and empty skin, and I could not—I was not. I have endometriosis, a disease that I was told, when I was first diagnosed at age twenty, meant I would probably never be able to get pregnant, and I am genderqueer and have gender dysphoria, the latter of which is also classified as a disorder. The fact that I have a uterus at all feels like a weird mistake, a curse nevertheless borne from my DNA. So, when I say that a small hole dilated, I'm referring not only to a hole that was the absence of an impossible fetus, but to a hole that existed at the very site of the impossibilities that are my self.

One night, bleeding blood that had turned to black ash, I was crying and could not stop, I was a mad dog trying to tear its way out of my own throat, I thrashed around like the female protagonists in Greek tragedy, a cursed woman who has had everything taken from her, so I cursed everyone I knew, and the most unkind curse I gave to myself. The man who'd fathered the baby that was now a hole thought I was a danger to myself because I could not stop crying and threw my head into the wall, so he called the police and had me involuntarily hospitalized in the psych ward.

They took me away in handcuffs and wouldn't let me bring my shoes. I tried to get them, and they said, "Ma'am, where you're going, you won't need your shoes."

On the way to the hospital, one of the cops looked over his shoulder through the metal fence that divided the front seat from the back and said to me in a quiet voice, "My girlfriend is pregnant right now, so I understand. I'm so sorry."

I looked at him calmly and in a clear voice said, "You don't have to take me, you know. I'm just grieving."

"I know," he said, "but we have to. It's the law."

This is not a representation of the patriarchy in practice. This is the practice of it. For a practice to become an institution, it has to be instituted and reinstituted. It's a doing that has to be done.

My boss, who was also my professor at the time, took it upon himself to be my medical "advocate." He supported the hospitalization and introduced the notion that came to dominate the discussion, which was that I "should have gotten over it by now," hence why hospitalization was necessary. I was hysterical, out of control. He wasn't wrong. But he left out the part that considered the question of how else, if not this, I should have been. How else, I kept asking, should I behave? What is the right way to grieve? And can it ever be lawful?

A friend, an older woman, upon my release from the hospital, told me, "Remember: Medea may have been hysterical, but she was right."

I met Z in June, a few months after I was released from the hospital. I was living alone in Chinatown, on Chung King Court—one block of a clean, spacious lane where cars aren't allowed to go. It was built in the 1930s, when LA was young, as part of something for tourists called the "New Chinatown" but which has since been drained of its commerce. In the 1990s, art galleries moved in and flourished for a few years, and I was staying in a studio owned by an artist whose career had had a similar trajectory. The scene was now empty, but the red paper lanterns strung across the alley were still turned on every night. It looked like the abandoned set of a racist movie: stray cats, people collecting bottles, an old Chinese woman carrying plastic bags of bruised vegetables, a pair of busboys on a smoke break from a Chinese restaurant, squatting at the foot of a crooked staircase.

I would sometimes walk barefoot at night down the lane. The air was warm and my body felt featherweight, capable of lifting into the air and tumbling away. I'd lift my arms up and sway under the paper lanterns. I'd feel as though my life and my self and my world and what I wanted and who I was were my own. This was the only thing I comprehended in the face of many often contradictory facts, untamed and teeming in their disparity. I had to turn away from them; in the face of too many things, I had to make only one: me. Nothing, of course, actually belonged to me, not least the entity I'd constructed and started calling "me," but I told myself it did because I live by the law, and that's what I've been taught to want: a "me" that I can own, like an object to keep in a pocket.

At the hospital, I had been prescribed medication which would turn out to be the wrong medication. I had been misdiagnosed with depression, because they saw in me only one thing in the face of many, because again, that is how the world is structured. Our collective delusion.

Is it for me to say where I stood, still stand, in relation to the line between the things that happened to me and deciding that those things were what I wanted? Let me put it another way: Is desire a thing that belongs to you—a thing you can own?

I should probably define "delusion," because it's hilarious. "Delude" comes from "*de*" and "*ludere*" (a form of ludicrous)—"*de*," meaning "down, to one's detriment," and "*ludere*," from the Latin, meaning "to play." So, a game you play to your detriment.

If it's a game, then there must be a winner and a loser, right?

When people with bipolar disorder are given antidepressants, it triggers mania, and this period would ignite in me my first and only true euphoric mania, the kind the textbooks and diagnostic codes call "classic." But I wouldn't learn that until six months later. For now, the medication was pulling me out of my grief. Reborn, I felt unspoiled by all that had happened. The chemicals in my body were cooking hypomania, the early stages of mania, and the charged, fertile wonderfulness of it hadn't yet turned treacherous. I felt buoyant, overflowing with visions, and untouched by time.

What I mean is that I could not grasp the thought that my actions had consequences, that my body was made of material, and that what I did with it was tethered to reality and its laws. What makes mania feel like mania is the feeling that the force which moves time in one direction has been suspended, making reality a lawless place where everything, past present future, is happening forever and always and right now. It's a kind of surging that feels both dispersed and radically concentrated, and because it is so extraordinary, the fact that you feel it seems to imply that something about you is extraordinary too.

I'm sympathetic to the notion that linear time is an illusion, so I'm always frustrated when things that get broken tend to stay broken.

I like to refer to this manic summer as "The Summer of My Twelve-Inch Cock."

My cock is twelve inches long and it's a gun and a Molotov cocktail and a megaphone and a long perfectly balanced sword and a power drill that can grind through bone and a really big hammer—a hammer that could crush one of Jupiter's moons—and a flamethrower longer than my body and a huge punishing stretch of silence and a ghost and a cave and a vase of bleeding hearts and easy sugar and a deep old forest with ancient mosses and a combustion ex nihilo and it stinks like very expensive perfume and when it lands on the face of my enemies it cracks through the air with a thwack *that registers at 150 fucking decibels.*

During manias, it is difficult to remember things you know are true. Lies are difficult to distinguish from desires; reality is impossible to locate amid what feels like a warm dream. It's easy to get lost and not feel like you're lost. Also, how can a person be lost if they went there because they wanted to?

There are many etymologies of the word "lost," the adjective of "lose," but my favorite is the transitive sense from the 1200s: "to part with accidentally, be deprived of, miss the possession or knowledge of." I like that it can be an accident, and I like the double meaning of the word "miss," that it is both a failure and a yearning.

Manias feel great. Doctors don't want you to know that. Manias are also encouraged in certain kinds of people in certain areas of life, but doctors don't want you to know that either, because it relies on the premise that sanity is a straw man. A delusion that the whole world believes in.

The *DSM-5* criteria for a classic manic episode includes "inflated self-esteem or grandiosity," "flight of ideas," and "excessive involvement in pleasurable or risky activities that have a high potential for painful consequences." Sounds like qualities that are especially encouraged in the *Malerschwein*, with the exception of the last part—the painful consequences—which sounds like what everyone else will feel when dealing with him.

You'd think there'd be a definition of "painful" in that diagnostic criteria, because locating the pain, and who will feel it, and why, and how, seems essential to distinguishing how exactly mania is different and deserving of pathology, than, say, the condition of masculinity at all. But, like its refusal to define "normal," the *DSM* lets this stay ambiguous.

There is another way of looking at it though (even, not one, but many). The *DSM* makes it seem as though inflated self-esteem, flights of ideas, and excessive involvement in pleasurable or risky activities necessarily *result* in painful consequences. As if causality equally affects everyone, no matter who you are, one of the laws of reality that binds us all. But the burden of causality is not everyone's burden.

For some, the shattered glass on the floor doesn't stay shattered. Well, it does, but it's not ascribed to be their fault. They are not expected to pick it up.

And what do we do when the shattered thing is a body? And your own? Who picks it up then?

Men are less often diagnosed with bipolar disorder than women, and when they are, it usually happens when they are in a depressive episode rather than a manic one. When depressed men are given anti-depressants, they swing into mania, but since manic men are hard to distinguish from Geniuses who are changing The World, society tends to support their manic behavior until it stops producing a culture that can be capitalized upon. Manic men often appear drunk on their own divinity or high on endorphins from the gym, all fired up in a legibly masculine way, so there's nothing to be alarmed about. If they cause too much trouble, manic men get dumped in jail for the night, and the enforcers of race and class take over from there in terms of where they end up. A certain kind of world is available to manic men—indeed, *The World* is available to him, not only to live in, but to change. People who are not straight cis white men are not afforded this, we do not belong to The World, but each to our own minority world, so our crazed behavior always looks provincial, limited.

When Robert Lowell applied for a teaching job at Cambridge University, one of his referrals listed the signs to look out for that would precipitate Lowell needing to be taken "to the bin," i.e., that he was in a manic episode. First, he would start a sexual relationship with a student, threatening to leave his wife, Elizabeth Hardwick, who'd nursed him through many manias and depressions. Second, he'd talk incessantly about Hitler and Napoleon and start referring to himself as one among them, a great world leader. Third, he'd throw a big party. No big deal, just a heads-up.

When a woman or femme person is manic, she is easily legible as violating the laws of reality: she often fucks a lot and insatiably, spends a lot of money on herself, abandons her duties as a mother or wife or servant of any kind, talks a lot—i.e., "too much"—and usually about herself, all of her potent ideas, the epiphanic discoveries she's made, and she seems to take great joy in herself, for she believes herself to be important and inspired—i.e., "inflated self-esteem." And if she's an artist, she feels as if she's in the throes of artistic production and worthy of the space and attention that Geniuses deserve. Obviously this is a sign of insanity, because insanity is simply a measure of how one has become untethered to reality and its laws.

"Can a woman be a *Malerschwein?*" is another way of asking what happens when inflated grandiosity collides with painful consequences, what happens when flights of ideas are brought down to the ground. Another asks, "But where would she live?" which is to foreclose the question altogether.

I want the world to allow me all my delusions about my own importance, to bend over backward to make my importance be true—not just for me, but for all of you too. I want to snap the jaws of people who get in my way and have the world applaud this and call it honor. I want to bellow with baseless anger and have the world hear it as a lullaby. I want to whine and mewl when someone wants to take up as much space as I do, and I want the police to shoot them in the back for their gross trespass. I want a secretary and a therapist and a nurse and a maid and a fucktoy in the same body who I never have to pay, and I want to blame everything on my mother, that cunt. Every evil should be blamed on every mother. When I'm asked to account for myself, I want to be silent, arms folded across my chest, jaw set indomitably, and have this act pull power away from my inquisitors and consolidate it within me. I want to call my inquisitors hysterical crazy bitches, and I want this to become the ideology in the water supply. I want my brittleness to legislate the wretched, but first, I want to declare their wretchedness and define it recursively, that they are wretched because they don't look like me. I want my wounds to be the reason we build prisons, tanks, and guns. I want the world to labor to secure me, and I want them to need no other reason to do it

other than because I said so. I want this reason to become a universal Truth with a capital T that constructs the World with a capital W. When I break someone else, I want the world to wag its finger not in my face, but in my victim's, tsk tsk, who should have known better, who was asking for it. I want children to be taught not to tempt me, and when they do, I want them to feel for their entire lives the dirty shame of their mistake. I want wealth such that the world has never seen, and then I want my face imprinted on all the coins.

Whose voice is this? Is it my own? No, it's not mine—but then why have I been taught to want it to be? Perhaps "I" is too limited a pronoun in these questions. What happens when it's changed to "we"?

When a person who is assigned female at birth comes to understand that they don't agree with that assignment, often the first gesture away from it is to wonder if they are in fact a man, a swing toward the perceived antipode. Some find solace there, indeed find themselves there: yes, actually, here I am! Some don't find themselves at either pole but at some errant ineffability between, and the question becomes whether a binary is an accurate framework for gender at all, even though The World insists that it is.

It's like Schrödinger's cat, the thought experiment of a cat locked in a box with a device that has a 50 percent chance of killing it. At the moment before opening the box, the cat is both alive and dead at the same time because of what's called its "quantum superposition." Schrödinger was trying to figure out when the cat would stop being its soupy mess of both states at once at the quantum level, and become, on the level of the cat itself, either a dead one or a live one.

Gender, for me, often feels like the moment right before opening the box when the cat is a blur of probability of *both* and therefore *neither*. Another way to say this is that during The Summer of My Twelve-Inch Cock, there was a kind of collapsing of the very binary that I thought I knew, and the site of the collapsing was me.

Z was hung, not twelve inches but at least nine, and thick, a real-life baby arm, and liked to think of himself as the top in our relationship, in the way that straight cis white boys assume the role because they believe it's what the cock ontologically decrees. It's what has built and paid for the house of their identity, so they feel obligated to live there. The possibility that they could gut-renovate the place, or burn it down, move away, and build a different house, in a different town, is not entertained, because it would require a premise that one can be homeless, be lost.

Getting lost is not something that exists for those who benefit from the patriarchy. It's impossible to be without your home when one is either the king of his land or has by divine right conquered and settled the land of his neighbor.

In other words, getting lost is impossible because everything already belongs to you. And if it doesn't yet, you can simply point at the teeming pile of unmanageable and savage things and make them ownable by declaring, "Mine."

A tentative conclusion: for some, but not everyone, yes, desire is a thing you can own.

There is the question of what happens when the Genius accidentally loses his way—how the machinations of the patriarchy work to either bring him back or reframe the detour to be included in his divine direction. This begs the question of what happens when those of us who are not considered Geniuses are steered off course, lost in the weeds, wayward. Are we ever heard from again?

The focus of our fucking was always Z's cock—his magnificent, god-given cock. The very fact of it. He would unfold his pants and hold out his arms like Jesus as the cock fell into the light, while in the background a choir was cued to sing awe. A whiff of that muddy mix of faith and delusion would come into the air. *Submit*, it seemed to say, as though there is only one universal truth and here it is, *I'll let you suck on it if you say please.*

He would tell me to "get it" because "that's what you need." I still laugh when I think of this line because of its blunt, bald truth. How he spoke the truth and how the trouble came because I didn't believe it. I kept insisting on a different truth, one where I didn't need that cock, I wanted to live in a world where that cock's power had sputtered out like a short, wet match. But remember, at the time, I was untethered to reality and its laws.

Why am I writing about cis-boy cocks? Why am I still thinking about them? Goddamn motherfuckers.

My time with Z overlapped with my reading the De Kooning biography, and during that summer I had the sense that, like the Holy Ghost hovering watchfully behind me, I was being followed by his *Woman I*

painting. I felt exposed to her, by her. When people looked at me, I saw that they saw her, my face scowling like hers, teeth bared, my body's outline jagged, threatening to shred into the bodies of others.

I cut my hair down to the scalp, drove too fast, cranked up the stereo to play the same song fifty times a day. I talked a lot, too much, about myself and my work and my soaring ambitions, and I had no hesitation in saying what I wanted and exactly how and when. I fucked a lot and enjoyed it all. I was hysterical and grandiose and confident and inspired. I flew high on my great ideas. I indulged in pleasurable and risky activities. I jerked off while driving on the free- way. I stayed up all night. Self-doubt and caution evaporated, which is a dream come true for an artist. I made new work every day, and it came whole and alive and sizzling with meaning, as if I'd simply walked to the top of a small hill and found god's word waiting there for me to pick up and hold.

Sometimes I think about how this one experience of mania might never have happened if I hadn't been misdiagnosed and given the wrong medication, because I'd been involuntarily hospitalized by a man who thought I was a danger to myself because I was cry- ing too loudly over an obvious grief, one that might have been pre- vented if I hadn't had a uterus, if I'd had gender confirmation surgery, if I'd understood who I was earlier rather than later. But it doesn't matter anymore; the cause and effect are muddled. That line between knowing who you are and knowing who you are not is never a straight one.

It has taken me five years to write this essay. I've had to set it aside for months, I've tried to abandon it, shove it to the back of the desk, it's as if I drive out into the desert, hours away from the city, and dig a big hole and bury it deep in the vehement hope that it will finally leave me alone. But it keeps crawling back. It keeps insisting on itself.

I am sympathetic to things that have been told by The World that their insistence on themselves is delusional, and yet, at the risk of embracing the sort of delusion that The World does not like as the very ontology of their existence, they keep on insisting.

Years later, I saw my ex, the man who'd had me institutionalized over our—my—our?—*my* miscarriage. By then, I was on the right medication, stable, going to bed at the same time every night. I was trying to forgive him. We met for coffee.

"I wished I'd seen it sooner. Maybe I could have helped," he said.

"Seen what?" I said.

"There were things you'd do that weren't right. But I just thought, she's a crazy artist chick. But if I had known you were sick, I would've tried to get you help."

"What things?"

"You would fuck strangers. And you were so confident about your work. I've never seen someone so confident about their art."

"But I only fucked a couple strangers. How many strangers have you fucked?"

"I wish *I* was that good of an artist."

During that Twelve-Inch Cock summer, I made a series of pieces called *Actually, It Happened a Moment Ago*, which consisted of poetic, fleeting performances in liminal sites like driveways and piers "for small audiences of one person or a few animals." I wanted to feel into the question of the audience, if it was important for an audience to be present or not, and if it was or wasn't, then why. Looking back on it now, I see that I was trying to come to terms with my work and my body being perceived according to laws that I didn't necessarily want to follow.

If a person whose body looks like a woman's dances in a driveway at night in front of three cats and calls this "art," what are we to make of it? Is she crazy? Does she know she's crazy? If she knows, does that mean she's actually crazy, or is she just performing being crazy, which, instead of negating the possibility that she is really crazy, means she's probably even more, pray, crazy than we thought?

But could this piece be about its audience—who they are, their values, desires, prejudices, gods, and monsters, and what, because of all that, they assume and decide about the artist? Which is another way of asking, is the audience crazy, how will we know if they are, and, critically, who gets to decide?

That summer was hot, dry, and dirty. Los Angeles summers are mythical. They often feel like the end of the world already happened thirty years ago, and this is the scorched, wasted aftermath. The survivors have persisted by pushing into the heat and the dust, singing to themselves, and belonging to cults of one. They travel in eggs of metal and glass, blasting their faces with artificially cold air created by draining resources from the dying earth. They persist on diets of grass and sticks, they dress themselves in flapping tents of fabric that cost half their rent.

After a few weeks, the medication swimming in my veins washed me ashore and, waterlogged and tossed, I rolled over in the flogging sunlight and didn't know where I was. One Sunday I took myself out for brunch, though I can't remember how I had any money. I went alone, I brought a book to read. I wore a skirt that a friend had given me, which depicted a tableau of an Aztec ceremony of virgin sacrifice outlined in sequins. I went to an expensive French restaurant in Los Feliz that had a sticky floor. Liv Tyler was there with her mom.

Z was my waiter. He was very, very handsome, in the LA way of someone who would call himself "an actor and a model too" but who is working as a waiter. Six foot four and slim, dark hair, impressively large hands, round blue eyes, a strong Superman jaw. His whole affect was Superman-like, gallant, shoulders straight, chest out. He had that old-fashioned kind of masculinity that is chivalrous, more powerful than any force on Earth, which seems to be held in check by an invisible code; we tell ourselves he will keep us safe and never turn against us. When he brought something to my table, he'd offer it with a bow of his head. He complimented my skirt.

I left my phone number on the bill, and he called two days later.

Because I've already told you that I was manic at the time, fresh out of the hospital and torrid with gendered trauma, am I not also casting myself as a casting director on speed dial would? The crazy hysterical bitch with her tawdry wounds, leaving her number for a stranger, like dropping a bloody rag into a sea of sharks.

He made me mix CDs. All but three of the tracks were by men. (He'd say, "It's great, right. He was great, right.")

On one mix, he included Karen Dalton's "In My Own Dream," a slow blues song about the line between dreams and insanity, how it feels to live there. Or, maybe she is talking about where she stands in relation to the line of choosing to be lost versus having no choice.

Dalton's voice is soft and furry, and I wanted to listen to it all the time. It became the soundtrack of that summer.

"I feel seen by that song," I told Z.

He nodded. "I know," he said. "I put it on there for a reason."

My sublet in Chinatown ended halfway into July, so I took a sublet in Hollywood, two blocks south of the Magic Castle. Parking was a bitch, but the neighborhood was lush with trees, close to the Hollywood foothills, and redolent with the feeling certain neighborhoods in LA can get around their fame and nostalgia for that fame. There was a building down the street with this quote painted on its side: "What's the fastest way to get into Hollywood? Take Franklin." I can't remember now who the quote is attributed to—Google tells me it's Mae West, Bette Davis, and Katharine Hepburn, all of them interchangeable as blunt old broads who used to be the beautiful talk of the town.

My sublet was in a cluster of bungalows, behind a decrepit iron gate with a broken buzzer that summoned *Mulholland Drive*. The apartments were aligned around a courtyard of bottlebrush trees and bougainvillea, and there were a few benches and slender metal cans in which to throw cigarette butts. This sublet was the place where I cut all my hair off and then cut his.

Late into the night we'd sit in the courtyard. Nights in summer are my favorite time in LA. The grueling heat of the day barely abates, and the air is fervid, in the high eighties or low nineties Fahrenheit, but in the dark it becomes erotic, charged, like Goya's painting of the witches' flight. Barefoot, we'd wear each other's clothes to go outside and smoke. I'd pull on Z's soft, worn-in T-shirt, he'd wear my long, thin sweater the color of blood. He looked elegant in it, that strong jaw, like a leading man from old Hollywood— Cary Grant, Marlon Brando, James Dean, they're interchangeable though we are nevertheless able to parse their distinctions. Sitting underneath the bougainvillea flowers and the bottlebrush, with this elegant man who couldn't take his eyes off me, I'd feel like the luckiest person on earth.

Earlier that year, I'd think, not even six months ago, I was in the psych ward of East LA County Hospital. Inside the locked ward, there were about forty patients housed in two rooms, the beds lined up in cramped rows. I had a bed closest to the wall, which was a kind of mercy, I could at least turn away from the room. People, almost all of them not white, shuffled up and down the corridor shouting obscenities, screaming someone's name, muttering to themselves, the backs of their hospital gowns untied, bare, flapping asses and gaunt legs on display. Behind a locked door in the hallway near the bathroom, for the entire seventy-two hours I was there, came the screams of a man. He shouted without stopping, "*Agua, por favor! Agua, por favor!*" I never saw him; he was never released from that room. I will never not hear his voice, swinging from enraged to pleading. He was still in there when I was released.

Visitors were not allowed more than five minutes; my aunt kept trying to see me, to bring me food, but they made her throw the food in the trash. There was a pay phone in the hallway where you could receive calls, but the cord attached to the phone was only six inches long, so you couldn't hang yourself with it. I could not stop laughing at how this caused you to assume a pose, stooped down, head close to the wall in order to speak into the receiver, that made you look unquestionably insane. Laughing about it didn't help me look any less insane, of course.

You were also not allowed to have any pens, pencils, or bound books—if the intention was there, they could all be used as weapons. Luckily, a friend of mine had just sent me the manuscript of his novel, which I asked another friend to bring so I'd have something to read. But once it was in my lap, a five-inch stack of loose paper, it also made me look unquestionably insane.

One of the nurses asked, "Whatcha readin'?"

"A friend of mine wrote a book."

"Oh, really? What's it about then?"

"It's a sci-fi psychedelic crime novel set in the 1960s."

"Is that right?"

"The detective is trying to solve a mystery with the help of mermaids he can talk to when he's on acid."

"Okay?"

I learned to keep my mouth shut. Being taught something is not the same thing as choosing to know it.

I've now become the person in my community who you call if your friend is talking with ghosts, or pronouncing themselves to be god while dancing without clothes on, or lying down in the middle of the street so that the aliens, who are on their way, will be able to find them easier to finally take them home. Because I've been there myself and somehow survived, I can function like a guide to uncharted territory. Know this, don't forget that, it will probably feel like this. I know who to call—I know who not to call. I wake up to texts and emails from concerned partners and parents. "We were hoping that we might speak to you for some guidance," they say. "Would you be willing to help us?"

In my responses, beneath the medical terminology and names of medications and links to resources and urgings that they know they are not alone, I try to smuggle in a little flame of a question: "How much of the world's perception of illness are you willing to forsake?"

In other words, *Don't call the fucking cops.*

Illness is not—despite The World telling you it is—only a personal, individual experience of pain, trauma, and limitation. It happens inside your individual body, and yet it is an index of the social body. It's the collision of a lawless body against a body of laws, your world being crashed into by The World. It produces an embodied experience that undoes who you think you are to such an extent that telling other people how it feels seems impossible, and at the same time, it produces a body that is read and deciphered in terms that are historical, systemic, and political. However, the social vector is usually ignored, so that illness becomes an index of one's own individual powerlessness rather than being seen as the experience of how we are all enmeshed within systems of power, how we are all interdependent, for better or worse, and how such enmeshment and interdependence shapes consequences and potentials, desires and rights, dreams and deaths, worlds and realities.

One afternoon that July, Z said he was going to sketch me. Though he didn't paint portraits, he'd been saying he would paint mine since our first date. It was one hundred degrees, too hot for clothes, so we opened all the windows in his apartment and I stretched out on his mattress, which was on the floor. He lived one block away from Alvarado Street, and the lapping sounds of traffic washed the room. I read the *New Yorker*, trying not to pay attention to the scratches of his pencil. In his drawing, my face is pugnacious, mouth twisted up and nose scrunched, De Kooning's *Woman*. I sneer at the magazine in my hands, which makes it seem like I'm sneering at the whole capital-w World.

"I look like some deranged goddess who eats men for breakfast," I said.

"Well, you are," he replied, and I saw that, instead of winking irony, his eyes were big and round and fragile with cruelty. I'd see this look on him often. I've seen it on children when they hit each other in revenge, sobbing, clutching the part of themselves that's been injured. It's the look of someone who feels humiliated but keen to turn his humiliation into a weapon.

Some titles for that drawing could be:

"Woman" Reading, Fresh Out of the Psych Ward

Goddess at Rest (Between Meals)

Crazy Artist Chick

Portrait of an Artist

How can I perceive myself as that which The World perceives but also that I insist on my own perception of myself, which The World does not perceive: impossible, probably, but, and, so why do I still want it?

A friend read a draft of this essay when I was ready to give up on it again. They asked me why, for so long, I kept wanting patriarchal power, for the patriarchy to perceive me in a way they deemed legitimate, why I kept needing to fit myself into such a world. The best answer I could summon was that, for nearly my entire life, I didn't understand that I could want something else.

The definition of masculinity is its capacity to be free of the labor of perception at all—it perceives, yes, but only one way. This is why it's devoid of pluralism. In a knife twist of cleverness, though, masculinity has devised its own philosophy to suit this arrangement: the philosophy of the subject and the object, which is a philosophy built on the idea that the object is constituted by the subject.

I've been told that philosophers call this "intersubjectivity," which Hegel "invented." Masculinity perceives, which means it is the subject, and everything else becomes the object. In other words, the very fact that Z, as the subject, perceived me, as the object, is what made me exist at all.

That I now feel compelled to cite Hegel to corroborate my argument is only more evidence of how I've been schooled by these laws. Yes, dear reader, as you presumed, Hegel's spooge is all over this essay, all over me, but since you can already see it everywhere, do I really need to say how it got there?

Can't I just, like a good little constituted object, spooge-faced, declare my face to be covered in spooge—QED?

I asked a friend who studied philosophy for the primary definitions of "the world"; he sent that earlier list of the main dudes—Plato, Hegel, Leibniz, etc. A few days later, I woke up to a text from him that said, "Came across a further bit of Wittgenstein today. 'The subject does not belong to the world; rather, it is a limit of the world.'"

When you paint my picture, paint it with strong colors that radiate valor. Make it a portrait of authority. Make my image synonymous with virtue, the Machiavellian kind, virtù, the tautological one that not only belongs to a man but is how we define men: moral strength, high character, goodness, excellence, courage. Give me the largest canvas you have. Then make it ten times bigger. Paint me in the center, my head high above the rest. Whoever it is that deigns to look at me will have to look up like a little bitch. Use thick, sure brushstrokes. Don't be a pussy. Get the light right, get it exactly right, and make it golden. Give me a red cloak the color of power and inflate it with the gales of the gods. Make me gesture out and up to the sky, where I am going, where I will take the people who follow me. Mount me on a stallion, risen up on its hind legs, eyes ablaze with righteousness; let us both stare out with impunity. Dare to give me a weak chin, and I will have your head on a plate. Get your symbolism to show that, if and when I want to, I can do anything because I can. Paint this and, if I like it, I will pay you to paint three more. My audience, my reader, my kingdom: look at me and let me tell you what to see. I am what you find on medals and money. I am who the world means when it says it needs a leader. I am a hero, and I can be yours, if you ask me nice, if you want it bad enough. I am how to define, how to know, what anything is, because I am how you know what you are not.

Masculinity is sitting on a throne on a pedestal in a spotlight at the top of the tallest hill in the land.

Femininity is the inverse of this: Chained to the floor in the cave at the bottom of the prison, but a prison that has a stage upon which the prisoners are required to perform. Femininity is this performance.

The guards are above you, around you, they can see you from all angles. They are your audience, and they have brutal opinions that they shout at you while you perform. The trouble with femininity is that it's hard to tell who exactly the guards are, which means it's hard to tell where you stand in relation to the line between prisoner and guard, reality and dream, student and teacher, subject and object, audience and artist, which means it's hard to tell who's going to love you the best.

Another knife twist: through its constitution by the subject, the object then necessarily belongs to the subject.

Which is why people like Z need people like me so badly.

Reader, no! I will not cite Hegel here either!

Anne Carson writes: "The mad state is, as [Artaud] emphasizes over and over again, empty. Teeming with emptiness. Knotted on emptiness. Immodest in its emptiness. You can pull emptiness out of it by the handful. 'I am not here. I am not here and never will be.' You can pull it out endlessly."

I agree with this emptiness, but I would qualify that it is empty only because it is empty of things The World values.

Anne Carson, again on Artaud: "For Artaud the real drawback of being mad is not that consciousness is crushed and torn but that he cannot say so, fascinating as this would be, while it is happening. But only later when somewhat 'recovered' and so much less convincingly. . . . A primary characteristic of pain is its demand for an explanation."

Let me propose that I did, while it was happening, say so, but I did it in a language that The World has decided it doesn't want to understand.

Another way of saying this is, in my relationship with Z, I encountered a crisis of representation, because any kind of representation is always a crisis. Maybe he encountered this too, but maybe it's easier for me to see it because I know representation can't be trusted.

Representation is always also a negation, and narrative is always a fiction. Morgan Parker has noted: "Fact is fiction with state power."

Some of us have been deemed unreliable narrators, and some of us have had our truths recast as fictions, and some of us have been defined not by our crises, but as crisis itself.

Just as quickly as I'd fallen into it, one day everything changed, and I came out of that summer and all of its mess in a flushed, lustral sweep. One of the comforts of bipolar disorder is that it's a reliable cycle. What goes up will come down.

Z helped break my fever dream. Not long into dating I told him I didn't want to be monogamous and that I wasn't straight and that I wasn't even a woman. Like many straight cis white boys, he understood the first two of my declarations to mean that I wouldn't sufficiently devote myself unto him alone, and he took the last to mean that his suspicions about me were right: I was unmanageable, unownable, beyond the law. He tried to own me outright, breaking into my email account, threatening his vulnerability, his fragile eyes trembling with vengeance.

"This is going to break me," Z said, not as a plea but as a warning.

When I tell the story of Z, I say, "My only regret is that I didn't throw more things *at* him."

The reader might wonder why exactly I was dating a straight cis white boy at all. Good fucking question! When I look back at that summer, this is the one and only bit of evidence that convinces me I was indeed mad at the time.

I never spoke to Z again. In the wake of our breakup, he wrote me several emails about the mistakes he'd made in our relationship, an attempt to try to "win" me back. He framed his mistakes as qualities of mine that I'd inflicted upon him.

You're a fucking she-devil who put a hex on me is one example.

I tried to do too much for you, right? I was good at the sweet, loving man but not good enough at the asshole. I flubbed my lines too many times, and you had the casting director on speed dial is another.

You laid out something that looked an awful lot like bait.

These are direct quotes, unchanged. How sweet perception must be when it's only subjective!

The last words he ever directed at me came in a drunken email sent at two in the morning: *I'll leave you alone now. You will always be simply magnificent.*

It is the singular talent of straight cis white boys to render into weapons lines that are offered as compliments. I wish I'd learned how to do this, but I could only be taught so much. Ultimately, I flunked out of this school.

What I think of most when I read these lines today is how close Z got to understanding the game we were both playing, how absolute it is, how damaging, how no one, not even the winner, is meant to win it, but how he never allowed himself to be released from the notion that he should be the one to win it. Wanting to win a game that's rigged to let you win—oh, the pity I can pull out of this by the handful.

Sometimes I refer to The Summer of My Twelve-Inch Cock as "The Summer When I Finally Learned My Lesson about the Patriarchy Because Its Theater of War Played Out in My Bed."

The fact that this summer coincided with my being mad should beg the question of whether madness is ever *not* insurrectionary.

Making a location in time and space and furnishing it with words and feelings and desires that could belong to me is an attempt to become a thing to which a location and a comportment belonged, which is to say there becomes an "I" to whom a desire belongs, which would mean I was not lost. I wanted so badly to be a subject that I was willing to own what didn't, couldn't, belong to me. But more than that, I was willing to believe in ownership at all.

When the whole world believes—*what do we do?*—in the same thing. A flight of ideas, upon which only some can soar while others are tethered to the ground?

Who am I to say where the line is between wanting to fly and only wanting to dream of it; between taking up a space because you like it there and being born into a territory that is supposed to belong to you? We all develop our own ways of insisting on ourselves, which is to say, of persisting in our prisons.

Am I defined by whether I win or lose the game I'm supposed to play? Or, can my definition come from how I've gotten lost, from my refusal to play at all?

A conclusion:
    I think it's that the world simply *is* the law; the law is the world.
    The question is whether you're willing to break it.

Can I Hit You?

They are face down and naked on the bed.

"Can I hit you?" I ask.

"Yes please," they say.

I straddle them and push my wet cunt into the small of their muscular back and make fists and swing. Not too hard on the first hits, but not fucking around either. They make little whimpering sounds. There is a lot of them that can take it.

"You like that?" I ask.

"Yes," they say.

"You want me to keep going?"

"Yes please," they say.

"Harder?"

"Yes *please*."

I time my exhales to push out of me when my fists land. Blasts of air. The smack of knuckles and skin on muscles and skin. I unload. Moan. Make combinations. One, one-two, one, one-two-three. Jabs. Hooks. Their body sounds, feels, like a heavy bag at a boxing gym.

"I think my right is better than my left," I say.

"No." Their breath is interrupted at my impact. "Your left is better."

We laugh. I hit them as hard as I can with my left over and over and over, and I try to get my right better too. I feel their skin get wet with sweat against the insides of my legs.

"God, I *love* this," I say.

"Me too," they say.

I hit them again.

"Thank you," they say.

"Oh, what was that now?" I command.

"*Thank you*," they say.

I hit them until I cannot hit them anymore, then I crumple into their back and pant against their ear. They are still whimpering beneath me. I love it. They are much bigger than me—six foot four—with a cock that I can't close my hand all the way around, but they are making themself small right now, and I am glad and very wet for it. Such a good little sub. I lie on top of them until my breathing slows, feel the heat and fatigue pulse down my arms, and then I wrap one hand around their throat and pull them into me, and they let me bend their neck, and I use my other hand to make myself cum against their back, and they whimper in time with my screaming.

Kink is care, and care is kink.

What do you want me to call you?

Do you like that? Is that what you want? How much do you want it?

Is it right? Not enough? What would make it better?

Tell me how you like it. Am I doing it how you like?

Are you okay? Are you good?

In Mexico City, my best friend and I go to Lucha Libre and get our lives. They have been living there a year, and we've promised each other that we'll get friend-tattoos once we're together in their new city. The day before going to Lucha Libre, we decide to get something that the crowd will chant in the arena because we know that the chants at pro wrestling shows are everything. In CDMX, the crowd doesn't stop yelling:

"*¡Ahhhh huevo!*" (technically "testicle" but means "fuck yes")

"*¡Esoooooo!*" ("that," when something is good)

"*¡Con fuerza!*" ("with force," my friend makes this one up)

"*¡Quiero ver sangre!*" ("I want to see blood!")

We love this one. Obviously it will save us. (Tattoos are both archive and aim.) The next day we tattoo it on our bodies in each other's handwriting. We have been friends for over a decade, we have seen each other's blood. And tears and sweat and spit and laughter— so much deranged rainbow laughter. We are both disabled, mentally ill, neuro-spicy, queer freaks, gothy punks, into kink, stomping around in combat boots, reaching for metaphysics and dirty jokes to cope, and we have been with each other during the days where it felt impossible to live, and we have helped each other keep living. We have been each other's archive and aim. At the tattooist, we touch each other's skin, give each other compliments. I order us a pizza even though they say they're not hungry. "You will be in an hour," I say, and they are.

The next night we go to a queer sex rave called Pervert, where— on the dance floor, blow job to the right, hand job to the left, encountering that particular kind of god who lurks in near-pitch-black rooms with very loud music and many sweating bodies—we get our lives again. Somehow, in a sea of leather daddy gay boys wearing bondage harnesses, I manage to find a twink on molly who's into me.

I mean, I definitely *am* a leather daddy gay boy in a harness, but I don't look like one, especially in a dark room. The twink speaks no English, so I yell various phrases—"You're so hot!" "Can I hit you?"—at my friend who then yells them in Spanish at the twink who nods and nods. I'm wearing black leather gloves, and the twink puts one of my hands on his jaw and indicates he wants me to shake the shit out of his head. So I do. The harder I grip his jaw, the harder I shake his head, the happier he is. I can feel his brain sloshing around in his skull. His grin is cute.

The next day I sleep until six p.m., then stay in bed watching TV and eating a fuck lot of food. I think about how everyone who was on the dance floor last night is doing the same thing right now. This is my favorite part of raves—the long, soft day after, the sleepy ache in your whole body, the necessary rest and repair. I can only drink or do drugs when I'm lucky, and I'm never lucky, so I am pretty much sober all the time. But I dance until four a.m., in six-inch Rick Owens platform heels, and the next day I can barely move. My chronic pain flames like a motherfucker whenever I use my body for too long and too hard. It happens after I perform music live, or travel, or have one drink, or don't sleep ten hours, or have sex, or take one drag of a cigarette, or eat chocolate, or walk for more than twenty minutes, or sit in an uncomfortable chair, or work more than four hours, or carry any weight, or feel intensely about something. I have learned that pain is the price I must pay to have such experiences, which is to say that pain is the price I must pay to be awake to life.

As I write this book, I become fevered with the fact that if there is a body, then it will hurt. It's the texture to existence. I wonder if I'm fucked up for being the sort of person who is not surprised by pain, who reaches into, for, starts, and ends with pain.

I tell my friend Uma Breakdown about Lucha Libre and Pervert, and my love of violence, and my kink for punching people who've been socialized as men, how there is something about all of these that feels similar in how they deal with the body being pushed to an extreme and the support required for that. Uma points out that the most well-built care networks, the most abundant allowances for care, tend to form around activities that are criminalized—taking drugs, having deviant sex, being trans, being poor, being disabled— because of the attendant danger. Here is where we build for each other mechanisms of shared knowledge, where we make room to look after each other, because we know we will need it most in these places. Uma notes that the decision is not to *not* engage in these activities but to find ways to do them that take into account the risk and help each other through.

There is an expectation that to be shown care is to not be harmed, or that the function of care is to diminish the pain of harm, bring it below its lower limen to where it is no longer perceived. I'm not sure I trust this expectation. Numbing, forgetting, erasing, diminishing— these are never my ambitions.

Suddenly I become aware that there's a causality to care, a reason for its existence, and this—the *because of* care—is pain. Why else would care be necessary? How else would we know to rush it in? Perhaps it's not that we should try to build care around ourselves. Perhaps it's that the architecture of care is already built by pain, and the task becomes to inhabit this place, to feel free to move around in all of its rooms. I'm worried about too much silence, about that which is silenced, in this house.

We must allow ourselves to be astonished by all the ways that care forms around, is birthed from, attendant to, and necessitated by pain; and we must revel, think hard, feel deeply into the abundances of pain, for there are so many different kinds! They boil lowly and at a roil. Their color palette, the poetics, the flavors—they propel us, already, and will continue to do so. I want to be awake to all of it.

What arrives like a trailing shadow loosed into this house of pain and care is the fact of the kind of violence we can hold hands with, one to one, skin to skin. There are, of course, violence's scaled-up parents—what our governments and systems of power inflict on us—and violence's many nonconsensual relatives. How these make themselves fit into our houses, alter and rearrange our spaces and furnishings, is the stuff of many stories whose tellings have been wrested from our authorship.

Right now, I want to write about what's beneath those violences, the slithering things refusing the light—the intimate kinds of violence that we ask for, that we want, that we invite in with our own mouths and hands. These are the kinds that make us know ourselves and each other in terms that are encoded into the most foundational of experiences and yet must often be disguised, blurred, and disarticulated because of the neurosis, the perversions they point to. I am talking about the kind of knowledge that lays the substratum to the architecture built by pain.

I should tell you how I remember my mother chasing a neighbor down the street with a kitchen knife. I don't know why she did this. But, now, after years of telling it in other tones, I tell this story admiringly.

When I was a child, the most violent people in my family were the women. Of my parents, my mother was the scary one, the raging, deranged demigod who broke furniture and trashed rooms. My dad tells a story of when I was a baby, crawling on the floor, and he scooped up my small body just in time to keep my mother's kick from landing. In most of my memories of my mother, her eyes are flashing red. She thrusts her jaw forward and her bottom teeth are sharp. She looks like a piranha, a wolverine. She careens into my room at three in the morning to shriek, throw things, break everything she could get her hands on, including me. The desperate need in her was heartbreaking. It was like watching someone try to contain a detonation the size of the universe inside her rib cage. Her rib cage was engineered by pain. No care lived inside it.

My father was docile, passive, suffering. Every now and then he'd explode and punch a wall or clobber my head, but mostly he'd just sit there and simmer. He was sensitive, a musician, a dreamer, someone who went on long walks alone during his lunch break, turning over rocks to see what lived underneath, bringing home snakes and lizards in his lunch bag to keep in aquariums for a few weeks before releasing them back where he'd found them. He speaks softly, smiles easily, giggles, like a child. He is kind but distant, solitary, and can turn hard. Sometimes, during the peaks of fights with my mother, he'd get in his car and drive away, but he always came back. Until the day he didn't. I've heard from other Koreans and Korean Americans that their families had similar dynamics: violent, mean, ruthless women, and men resenting them silently, closing in on themselves. My father would shake his head with disdain and insult my mother under his breath, not listen to her, slowly and steadily and over many years erode her sense of herself, which only made her more heartsick and volatile. Once he drove away for good, the story he told about her was as if she'd been a wicked ogre who'd held him captive in a dungeon for thirty years, from which he'd finally escaped. He'd shiver in disgust whenever we talked about her. He'd make a retching sound.

If you have been asking yourself why, how, I could possibly admire my mother, butcher knife in hand, for letting her rage electrify her so much as to throttle her down the street after someone, then you haven't been paying attention. To me, or to her.

Yes, obviously, it's bad to chase someone down the street with a knife, but also, to be a child and watch a woman do this, to have this as a female role model—kind of fierce, no?

My father had been twenty-three years old for barely three weeks when I was born. Which meant he never really felt like a father but was more a big brother. He'd say we were growing up together. One of the things we'd do together was watch boxing, which I still love to do. He'd narrate. He'd show me how to hold my fists in front of my face. I have a vivid memory of playing baseball at school, around the age of nine or ten, and one of the coaches was teasing me, being a real dick. He was a large, hulking dude in a baseball hat and hoodie, and I put my fists up like my dad had taught me, and launched a series of jabs at the guy's bulk, and I could feel my wrists collapse, he was a stone wall, and he chortled at me, I made absolutely zero impact, and I understood something in my body then—a terrifying fact—how small I was, how weak, compared to men.

A recurring nightmare I've had for thirty-five years: a strange man I've never seen before (he's different in each dream) is threatening to rape and murder my mother, my sibling, my aunt, my grandmothers, my girlfriend. The man is naked to the waist, flabby or lean, hairy or smooth, old or young. His torso shines with sweat. He has a knife or a baseball bat or a club or sometimes only fists, but they are bigger than my head. He is always smiling. He can't wait to ruin us. I stand between him and the woman I need to protect. I fight him off for a few struggling minutes. He does not slow down or back off. I keep fighting. At some point in the dream, I realize I will need to murder him, that he won't stop until he's dead. Then I realize that I will have to do this with my bare hands. It is a staggering realization that spreads through everything and makes the world of the dream feel so cold it burns. My fingers can already feel the ropes of his muscles beneath his skin, the way they worm and wriggle, but I realize that I will need to claw even deeper into his body, I will need to tear the skin and muscle off his bones. That it's remarkably difficult to tear living tissue off bones is an epiphany that stuns me, but I persevere and accomplish it. I rip his hair from his scalp, feel the roots of it come out as if his head is dirt. I push my fist into his mouth, pull on his jaw until it cracks apart. I'm covered in his spit, blood, and sweat, and his tongue bucks against my hand, and he gags and I keep going. The dream goes on and on like this. In equal measure, I become more afraid and determined. How committed one has to be to murder a man with their bare hands. I am committed. This is my task. I will do it. And I do. It takes a very, very, very long time, but I always kill the man in these nightmares. Even as a child, when the dream first appeared in my night, I won. I am exhausted when I wake from them, I taste blood in my mouth, I can't move my hands. I have been fighting all night. And now I get to fight all day.

One of the most universal languages is the language of fists and power and dominance and aggression and violence. I was socialized as a woman, which means I learned this language but was told to never speak it. I was told that *when* I spoke it, this was evidence that I was beyond the bounds of the acceptable, legible, governable, and ought to be punished for my transgression. The fact that this language is always spoken first at home, in living rooms, bedrooms, across dinner tables—and is so often spoken *at* women, queers, femmes, and the sick—reveals the fantastic disingenuousness, the ostentatious hypocrisy, that architects the gender of our language.

As a child I never identified with girls. I felt closer to boys, but everything about my body and the way I was treated and talked to blared that I wasn't one of them either. I always felt closer to nonhuman creatures from fairy tales: witches, hags, vampires, ghosts, monsters, dragons. These beasts were the wrath-fueled, powerful ones, and I loved them for it. I was Maleficent transforming into the obsidian-colored dragon as tall as the sky, exhaling waves of green fire onto the tiny prince. He swung his little sword at her, and it looked like a toothpick.

For many years, I could not differentiate between fighting, violence, rage, and the pain they caused because they felt like a hot, sticky, grimy ball of worms that leaked, made messes, got me in trouble, did damage, stained everything, ruined my house. I did not know that rage can be an emotion that passes through you, no different than curiosity or joy, that it can even sometimes be a bed to rest in; that fighting can be fun and respectful, just push the furniture toward the walls to make room for sparring; that violence can be propelled by desire and choice, contained in ritual and ceremony, and there is ample, imaginative, and romantic language for all the ways in which we can say yes to it. Perhaps I could not make these distinctions— conceptually, linguistically, or practically—because for so long I did not think I was allowed to speak this language, hold it in my mouth with any sort of authority or choice.

When I got sick, I arrived into many a strange land, but perhaps the strangest was the marketplace of healing, that bazaar of quackery trying to sell me wellness in a sixty-dollar tube of cream, which is a place that predominantly peddles the idea that the rage which breaks us open, however legitimate it might be, ought to be mistrusted and ultimately mollified. Healers proclaim that anger causes cancer, that only the unenlightened hold a grudge. In this place, I've been told that the anger I carry at those who've abused me is evidence that in this life cycle I will not ascend to wisdom but will only be doomed to suffer the limits of my own ego. I've been told by a medical doctor that maybe I have chronic shingles because some part of my psyche wants to have them. When I am not an amenable patient, when I insist on my pain and agitation and fury, therapists have told me to close my eyes and breathe slowly and let go of my grudges because they only poison myself. In the marketplace of healing, there are large billboards with stock photos of (always white) women with innocuous smiles surrounded by flowers and pastels and phrases like, "Thank you for taking care of yourself."

Fuck that. I don't want to talk about healing unless we talk about never getting better and staying broken and what to do with all that hurt. I don't want to talk about care unless we also talk about how messy and painful and unfillable is the hole that our needs make in us. Do not speak to me about self-care unless you also speak to me of revenge. Do not tell me to rid my house of the demons in the basement—where would they live if I kicked them out?

Of course, there should be something psychoanalytic here about the violence my mother instantiated in me, the power of her that I myself crave, and the dynamic of she and my father that I continue to reenact in kink and elsewhere, but I'm sure you can get there on your own. My mother's violence wasn't something she directed at me because she wanted to dominate me; it looked like it was dominating *her* as much as it was me. For this reason, it did not taste like patriarchal violence, which always smacks of the will to dominate. It was a convulsing thrash that came out of her as a way of coping with the wreck of how she felt. There was no cruelty in it. There was the house she lived in, and it did not protect her, and so how could she be tasked to build one for me?

I do not hold my mother's violence against her—or, I no longer do. It's taken me two decades of all kinds of therapies to find a way to see her not only as a monster. The therapy that worked the best was kink, because, in kink, monsters are not kept outside our houses of pain and care but invited in and given a room of their own. When violence is understood as a free agent, moving through the house of pain and care, spilling its slime on the rug while also having a seat at the dinner table, the metaphors, the symbolism, can move beyond light and shadow, disgusting and pure, what we keep hidden, what lurks against us at night, what has its place in the sun. Not only is it not useful to limit ourselves into the binary of care and pain, when there are so many rooms we can go to with each other, it's not very fun.

Despite myself, my metaphor of the house brings me to a Freudian ground zero: Daddy, Mommy, Baby. Man, Woman, Orifices. Bedroom, Basement. I am bored by Freud, but I do appreciate how much space he made for resentment and jealousy, especially toward one's parents. I also like how much emphasis he placed on genitals being the seat of the problem. My problem is not only that I long for a cock of my own—my problem is that my ultimate dream is to make a cis man want to disown and remove his cock by his own hand. This has proven hard to accomplish, but a "girl" can dream, can't "she"?

The house needn't only be built by pain. Bachelard, when thinking of the chief benefit of the house, proposed: "The house shelters day-dreaming, the house protects the dreamer."

When I came out at age fourteen, it was 1998, so the only options available at the time were to be "gay" or "lesbian." It would take me another fifteen years before I had language to articulate that I was also not a cis woman, but even then, from my teenaged vantage point, I already knew that "gay" was both more accurate and pro-spective, what felt true then and what I wanted to grow even more true as a thing to reach for. I not only felt more like a man than a woman, but I preferred to fuck men. I also preferred to fight them (forgive me my spiritual smallness, but there is little difference, when it comes to men, between these two for me), and I liked how it felt to let this blurring spread through me, steel my tone, heat my gait, infuse my hands, fists, and aim with a sort of purloined priapism. It wasn't something I was allowed to do, be, or want, so of course I wanted it.

Kink, to me, is about the deviations that arise around power and pleasure; kink is anything that ruptures the seemingly impervious actions, rules, and choreographies that stabilize power—and the pleasure that comes from this rupture. It doesn't have to only be about sexual power and pleasure, but the sexual is often the site where both power and pleasure feel the most potently echoic of each other. (Sometimes I think heterosexuality is the kinkiest thing there is because it's always about how the most normie power represses pleasure, and the pleasure is in the repression itself. Ugh!)

I like rare, precious prizes; sights and sensualities that are unusual. I want fantasy to live up to its name, to show me something not common to everyday life. It felt, and still feels, defiantly profligate that I look like a woman but am not one, body as *trompe l'eoil*. I like serving hard femme cunt while using he/him pronouns. Call me Daddy, get on your knees, be prepared for humiliation if you bore me, and note, if you are a cis man, I am already bored. My favorite delicacy is the one of having a man on a leash, begging me to hit him and thanking me when I do. I like the ones who look a little uncomfortable in their own skin; they are sometimes disturbed by the residency of their cocks or curious about what other genitals might sprout from their bodies; they feel allegiance to aliens, they/thems who wear pearls, eye shadow, frail and gaunt; maybe their moms smoked cigarettes when they were enwombed. My first boyfriend wore black dresses and pushed safety pins through his face, and I began my liberation, started to form that language which had been in my mouth for years but which I'd never uttered, when, at sixteen, I informed him that the best work he'd ever do was being of service to my cunt.

The sex I've had that's felt most cathartic, magical, an iridescent transformation, were the instances where we loosed into the open space between us the desires we'd long sheltered that felt most dangerous. Until then, we'd buried them, shamed them. Now we made a container for these messes by facing our sternums toward each other, making a little auditorium out of our open mouths. We had towels nearby to clean up the fluids. We ate a lot of cake. We wept. Made noises not fit for public. We took pleasure in how desire parries the platitudes of living, we let it take us places we'd never been, were afraid to go alone. Pleasure is an infinite grammar: its expansiveness stuns, articulates beyond what feels only "good." What happens when we help each other speak this language together, let the rules of its grammar, the syntax it births, shape our insides, in turn shape our outside?

Let's start by telling each other stories of the fights we've been in. The fights I've been in are elemental to who I am. There are the stories—too many—of when I did not fight back. What I lost then. What I learned. What these lessons make me do now. Tell me about the fights you've been in, including the ones that didn't have fists. Where are the scars? Can I see them? Tell me about the most you've ever hurt and the most hurt you've inflicted. Tell me what it felt like to win those fights and what it felt like to lose. I want to know what you're like when you lose, what I get if I win. Do you want to know the same about me?

Some might disapprove of my wanting us to speak this language together. They might warn against the risk. They might be worried that I'm moving us in the opposite direction of a safe space. Except, whenever I hear the phrase "safe space," as a goal, as a promise, I flinch. When I hear people talk about trying to minimize, reduce, even eradicate harm within society, I flinch. I don't know how they purport to go about this, because it sounds to me like saying we can fix society if we just liquify all the bones in the human body. Perhaps this is a failure of my imagination, but I cannot imagine being alive in a body on this planet without violence, without pain. Even if everyone in the room agrees to reach for safety, trust, consent, care, what about all the ways that, despite ourselves, our animal parts can feel threatened, attacked, in danger, and move to break themselves open against that which violates us? And what about the hot and dark and craving ways that our animal parts wake up without being threatened? What about when we crave blood and pain and our craving is gleeful? What about the desire to tear and be torn that is not animal but human?

One of my favorite moments of my erotic life happened with The Goblin. I met him on Feeld, where the opening of my profile says: *You know how in sci-fi stories the village prospers because they keep a child chained in the basement? I'm the child.* I also say, *Go right ahead and sext me if you look like a mythological creature, especially a sick one from the underworld,* and this yields lively results. The Goblin was a queer boy from Iowa, who, yes, looked like a goblin but a sexy one (think young Willem Dafoe). He was dressed as Carrie in one of his profile photos—white prom dress, blonde wig, covered in blood (swipe right). He lived in a cave-like room in East Hollywood (uh oh) with dozens of action figures (*uh oh*), at least seven of which were the xenomorph from the *Alien* franchise (hmm), but there was a large flag, covering one wall, of Nicole Kidman's face from the AMC ads (okay, swipe right). He was trying to fist me, but as he moved his hand, something caught and cut me, and the pain flashed through my entire body. I cried out and contracted myself into a question mark. The throb in me was awful as it spread everywhere, and I closed my eyes and tried to breathe through it. That's not my favorite part.

My favorite part was his reaction. He looked suddenly afraid and worried and sad. Only a moment before, his eyes had been glazed with a dark, focused hunger. I loved making his eyes look like that, even if it was easy. How eager he had been to get his entire hand inside, making it into the shape of a swan's head, up to the hilt of the fingers. The hand was a burrowing, needy, greedy thing. But it was an accident. He'd moved his hand when I'd moved my hips in the wrong direction. When I cried, he removed his hand immediately and started to apologize. "Are you okay? I'm so sorry." His hand was now nervous, hovering over me like a frightened bird that was trying to gauge if it was safe to land. "Are you okay?" Tentatively, very gently, with fear and concern making it tremble, he lay the hand flat on my stomach. It felt like the softest thing in the world. He held up the other hand in that gesture humans do to indicate they mean no harm. It can be that sex makes a rupture, and bodies must deal with it before brains know what to do. It can be that care happens in the body before language consolidates it with intention; it can be an instinct, a compulsion, a spurt. It can be a child stepping between a smaller child and the fist of their mother. It can be a man making his hand something other than a fist.

"Are you okay?" The Goblin asked four, five times, and I said yes, even though I was not, because it can also be true that language obscures care, that words fail us, that we say what we don't mean, that we say what we wish were true but isn't yet, which is why we say and say it, trying to will it into being.

I shut my eyes and shivered, and I could feel him watching me feel my pain. This was different than the pain he was making me feel moments before, the pain that I'd wanted, how he'd watched with those hungry eyes as that happened in me. This was now our pain, something we shared, and we'd had to start sharing it because there was suddenly too much to be held by only one person. He'd given me more than I'd consented to, and now he was consenting to feeling the guilt of that in return, to participating in the repair it compelled. It became an exchange, a field in which we were both located, a kind of plenitude around both of us, rather than a force moving in one direction. I liked that. I liked how it changed him. I liked how, in an instant, from somewhere deep inside him, everything in his body agreed to hold it, to hold me. It made us try to find language to speak together. *Please*, my body said to him, *fix this. Make me feel better in the place where you made me feel bad. Learn with me that I'd asked you to make me hurt, but you gave me too much, so let's now learn together how to hold all this hurt.*

People don't always say yes when you ask for this. People often say no. He'd said yes.

A few weeks later, our fling soured. I was going home to my partner of ten years, the love of my life, and I'd never indicated that I'd want anything otherwise. The Goblin, in what I suspected was a move to keep himself from becoming too vulnerable, became unrelentingly derisive. Lots of cutting little insults. When I said it didn't feel great, he called me needy and dramatic. On our last night, I straddled his back. I was naked, he was clothed. He sort of fell asleep. It took a long time, but I made myself cum with my hand. While I was cumming, I bit his shoulder as hard as I could. I could feel the flesh between my teeth. "Ow!" he yelled, and he was angry. "*Stop!*" I stopped and rolled off him. I apologized profusely and he said, "Okay, okay, it's fine." Like him, I didn't fully mean what I said. We can say things we don't mean. We can use acts of vengeance, of violence, to ask for care.

Understanding my mother's fists on my body does not diminish the pain they caused, then or now, but knowing that they were her disconsolate attempts at putting language to her own pain, her way of asking for recognition, validation, and help the only way she knew how—in the only language in which she herself had been spoken to—offers me another meaning, which is to say, more room.

If I make room for pain to architect care, and violence to dilate and deepen meaning, and I have nightmares residing alongside my other domestic occupants, not in the basement but in whichever room they prefer, then don't I live in a house that protects dreaming of all kinds?

As many of us have, I've had to learn the hard way that, in order to encounter healing, there first must be damage that necessitates it. I've had to learn the hard way that healing is *birthed from* damage, that healing *succeeds* damage. It's that pain must already be there for us to be compelled to care.

What a cruel law of the universe. How terrifying that is. What it means we have to risk, to endure.

The blood stains that accumulate. But also, the blood stains that remind us of our shared condition—our archives and our aims.

I don't think we can plan for a better world without including, giving language to, finding ways to house all the ways we like to push each other's faces into the dirt.

It's that I can think of no greater intent to do care together than a willingness to do pain together, to invite our monstrosities, our leaking guts, our violences to find ways to live under the same roof. Turn your sternum toward mine, risk your rib cage, open your mouth. Make that little auditorium with me, a house, a stage, a dream.

The Freak

*"Haunting, or being haunted,
might indeed be another word for writing."*

JACQUELINE ROSE

Part One

I was smoking outside the café at the intersection in East LA that feels like a portal to hell when I saw them for the third time. The neighborhood weirdo, I'd heard them called. On their left arm was a large, severe, and bizarre cast: stiff and heavy over the forearm, almost up to the shoulder, freezing the elbow bent, with an elaborate rigging system that included a metal rod buttressed to their torso to keep the elbow aloft, ace bandages coiled and lashed around it all, safety pins, a rubber band tied to fishing line that looped around a hook attached to the nail of their forefinger with glue. They had a strange head that was both round and square, knuckle-sharp points of jawbone, most of the hair shaved, with a ridge in the center hanging to one side in soft spears of dark brown. A long lithe body, tapered like a pencil, taut, tall. Simple, feral clothes in various states of decay: the one outfit of black clothes worn every day for years so that everything was the color of mud, and it was their skin. Their feet curved upward in controlled flaps as they walked, a choreography I've seen only in Noh theater actors. Their walk was what I'd noticed first. A strap crossed their chest, holding a large black bag high on their back. They walked fast and stiffly, intent, not turning their head. Their back was always rail-straight, even when I had seen them reading in the café. The damaged arm was always out in front of them, a weird shield.

They walked past me, that day, in the late afternoon, and I thought, *Now*.

"Hey. I have to ask you. What happened to your arm?"

In the time it took me to speak, they halted and whipped around to face me and held up their good hand. They moved their body close, shadow looming, they were blocking the sun from my face, and when I was dark in it, they said, "I don't know you well enough to tell you that yet."

It went easily like this.

We went inside, sat across a table. They were my age, Latinx, dark skin, an intense stare. At one point they reached over and picked up my necklace in their good hand. It was one red wooden bead the size of a tiny lime. "It's heavier than I thought," they said.

"I've been joking that it's a ball gag for kids," I said.

Without a beat, they said, "You have a little mouth."

Appreciated my naming things miserable because "most of them are." Called Americans "anodyne." Won't sit on Sunset Boulevard under a sign that says *Intelligentsia*—would rather be shot. "Don't they know who the intelligentsia were?" Had a long, elegant name that was dispensed with immediately: "But you can call me whatever you want."

No phone, no car, no computer, no email address, no social media, but also no roommate, no college education, no friends, no inquiries about me beyond my name. Long, long silences during which they stared at my eyes, blinking calmly, with an expression blank with want. They worked next door and lived a couple of blocks away, that little corner, portal, theirs. Asked for my number and said, "If you see a strange number calling you at a strange time, that's me."

We talked at the café until it closed at dusk. I watched the one-handed injured endeavor of putting on a disintegrating mud-colored sweater. It got clasped at the front with a butterfly clip they slid over a strip of masking tape that was folded around the hem and burnished gray. One sweater sleeve was torn by the rough thumb of the cast, and the whole thing had been mended often, with craggy stitches, pieces of other fabrics notched into it with rough sutures, but the sweater was not scary-looking; it just looked like the only sweater.

We went for a walk. A young woman carrying a prop witch broom walked past us. I said, "I wonder what she's going to do with that."

They grinned with teeth and said, "I hope she rides it."

Pulled me out of the way of a car so that I understood they were capable of taking me by the soft neck and throwing me somewhere else. On our march up a side street to the top of the hill, they grew hoarse, breathing as though to win the race. I saw a hot wire under their skin, what made them look so stiff and charged and determined. Tried to match their gait, where they put their feet. My legs were little. They sped ahead.

"Why do you walk so fast?" I called after them.

"Oh I wasn't thinking about that."

"What were you thinking about?"

Stopped to say it face-to-face. "Maybe you." The kiss was strangely soft, and they were already hard.

A strange number called me at a strange time a week or two later. We met at a bar. There was a band playing, and it was too loud. They yelled over it, "I want to go somewhere where I can hear your voice."

I drove. In an intersection ahead of us, a pair of cars barely missed crashing into each other. "I thought we were going to get a show," they said with disappointment. Their smell stayed in my car for weeks.

At the quiet bar I took us to, they looked around the room and nodded. "You did good, babe." Sometimes when I tell this story, a certain kind of straight woman will roll her eyes. The bar specialized in imported beer, and they talked far too long at the waiter about the differences between German and Austrian and Belgian beer. The waiter was bored and polite, and I was annoyed. But I always fall for the neuro-spicy ones. I don't remember anything of what we talked about, only that there was another staring silence, a very, very long one. We sat there for minutes, saying nothing, looking into each other's eyes and around each other's faces, not battling, not smiling, just looking. Generally, I think I am most charming when I talk, so I use it as armor, wit as a charismatic weapon. Being still and wordless is dangerous, someone can see right in. But with them, my breath slowed. I have never been so quiet, felt so calm in the presence of a stranger, and I have never stared at someone who was staring back at me for so long. Such bald eye contact, bare and plain in what it meant.

They raised their good hand, and in slow, steady motion brought it over to my face. They held it there for a while, I could feel the heat of it on my skin. I did not close my eyes but watched them through their fingers, they watched me back, a minute passed, and then they dragged a gentle middle finger from my temple to my chin and held me.

I drove them home. We sat in the car for a moment, then they said, "I'm going to invite you in. But I promise I won't do things like rub my thumb in circles around your thumb to indicate that I want something from you." They were extra careful to check that I could leave my car parked where it was, hopping into the street to read the signs.

They lived in a complex of worn-down stucco bungalows. A tall wooden gate guarded a steep staircase that went crookedly up the hill, the dwellings on either side of it facing each other, with bars on all the windows. A datura tree threw its scent at their front door. I wanted to remember these details because they anchored this person.

All the walls inside their studio apartment were painted brown, and so was the ceiling. The carpet was dirty, stained, and brown. In the back corner of the room was a thin mattress on the floor, covered with a bunched-up sheet that was brown. There were a few bare light bulbs in crooked wall sconces, lighting the room a dark yellowy brown. Their skin and hair and clothes and everything in their house—brown. Dark brown bookcases were crowded together along the walls, and a wood table took up most of the room, and these were all crammed with mounds of papers and books. On the table was a large electric typewriter from the 1980s with a page in it covered in words. On the floor were more books and papers, stacked precariously, waist-high, so there was no space to walk, and I thought of Henry Darger. Yellow Post-it notes scribbled with words and phrases dotted the whole place, stuck on the bookshelves, the walls, typewriter, table. I tried to read the ones on the typewriter, but the writing looked like hieroglyphics. They saw me looking and said, "You can't read those." I wondered if they meant I couldn't understand them or that I wasn't allowed to. I noticed a single black leather glove on top of a stack of books. The cover of the book beneath it peeked out: a biography of Louise Brooks. Other titles I remember seeing: *History of Nomadic Peoples, Boxing Techniques, The Book of Ass and Legs.*

There was one Post-it I did manage to read. It was stuck on the back of the front door, the last thing they would see upon leaving. It said, *Bring home the bacon.*

I used the bathroom. The bathtub had long streaks of rust and a bucket in it. I turned on the hot water tap of the sink, which was black with mildew, but only cold water came out.

"There's no hot water," they said when I returned. In the kitchen was a rusted bicycle upside down on the floor, and the walls and shelves were lined with empty beer bottles, all brown. I noticed the only window was blocked by a bookshelf.

I had a thought that rang inside me like a bell: *This person is going to kill me.*

Then I thought, *This is going to be great.*

I don't know how to explain this other than to say, as someone who has felt their body pushed into the possibility of death (my own, my mother's) without their consent, and who has reached for my own death and found it to be pretty boring, it was thrilling to realize that I might have reached into a wet, hot, extinguishing darkness that, rather than be a mundane removal of life, could be a removal from it that went out with a bang.

They put on a CD that sounded as though someone had recorded a lumberyard. It clanged and buzzed on loop for the entire night. At some point I asked what it was, and they answered, "Noise."

They stood in the middle of the room and stared at me. I stared back.

We met.

I felt around under their shirt, tapping at their hard, thin body. When I flattened my hands on them, I flinched. Their skin was rough. They were covered in scars.

"Why do you have these scars?"

"I do a lot of extreme sports."

"What do you mean, extreme sports?"

"I mean I do a lot of extreme things with my body."

"Like what?"

"Like I use my body for extreme things."

"What do you mean? Like BMX?"

They laughed.

"Like you jump between buildings?"

They laughed again.

I felt around some more. The scars covered their torso, shoulders, arms, and back. They were violent scars, irregular, many, little nicks, long cuts, seams and lines and gashes and patches of raised skin. They were not the carefully designed kind of the self-inflicted.

It jolted me when I thought it. "Are you in a fight club?"

They were quiet.

"You're in something like a fight club, aren't you?"

Quiet.

"Is that how you hurt your arm?"

"I can't," they paused, then their voice became a whisper, "tell you about it."

There was more silence while I touched them with this new knowledge and decided to believe in whatever sort of fight club it could be.

After a while, I said, "You're very tall."

They sank to their knees in front of me and said, "I could be like this for you."

When I pulled off their shirt, they raised their arms but it was awkward with the cast. They noticed my tattoo of a line that rings the inside of my right ear. "What's this?" they said and tilted my head, holding my face again. I started to say, "I got it because," but they figured it out quickly and put their good hand gently over my mouth and said, "Oh I see. It's a kind of instruction." They followed it. It was as if they could already read the language of me, they could anticipate me, hold me in the way I wanted to be held, even if I didn't know how to ask for it yet. They had shaved all their body hair. When I saw that they were eleven inches and uncut, another thought jolted me and I finally understood.

"Do you do porn?"

Without a pause—they never paused to think about their responses—they said, "I'm not known though, because if I wanted to make real money I'd have to do what I don't want to do." They blinked, their eyes wet.

I didn't ask what they wanted to do. I could already guess, how quickly they'd sunk to their knees, how they'd told me to call them whatever I wanted. I saw what must be done to them on set, how they must be hurt, how they must want to be.

When we first got into the bed, they turned off the lights, but after a while, they got up and started lighting tealight candles. "You might think I'm crazy, but I'd like to see your face."

It was then that I realized, rather than kill me, they probably just wanted to love me.

We had to maneuver around their cast. They apologized.

I said, "You'll have to demonstrate how dexterous you are with one hand."

They said, "Baby, that's what I've been doing." They said, "Both of your mouths are petite."

They warned me that they'd make "odd sounds," which they did when they buried their face in me for an hour and whimpered like a dog. They looked like the broken Christ in the arms of the Pietà when I made them cum beneath me without a sound, head fallen back.

Afterward, they told me, "I feel like I've been waiting for you for a long time." Then I told them I had a condition, an illness, and they looked at me like I was disgusting. "No," they said and turned away.

We slept without touching. When I got up to leave in the morning, they said quietly, "I'm sorry if I was mean at the end."

Two weeks later, they called me to say they would call me again in three weeks. It was the last time we spoke. When they did call three weeks later, three times in two days, I didn't answer.

Part Two

A few months later, I started working at an art space next door to the café where I met them. They worked in the building a few over, so close, I would imagine them in there, a couple walls away. I spent every day expecting to see them, and I could not breathe for this possibility. The art space had a large storefront window that looked out onto one of the busiest streets in LA, and I worked at a table inside facing the street. All day, as I sat there, I would look up with fear and thrill and shivering lust each time I saw a dark figure walk by, anyone who moved fast, anyone who was slim and stark, my stomach would surge. I'd hurry to my car at the end of the day, and I never, ever, ever went into the café next door. I imagined that if they came around the corner while I was walking to work, I would turn around and go the other way, or I would become unable to move, I would suffocate in myself, but I didn't know why.

As obvious as it may be now, for ten years I didn't know why I didn't answer when they'd called, why I was both so afraid to see them again and why I wanted nothing more. It's that they were a kind of representative of my own underworld, my depravity, my morbidity, my death wish, my demons, and to want to be face-to-face with that again, to want to hold it in my hands beneath me again, was incomprehensible. Also, I was just crushing pathetically.

But I didn't see them for the rest of the summer or that fall.

They became a story I told to friends. I named them The Freak. They were a good story.

At the end of December, I sublet an apartment about a mile away. There was a café on the corner. One late afternoon, I took a break from writing, not bothering to change out of my lumpy housedress, to come downstairs, smoke, get a coffee. The Freak was standing on the sidewalk, locking up their bicycle. I ran back inside, up the stairs, and breathed into my hands. They still had a cast on their arm, but it was much smaller, smoother, and they didn't have to hold it in front of their body like before. Otherwise, they looked the same, their muddy-black, sharp head, large bag strapped to their back, body like a lash.

So began the sightings. They were always precipitated by a kind of psychic flash, as soon as I'd wake up I'd be struck by the thought: *I'm going to see The Freak today*. And then I would.

A few weeks later, for instance, I woke up and that thought sparked through me and then I was driving to work and saw them sitting outside a café, leaning against the red brick, eyes closed to the sun. I had the thought rush me as I awoke on an unseasonably hot morning and then I saw them walking near the river that afternoon; the cast was now a brace on their wrist. Twice, I'd get an itch up my spine, a sting would spread through my scalp, and then moments later they rode past the art space's window on their bike, the bag on their back. What did they have in there? Books? Boxing gloves? Whips? Once, I was standing outside a restaurant, waiting to meet a friend. It was night. I faced the street. Someone walked behind me. I could hear the footsteps—it was like there was greedy breath on my neck—and then their tall frame slipped by. Did they see me? How could they not see me? One night, nearing two in the morning, I was driving home from drinks with a friend. Near the underpass, I thought I saw a slender shadow walking quickly on the sidewalk. I flipped the car around and drove back, determined that I would stop and get out and see them. I would say something.

There was no one.

It occurred to me that they might be a ghost. My ghost. A figment of my underworld who got loose. Maybe they didn't exist up here.

Months passed without a sighting. It became a new year. The streets stopped humming when I walked on them, and when I woke up there was no tingly spark. I calmed down at work, went into the café, loitered outside it, smoking with my colleagues or alone. The summer came. I spent an afternoon walking around with a friend, putting up posters for an event. When I was inside a restaurant, taping the poster to the window, I looked out the glass to see The Freak standing there, a few feet away. They were still, their face arrogant and strange, scanning the street. There was a carnal hunger in their expression, like they were calculating some kind of destruction they could bring to the scene. I hid behind my poster and watched as they walked past. They wore black leather gloves without fingers and their cast was gone. They had the big bag on their back. They strutted like a rooster, skating their gaze back and forth. I thought they saw me, were looking right at me, but then I realized they were making eye contact with their own reflection in the glass.

My friend and I walked on, stopping at the farmers market for tacos. While sitting at the tables, The Freak roamed by, still scanning everything like it was prey. I hunched over and tried to explain what I could to my friend, who responded by saying, "I don't see what the big deal is." How to explain that a demon from your own underworld has managed to walk through the farmers market?

We went back to my friend's car and drove on, but while waiting to turn right at the intersection at the portal to hell, The Freak walked up to my side of the car. My window was rolled down. They were twelve (eleven?) inches away from me. So close that I could see only their mud-black T-shirt that I recognized. And I could smell them again, I loved it, that smell. I screeched and covered my face. My friend drove us away, saying, "You're acting really weird."

In July, there was an opening at the art space for a collective I was in. I stood outside with the crowd, in the hot night, speaking with a close friend who had heard me tell the story of The Freak many times. Over my friend's shoulder, I saw a figure in black dart across the street.

"Oh my god," I hissed, interrupting my friend, leaping behind him to hide. "It's The Freak!"

My friend, an old bitch, tossed a glance over his shoulder, turning lazily while taking a drag of his cigarette, then said, "You didn't say The Freak was hot."

In August, I was standing outside the art space in a small group, speaking to someone on my right. I faced north, the busy street on my left, droning its river of traffic sounds. I felt someone soundlessly walk by me. I looked. It was The Freak. A few paces ahead, they turned to look at me over their shoulder. Our eyes met. I couldn't read their expression, and I did not move my face and it was similar to when they weren't looking at me but at their own reflection in the glass, but this time they saw me and I saw them, and we looked at each other, and what we saw then is the reason I've spent more than ten years trying to write this essay.

They turned away and kept walking. I didn't see them again for a year.

Part Three

In January 2013, my illnesses crested, and my body and my mind broke. I fell out of the world, out of time. I forgot many things and wasn't capable of doing those that I could remember. I spent all day and night in the bed and months passed this way. I retreated to the exceptional world of my dreams, preferring them to my waking hours, and The Freak appeared several times there. So did everyone else, but The Freak's appearances weren't like the others. In the dreams, we were happy together, laughing, carrying each other in yellow afternoon light, warm with love. In the dreams I was safe with them. In the dreams The Freak would giggle like a child.

In June, I began writing a novel, trying to conjure an Icarus-like character who builds a flying machine into himself, hacking his own flesh. I thought of The Freak, their bionic cast, their scarred body, and started to make the character from flashes of memory of that evening in their brown room. By then, the memories had dimmed to only the sharpest shards, so I searched my past writing for any notes I might have taken. I found a long paragraph in a folder on my computer from 2011. The details I had forgotten rushed back, and I felt an immense and disturbing amount of pleasure at the story of The Freak washing over me. I told a friend, and she was instantly fascinated, which felt validating, it wasn't only me. "The Freak!" she said, rubbing her hands together. She kept trying to guess what they had in their bag.

A week after I found the paragraph, I was cleaning out my car. Under the seat with a load of trash was a notebook I didn't even know I'd lost from the summer of 2011. I opened it and found several passages about The Freak, breathless and electric, written in the days after our two encounters. I had written down many things that hadn't made it onto the computer—their comment about both of my mouths, for example. How could I have forgotten that? I'd also written down their address—the only way I had to reach them. When I read the numbers, I felt the jolt, the sting, the itch.

In the notebook, there were descriptions of the five weeks between our final phone calls. I had been wild trying to get in contact. Since I had no way to call, text, or email them, and I'd thought it'd be a douche move to show up at their work, I'd gone the creepy route and left a note on the gate of their complex, saying "And so?" I'd driven to their house one night to find the gate open and amazingly summoned the courage to climb the stairs and knock on the door. I climbed up and down several times before knocking, and when there had been no answer, despite the dim light coming from the blocked window, I snapped off a branch of the datura and left.

I think I had forgotten how badly I'd wanted them because I didn't know why I so badly wanted them, only that desire like this had never taken me over, it wasn't a kind I had felt before. It was only partially about sex. We had spent just one afternoon and one night together. We had talked on the phone twice, for only a few minutes, and the last time they'd breathed one sentence at me, then hung up. They gave me no backstory, asked nothing about mine, and they only ever complimented me. I knew nothing about them except what they'd shown me, but what they'd shown me had been unlike anything else.

And I knew that I had seen The Freak in a way they'd never been seen before. I could see why they wanted all those scars to accumulate on their skin, why they sought and reached for pain, why they hid from the world, why they dispensed with their given name, got on their knees without needing to be told to. My joke to friends was that if The Freak had the internet, they'd be trans by now. They'd claim their neurodivergence. They'd have a killer Tumblr. Know where to download the weirdest hentai. But they didn't have the internet, or friends, or a community. So instead, they had their solitude, their injury, the chronic pain and disability it gave them, and they had their peculiarity, specificity, their kink. They rented DVDs of black-and-white movies and watched them over and over. Their favorite was Marlene Dietrich; she was The Freak's mirror. They covered the walls of their home with little notes because their brain spilled over the edges of itself. I could see them going to bars to dance alone, drinking too much, getting in fights at closing time, and when someone made them taste their own blood, I could see the ground it put beneath them, the only time they felt they were standing on something stable.

When I first touched their skin and felt their scars, how many there were, how alive, I felt as if I were touching my own insides. I knew what these scars meant and memorialized. My skin does not itself look like The Freak's, but I have cut it, scratched it, bruised it on purpose. I have bashed my head into a wall, thrown myself out of a moving car, had myself tattooed, known the pleasure of having a needle and other things hammer into me. The kink, for me, is when it gets psychologically complicated, goes past the expected, brings you to your fear in such a way that you cannot look away from it. One of my favorite things is to demand my subs look me in the eye while I'm topping them. When they squirm and say, "I can't, I'm afraid of you," I hold their face, like The Freak held mine, gently, exactly. "Open your eyes and look at me," I command.

The Freak never looked away, never said I'm afraid of you. Instead, they stared right back.

They saw me the same way I'd seen them. They were a version of myself that for so long I could not show anyone, could rarely even show myself, but it was more honest than the costume I wore.

Over the years I wrote them into my novel, I watched them appear in other characters I created, I used part of this text for a video series I made about memory and myth, and when I describe my type, I describe The Freak, when I fantasize I see their body, when I see the parts of myself I keep hidden, the illegible parts, the fucked-up shit, I see them, I am them, my masculinity sitting awkwardly on my frame, my vengeance and carnality moving against the ways I tremble and whimper, the ways I am expanded by rage and pain in parallel with how often I feel fragile, small, and beneath, I see—I am—The Freak. The Freak is looking up at me from on their knees, I am standing over them. The Freak is beneath me, looking divine while I make them spurt into my hand. The Freak is looking at me, into me, and seeing themself. Mirrors.

It has been years since I have seen The Freak, but I cannot now be in that part of LA without thinking that this nook in the world still belongs to them. At least, I hope it does. They have come to represent a time and place in Los Angeles, of what LA could make, whom it could birth. They are an LA that freaks could live in, with no phone or computer, with only a typewriter, no car, a punk kid who did brutal, underground porn and rented Marlene Dietrich DVDs at the library, and alone, they were always alone. I don't think that version of LA exists anymore. Now, the lake has a fence around it.

A few days after finding the lost notebook in my car, almost two years to the day of our first meeting, I was driving by chance near their place and saw a dark figure on a bicycle. I said out loud to myself, "Oh my god, is it The Freak?" And when I saw that it was, I shrieked and clapped and said their full name out loud. I'd remembered it even though they told me not to. I watched in my rearview mirror as they pulled their bike up to the tall gate. They still lived there, and I had the address.

The next day, I sent them a letter.

It said: *Sometimes you've appeared near me on the street, and I've often wondered about you. Recently I found this bit of writing from two years ago. They were just notes so I could remember. I'd like you to have it. And I'd like to get a letter from you.*

Now, still, I am waiting.

A friend, after I told him the story of The Freak, said, "You recognized in The Freak a place where your own freak could finally rest."

My own freak.

Obviously, I call The Freak "The Freak" out of love.

Obviously, The Freak in this story is me.

Part Four

Over the years a lot of people have asked me what care is. The words I've written on care have gone around the internet, someone even embroidered them in needlepoint. When I answer, I try to explain that care is not usually what you think it is: it's not someone bringing you soup while you're sick, and it's not someone brushing your hair because you're too weak to do it yourself. Well, it's not only that. Those normative moments can be full of care, sure, but they can also be completely devoid of it. They can be moments of manipulation, infantilization, exploitation, struggles and imbalances of power, of need turned rank and bent into a tool of control. Think of the many mothers and wives of gothic melodrama smothering their dependents with oppressive love. Think of someone punching you in the face while also claiming to care about you. Think of the weapons the state trots out in the name of care.

The example of care that I prefer to offer is this: One of my favorite concerts to go to in LA was the annual Metal and Beer Festival, held for several years at the Regent Theater downtown. It was a multi-night event, with many bands a night, and all their logos looked like the cracks in the back of an ancient leather chair. The crowd was adorable: spikes, tattoos, piercings, dog collars, leather, hoodies, fish nets, platform boots. At the door, as I do at every concert, I'd ask for ADA seating, and what it meant at the Metal and Beer Festival was that a security person would come to personally escort me inside, carrying a barstool, which they'd then tell me to "put wherever you want." I'd put it in a back corner, where the floor sloped up, so I could see above the crowd. But the Regent Theater was small, so I would never be far from the mosh pit—no one was.

Once, when I was sitting on my barstool and the friend I'd come with had gone to get a beer, the pit started to really fume. Boots floated by my head, and I struggled to stay upright. A couple standing nearby, very tall and fat, much bigger than me, wearing leather jackets with spikes, saw me, clocked the situation, and without words moved to flank me, standing on either side. The song roared and everyone screamed on cue, and the couple used their bodies to protect me from any damage that might get too close, and we raised our fists and punched the air in time with the double-bass drum, and that's what I think about when I think about care.

One of my most beloved details about the story of The Freak is that the first thing they said to me inscribed a boundary that could not be breached but was wonderfully enterable—*I don't know you well enough to tell you that yet.* What a great first line. I love the "yet." In a way, the last thing they ever said to me was also like this: "I'm calling to say I will call you again in three weeks." The part of the story that hurts the most, when they became disgusted at the fact of my illness, is another reason why—and here I finally realized that this is what it was—I respect them. It hurt, and at the time it ruined the best one-night stand of my life, and maybe that's why I didn't answer the phone when they called me later, but it also made me respect them. Am I saying that it made me love them?

This is the hardest part of the story to explain. It's the part that doesn't fit, that kinks the narrative.

I have had to tell many about my disability—family, friends, strangers, teachers, bosses; fuck, I have to tell the door guy at the Metal and Beer Festival—and I have received the gamut of responses, the majority of which were some shade of negative. With some I've had to dramatically cut cords when they couldn't hang, but with most, they just disappeared when things got real. I used to get angry about this, turning it over in my mind for years, how they abandoned me, how I must have deserved it, what sort of hex was suitable revenge. Yet, it is also true that, with those friends who are no longer my friends because of the care I needed, when I try to think of them as people who said no to me out of respect, out of care, for both of us, even if that's not what they meant or how it felt at the time, I know it feels better, takes away the burn. It is also true that, when I have shamed someone into caring for me, the results were disastrous and hurt much worse. Another side of this truth is that the best it's ever felt is when people say yes to caring for me because they want to.

This means that we can do care together, that I can care for, and with, them too.

Let me put it like this: a core fact about care, and kink, is that it requires strong boundaries to work well. Although everyone understands that about kink, this fact is not included in how we understand care. This is because we understand kink as a choice, a preference, an expression of desire, something to say yes or no to. And although we should, for it is all those things that kink is, instead we understand care as a provision, a supply, a resource to be mined—which means it can be depleted, turned into something inert. We make care into the sort of transaction that we have with an ATM. It is not something we can want together but what one of us concedes to give or to take, and only within limit. Rather than see care as an act that is brought to life because of and through the relationships it animates and sustains, our normative understanding of care is determined by *whom* it defines: who gave too much, who took too much. This erases the fact that everyone engages in, uses, needs, gives, and takes care all the time.

Yes, without the word "care" in front of them, the words "taker" and "giver" form a binary of opposites. So what, then, is to be gleaned from the fact that when we add "care," caretaker and caregiver become equivalent?

What gets me hard is the commutativity of human entanglements, the fluidity of let x equal y. How we can be moved, how we can swap positions, how the order can be changed but the value won't.

What I love about kink is that it starts from the premise that we're all freaks and then asks how to support that. Care starts from the opposite place, framing illness, disability, and debility as freak moments out of the ordinary that must be managed back into normalcy. Where kink foregrounds desire, choice, agency, and consent, care is incarcerated in duty, obligation, and burden, so no wonder care feels like a drag and kink is way more fun. At the heart of both kink and care is the darkly throbbing fact of power: in order for kink to work, power has to not only be acknowledged but engaged with, kept close, within sight and mouth at all times—but power is nowhere discussed in the context of care, and I don't need to tell you why that is a mistake.

In the disabled community, we prefer the word "capacity" to "capability." Yes, you might be capable of doing something, but do you have the capacity for it in this moment? This barometer works for everyone, disabled or not yet disabled. What do you want? What do you need? How do you want it? Are you okay right now? If not, what could help? These questions can be asked of everyone involved— let x equal y—not only the ones whom we perceive to be on the receiving end. Care *could* start from the same premise and fore-ground the same things that kink does: it could be voluminous enough to contain what someone wants and how they want it, what they need and why, and for everyone involved to flaunt this wetly for and with each other. We could understand that the person "taking" care is not the only one taking it, nor is the person "giving" care the only one offering themselves—just like the person getting off on being spanked is not the only person in the room who is cumming. As there is any kind of porn available on the internet for any possible kink, care can look a million different ways too. It can be dirty, it can be full of rage, it can happen in a mosh pit, it can leave shit stains on the sheets.

What I am trying to say is that the story of The Freak is about the fact that you cannot tell a story about care without kink, pain, and scars. Without someone on their knees. Hiding from themselves and whoever's watching and also unzipping themselves completely to fall into the open. You cannot tell a story about care that is not also a ghost story, an account of being haunted by someone you've been waiting for, or by someone, maybe yourself, who is no longer there. A story of care is about something twisted sharply away from where we think it is supposed to be and how fascinating that is. A story about care must include death getting close, the thrill of wanting it, the way the smell of a body stays, and someone whimpering like a dog. The strangeness, the hunger and need, the deviance—these are the things that make it a story about care.

For what kind of story is it of a young person socialized as a man, with skin they've decorated with scars, sinking to their knees in front of a stranger who knows who they are? Of wanting this stranger to call them anything but their name? What kind of character, in which kind of story, wants to be hurt so that it leaves a mark, and wants that and wants that again and again? Wants to give their body over to someone else because that gives them a way into who they are? What kind of story is it of two people staring at each other in silence and being seen—mirrors inverted, cloudy, defiant, waiting, wanting, sweet? What kind of story is the one about a freak who waits years to see a freak and then runs away when the other gets close?

The last time I saw The Freak was in 2016, a few weeks before I moved to Berlin. I was in the car with my sibling, going east, nearing the intersection at the portal to hell. We were backed up at the light, waiting to turn left. The Freak was sitting on a bench outside a store that had gone out of business. They were directly across the street from our car.

"Oh my god," I said, pointing. "It's The Freak." I'd told my sibling the story many times.

"Oh fuck, what?!" They were thrilled. "I can't believe I finally get to see them!"

We sat there, staring at them, just a few feet away. I don't know if The Freak saw us. I don't know if they ever saw me staring at them over the years, but I like to think they did. I like to think that they saw me watching and so, just for me, they put on a show.

They were in black, sitting with their back rail-straight, alone. Their hand, the one that had been in the cast, was open in their lap, and they bent their head ever so slightly over it. We watched them purse their lips and spit a long gob of saliva into their open palm. It left their mouth slowly, the string of it lengthening with gravity, and their hand was waiting for it, then holding it. My sibling cracked up. I screamed. Then the light turned green, and we drove toward the portal to hell and turned left.

Notes on Trash Talk
(aka Notes on Community)

You should know that I am a huge fan of UFC. I watch it every week. I am not being ironic. I find fighting in general to be one of the most exhilarating and erotic things to witness, and I love MMA in particular because there are very few rules (no punching the spine or the back of the head), so any savagery is up for grabs. I love the language of it—that a fighter's fists are "weapons" they "must control," that a knockout is "being separated from consciousness," that a fighter can lose by "submission." I love seeing the bloodstains accumulate on the floor of the cage over the course of a night. Watching bodies make themselves and each other sweat and bleed and pant and get red and broken and hurt together is a language that makes me feel connected, alive, with other people.

One of the things I love most about UFC, like drag (my other favorite thing), is the trash talk. For my money, it's contemporary Shakespeare. In drag, it's the library being open, reading a bitch, being read for filth: "You are so old that your colostomy bag is made of wood." "When asked to act her age, she died." In pro wrestling, a wrestler is valued for their "mic skills," for being a good "mic worker," grabbing the mic in a beefy paw and elucidating why exactly their opponent should be cowering in their booty shorts: "Understand, when you step in the ring, your arms are just too short to box with god."

Some of my favorite moments of UFC trash talk: Khabib Nurmagomedov saying of his opponent, the whippersnapper Conor McGregor, "I want to change his face." My beloved Israel Adesanya shrugging, unbothered, and saying his opponent Marvin Vettori would, by the end of round one, be "breathing through his mouth a lot."

A good insult is worth the cost of the earth.

What I want to make sure of is that, when we dream our political dreams that envision a society better than this one, trying to imagine a future better than the now, we make space for insults.

It's not lost on me that insulting your opponent in an ableist way is often the most lacerating. Any non-white non-straight-cis-man on the internet knows that being insulted for one's body is a special wickedness. If it's coming from an outright enemy—a troll on the right, a transphobe, a white supremacist, etc.—it's easier to funnel this into the bucket in our brains that holds nonsense. I have felt acutely the sting when words from enemies aimed with malice about my condition, my lack of ability, what I cannot do, how I move weird, find their mark and land—the times when strangers shout at me in the street about my cane, my hobbling walk. Yet, this happens far less than remarks about my disability that have been obfuscated with good intentions—the times when a judgment is snuck into a comment coated in politeness, an opinion smuggled into a passive aggression—and these are the insults that wriggle deeper and throb. Often, these come from people I know, or who seemingly mean well. I would much prefer that we could just have it out openly in a roast, where they can dish it and I can dish right back. I'm not saying I want us to hurt each other more effectively; I'm saying I want to make space for language to move in the open, to not prevaricate around the truth. My hunch is that, in doing this, language will be made both more precise and honed while it will also be expanded to contain more about what is difficult, painful, and messy.

Also, I want to laugh. More and always.

As we all know, one of the best ways to deflate an insult is to meet it head-on: to laugh at it, to be unbothered, to shrug it away as unimportant. Another way to deflate an insult is to agree with it. What punk glory there is in taking the slur lobbed at you and smearing it all over your grinning face. Bitch, that's *right* I'm disabled! You want to see exactly *why* I need a special toilet?

In Los Angeles, The Goblin (with the action figures and Nicole Kidman flag) takes me to a pro wrestling show at the Forum. I've never been to a show like this but have always wanted to. I dress up, wear black latex and red lipstick, and I masturbate in the car on the drive there. I scream during the orgasm and scare The Goblin a little bit, and this makes me even more cheerful.

The Goblin has explained to me that pro wrestling is masculinity drag. Drag is femininity drag. "Oh fuck," I say. "I cannot wait."

I always say that the best drag show on TV is not *RuPaul's Drag Race* but the UFC. I love the pageantry, the ceremony, how the fighters walk in to their song, slowly take off their clothes, get smeared with Vaseline. The Goblin is right—I cannot believe how fucking gay pro wrestling is. The spectacle, the costumes (leotards, tights!), the hair! And oh, so *much* homoeroticism. All the men sitting on the shoulders of other men, crotches shoved into faces. The Goblin makes a slurping sound every time this happens. "Mmm," he says, "all these sweaty boys," and chews his mouth.

It's a Wednesday, a sold-out crowd of 17,500 people. The head-liner of the night is a duo, The Acclaimed, who are a pair of gay boys in neon-pink spandex. Their slogan, which the entire crowd erupts to chant when they appear on stage, is "Scissor me, Daddy Ass!" There is a long story as to how this slogan came about, but it doesn't matter. All that matters is for you to imagine a crowd of 17,500 people, shooting to their feet, overjoyed, entire families brandishing home-made cardboard and aluminum foil scissors, men and women of all shapes and sizes and stations of life and sexualities, and people like me and The Goblin and his friends, two nerdy trans girls, all of us, making a hand gesture to go along with the chant, screaming at the top of our lungs, "Scissor me, Daddy Ass! Scissor me, Daddy Ass!"

The Acclaimed run onstage to a marvel of pyrotechnics and commence a song and dance. But one of them fucks up the lyrics. He waves his hands and stops the song. "Wait! I'm sorry, I messed up. We gotta do it again!" They scamper offstage, and the camera operators and MC reset, and the crowd erupts in laughter and applause. Everyone starts chanting, "You fucked up! You fucked up! You fucked up!"

I look around the arena, amazed. Everyone is happy, giggling, clapping. There is chiding, yes, but no malice, nothing cruel. I realize I have never been in a more supportive environment. I have never been in a collective of this many people who wanted so enthusiasti-cally for someone else to succeed, who held the space for a mistake with levity and benevolence. I could never have imagined feeling this way at a place like this. My wig is snatched.

Not me at a WWE event on a Wednesday having a vision of polit-ical utopia.

Can you imagine how the world would be different if this was the reaction when someone made a mistake? Online, at a work meeting, at the demonstration, in the classroom—what if fuckups were com-munally encouraged, amiably laughed about, even applauded? If, say, someone is trying to do something they've never done before, thinking a new thought out loud for the first time, presenting a project they've been working on, stepping into a new position of visibility—what if the fuckups they will inevitably make in those moments were met, not with shame or punishment, but a good-natured guffaw? And in political terms, if someone uses an offensive word unknowingly, if an opinion is expressed that is ignorant, outdated, perhaps was once accepted (even revolutionary for its time) but has now become problematic and cringey—what might our political life feel like if we all started clapping and chanting, *You fucked up*? What might it feel like to go forward together knowing that we could fall and fail and flail and laugh about it together, and everyone would be there to catch everyone?

Once, at an event of mine, an audience member asked me what possible third, other concept might offer respite from the binary I'd set up between care and pain. The first thing that came to mind was humor. Being able to laugh, joke, tease, and roast each other, it seems to me, is the easiest way to disrupt the endless seesawing back and forth between the grim certainty of pain and how it necessitates the earnest monolith of care.

Over the years, I've noticed that when topics of disability make their way into a mainstream place of discussion, it's often around terminology, what the disabled community wants or doesn't want to be called. The abled community usually responds that we should not take such things so seriously, and the disabled community can only reply by doubling down. I am not very stirred by this as progress. I don't want the abled community to think that all we care about is *words*. As if the greatest challenge, the greatest harm, to the disabled community starts and stops there.

On the other side of this, I think of how many newly disabled people are shamed and criticized by those of us who've been here longer because they don't yet know the community's preferred language. I often think of something a crip friend said about their disability justice activism: "I don't want to leave anyone behind because they use the wrong word."

I wonder what would happen if all the mistakes and the things we don't yet know, the ways in which we fumble and fuck up, were the moments that we let build us into an us?

I want all of it to be included, not just the moments where everyone behaved the "right" way, said the "right" thing. I want my activism to also include booty shorts, fuckups, homemade cardboard signs with scissoring jokes.

It's that I want language—and by extension, political rhetoric—to contain paradox. No, I *need* it to contain paradox. This is because paradox exists, and I need language to reflect that. In an interview on the *Between the Covers* podcast in 2023, the writer Mattilda Bernstein Sycamore (whom I consider an actual deity alive on Earth right now) said: "I write *toward* paradox. And I want it *all* to exist *because* it [all] exists. . . . If there is a paradox, we can't solve it because it's a paradox—but we can go to all the complications, all the levels, all the intimacies, all of the impossibilities that exist. . . . For me, holding all the contradictions . . . is a way of surviving."

Later in that same interview, she says, "I want a sentence to be a living, breathing thing. When the sentence takes me somewhere, I go there." Following from Mattilda, as I have often done, I would propose that we let our language be alive, let it take us places, rather than ossify it into regulations, rules, what should not be said, what is not allowed. I always want *more* space, more meaning, more truth at the risk of mess, rather than less.

Obviously, this will mean that we must become, in order to hold all this, even more attentive, open, forgiving, curious—caring. That's my point. I want more than careful versus careless. I want care as a verb, not an adjective; action over condition. I want everything that language can do, and so included in that capacity must be the ways in which we are changed because of it. I think of something the artist Lily Cox-Richard said when I asked her what she meant by care: "It's the intersection of attention and intention." This has become my favorite way to define care.*

The other reason I love professional fighting is because I can think of no other public event where, included as part of the show, integral to the entertainment factor, are the moments where care is necessary and where we can see it in action. The intense, embattled moments of care between rounds, the little breaks in between the blows when the fighter goes to their corner, are as important as what happens in the ring. I love watching the fighter's team swarm them with water and ice packs and a chair to sit in and advice. The cutman has gauze and towels and Q-tips to stop the bleeding, enswells to diminish the swelling. There are four or five coaches shouting strategy: "When she comes at you with her left, go up the middle." One thing that is almost always said to the fighter is: "Breathe. I need you to remember to breathe. All that's happening now is breathing."

You can tell a lot about how the fight is going in these moments. Some fighters immediately slump on the stool the minute it appears; some are too riled up to sit down. Some look dazed; their coaches

---

* The intersection of attention and intention has a capaciousness, a requirement that both words be qualified, that can of course be leveraged for nefarious ends. I think of a friend who got doxed by neo-Nazis for making a critical piece of art about the US Immigration and Customs Enforcement. Because of the attention and intentions of a bunch of internet trolls, his life was made into hell for months. Care always requires contextual, qualitative value.

repeat themselves in simple blasts: "Kick more!" "Go for her head!" Some fighters ask questions, almost hopelessly: "What do I *do* about his right hook?" What so impressed me about Israel Adesanya was how gracefully and calmly he stands in his corner, eschewing sitting at all. He breathes through his nose. His coach speaks to him in full sentences, quietly, with Adesanya nodding and responding as if they are having a serious conversation about an idea.

I particularly love watching the different ways coaches speak to their fighters when they're losing. After losing his first two rounds in a fight against Cory Sandhagen, Marlon "Chito" Vera goes to his corner and doesn't want to sit down. His team rushes at him, and his main coach, Jason Parillo, starts in with strategy, but when Parillo looks at Vera, he stops. The coach sees a faraway look in his fighter's eyes. Parillo puts his finger on Vera's sternum and says, "Are you okay? What's going on?" And then he pauses, to let Vera answer, a mumbling of confusion. Parillo continues, "Because you're starting to bum me out a little bit, alright? Don't do that. You can beat this guy." He pours water into Vera's mouth, a small moment of gorgeous care. "Is your mind there now?" Vera nods, then heads back to the center of the cage.

I wish I had this in real life. I wish all of us did. Not only someone in my corner, talking to me honestly, telling me what I need to hear, but that these moments were considered as much a part of the action as when I'm in the ring.

Look for the handles, ramps, and pillows.

Even the smallest ones help.

What Can Be Seen Farther Than Any Color on Earth

On P. Staff

I still dream about the shade of yellow in P. Staff's *On Venus*, the yellow of radioactive piss, corrosive light, the color of jaundice, as much the sun as the moon. Wallace Stevens called yellow the "first color," but for Staff it is the last, the final color at the end of the world, too late, post doom, now what.

A more romantic artist might balloon this into a cathartic break, a crack in the world that everything falls through. The primary feeling of *On Venus*, though, which was first on view at Serpentine Galleries, in London, November 2019 through February 2020, then traveled internationally, was that the yellow light was awake, breathing, something that held you. I walked through it, and it took me over, but gently. It soaked me like a liquid, warm and calm. I had the impression that if I were to open the skin of my wrists, a glowing yellow blood would trickle out, matching the color the light had made of me and everything else. I didn't want to stay long in the dark room at the center of the gallery—which showed a thirteen-minute video of the various animal brutalities (snakes cut open with scissors, a dying chicken's eye staring flatly into the camera) that motor our society's agricultural- and medical-industrial complexes—because I didn't need to; the images in there followed me out. I was irradiated by them. Staff has said *On Venus* "is about how to live with violence, continuous ambient violence all around us," and I think the liquid light that glared through it, comfortless but soft, still sheathes me, a warning, and a bath, and a sky, and—

Alexander Theroux wrote of yellow: "It is the color of butter, arsenic, sponges, candlelight, starving lawns, translucent amber, and cathode transmission-emitters in electrical chassis wiring. It represents wisdom, illumination . . . the hue of confessors . . . ripening grain, eternity, and the gates of heaven." Maybe I felt a special recognition in finding that Staff had drenched their show in yellow. It's my favorite color because it can be so many different things: toxicity and illness and gold and honey, the sun and the moon. It's the color that threatens acid rain despite, or because of, its softness. This versatility can tilt it toward vagueness, unlink it from meaning—this is why it's so cool. Unlike red or blue or purple or green, yellow has no dominant allegiances (it's not the color of blood or Mary or royalty or envy), only disguises, mutations. I once made an entire exhibition about the color yellow, during a period of three months in which I wore only yellow (a feat for a goth). The witch I was working with at the time told me to visualize that I was inhaling yellow light, that a beam of it was shooting out of my third eye. She wanted me to heal. But not too hard, not too fast.

When I walked into *On Venus*, stepping out of a cold London night in November, I said, "of course" out loud as Staff's yellow slithered into me and started to hum. Yellow's power is cunning. In Staff's work it was not a big fist pounding a table but a hand sliding around yours and pulling you in. On the surface, it was the color of Venus, her burning sulfur, but this asphyxiation quickly became political. It was the air we all breathe that is also suffocating, quickly for some, slowly for others. Yellow also appears in Staff's 2017 work *Weed Killer* as part of its vivid palette—ultramarine blue, cerulean, vermillion red—created through high-definition thermal imagery. The irradiation of *Weed Killer* is one of contamination, also slow and seeping and permanent. The film is propelled by actress Debra Soshoux reciting a monologue from Catherine Lord's memoir *The Summer of Her Baldness*, which describes the annihilating effects of chemotherapy on the body. She begins by noting it's "not quite right" to say that she feels like shit or has the flu: "The flu is like something is borrowing nourishment from your body. You don't want to make the loan but you can. This is different. Something has broken into your body with murder on its mind." Yet she needs the chemotherapy, paradoxically, in order to live. Over the course of *Weed Killer*, this intruder breaches and penetrates and plunders her body without mercy, and then it coils up and sleeps there, home. I think of the pharmacon: the poison that is also the cure. I wonder if the pharmacon is inherent to the body itself—that the body gets depleted simply by doing what it is meant to do, that pain rushes into your joints after moving, that your teeth get chipped from chewing, that seeing and looking and watching weakens your eyes. Sometimes I think that the history of the world is the history of trying to cope with this thing called the body.

In interviews Staff strategizes Venus, "a sister planet to Earth that is completely inhospitable," as a metaphor (metonym?) to describe a primary alienation that "the world around me is normal, but things are absolutely not okay." About the conceptual framework, they called *On Venus* "a parallel form of life, a parallel space of not quite being alive, not quite being dead, a sister planet, a sister reality." This idea animates all of Staff's work: it's the premise that dysphoria is an intrinsic condition. It's like their yellow—it's not blazing and loud but oozing, sinking, it snuck into my dreams. It's the suggestion that dislocation, rather than being an inciting event, is simply the default, because to be located—by what, and for whom—is a rare privilege, afforded only a few who've conformed to a world not made for most of us. Staff has called it a lens: "If my body is the prime mediator between some sense of myself and the outer world, then it's an inherently dysphoric lens." In this quote (from an interview with Claude Adjil), Staff is speaking specifically about gender dysphoria, but the next sentences expand: "It could also be like living in a nation state that's actively murdering, bombing, slaughtering others, elsewhere. It could also exist in relation to being a 'free' person knowing that there are ever more imprisoned people in this country."

The "alsos" here are what catch me, braid me into an atmosphere that I recognize—this list could be added to ad infinitum. It's the weather of our world, a climate we cannot control. We can only hope to cope with it, we can bring an umbrella if it looks like rain, but we cannot stop ourselves from getting wet. In an interview with CAConrad, Staff said of *On Venus*: "I try to use the idea of being on Venus as a way to describe a slow but perpetual or consistent state of being, a sort of pushing through this liquid, a sort of shorthand to or for describing parallel forms of life, dispossessed living, or ulterior states of near-death, non life, non death."

In other interviews, they repeat these three phrases—*near-death*, *non life*, *non death*—and I think that such states, rather than being bloodied or rotted or putrefied, are flavescent: clear, cautionary, well-lit.

P. and I first met one winter in Minneapolis, when we were both residents with FD13. We stayed in a place that was called "The Cloud House" because of its all-white interior and frosted windows. I remember waking up my first morning there and smelling P.'s perfume in the air. Later that night, we stayed up talking until five a.m. At FD13, Staff began work that would become the 2018 film *Bathing*, which depicts a lone dancer in an empty warehouse, moving in and out of a shallow basin of water. The dancer stumbles and lurches, sometimes bent over and growling like a dog, under fluorescent tube lamps. There is the occasional flash of an image of oil, the US border patrol, a dog playing at night, but the palette of the dancer is soft, pale, a Pre-Raphaelite white girl with cheeks flushed pink. The choreographic language of drunkenness hints at questions about cleanliness, as the water becomes more and more stagnant, eventually to be pissed in, and despite the dancer's thrashing and flailing, she is somnambulant, this is not rage or lunacy, this is just some evening somewhere.

In astrology, the asteroid Chiron is said to represent one's greatest wound, a wound that will never heal. The only respite from Chiron is that one might heal others through the knowledge the wound has given. In ancient Greek mythology, one of the stories finds the immortal centaur Chiron pierced by a poisoned arrow, but he cannot die because of his immortality, so he willingly takes the place of Prometheus, who is being punished for stealing from the gods, chained to a rock, his liver eaten every night by an eagle. Prometheus has his own wound that will never heal—he and Chiron are sisters. With his sacrifice, Chiron is granted reprieve from his pain and allowed to enter the underworld; in some endings, his body dissolves into stars to become a constellation. I tell my astrology clients this story and locate the Chiron in their own charts so I can speak about healing and fate, so I can tell them that they may never heal. I also tell them that the definition of the word "*kairos*" in modern Greek is merely "weather." The Chiron in your natal chart will show the wound of your life that will never heal, but like the weather, it is your background, your atmosphere, the air you breathe; you can lean against it, its rhythm; you can bring an umbrella. In some clients, this mitigates the shock of being told that your greatest wound will never heal. In others, though, hearing about Chiron is validating—I *knew* something was wrong this whole time! I know that if I were to tell P. Staff about their Chiron they'd already know about it, they'd probably laugh and shrug. Of course.

Perhaps the recognition of yellow that zapped me in *On Venus* is because I understand gender dysphoria as someone who is gender-queer, that I know transness is the chasing of an embodiment at which one will never arrive; or how, no matter my ethical rejection of it, I'm dependent as a disabled person on the capitalist medical-industrial complex; or perhaps it's because I'm a citizen of a country who proclaims itself to be the greatest in the world while it disappears people from the streets of its cities, locks children in cages, and supports the swell of wealth among billionaires while its people starve and suffer and die during atrocities that it perpetuates and aids: a pandemic, genocide, climate apocalypse. This list of atrocities could go on. It is merely the weather of our world, of our time. Chrome yellow is the color that can be seen at the farthest distance on Earth. Subtitles and captions are yellow because, over the course of becoming blind, yellow is the last color you can see.

In ancient Greek, the word "*kairos*" had a different meaning: it referred to a kind of time. Rather than chronological time, *kaironic* time was cyclical; something like the right moment; a measure of fate. Unlike chronic time, it cannot be quantitatively counted, it has to arrive when the time is right. How this shifted over the centuries to mean the weather is something I wondered about while moving through *On Venus*.

As I've revisited Staff's work to write this text, yellow has crept into my life again: last night I made dal with red lentils (which turn yellow when cooked) and turmeric, and I painted my nails gold; it was a weather, an atmosphere, while I read the news that Beirut was in a state of emergency after two explosions wounded more than five thousand people, but the hospitals, already over capacity with COVID-19 patients, had to treat them on the sidewalk. There was the color the fire and smoke made of the sky, the dark yellow of sallow skin lying on cracked concrete. I watched the death toll rise with Jeff Bezos's income. It is said that yellow is the least commercial color, not to be used on book covers or paintings if you want them to sell. How we keep buying things in the apocalypse, how nothing, even color, is free. I think of the farthest color that can be seen, the first color that is also the last. The color of illness and saints. Fate that is simply the weather.

White Nightgowns
Covered in Blood

On *Kier-La Janisse's* House
of Psychotic Women

favorite recent meme: *I'm only friends with people who would have been lobotomized in the 1950s.* I'd be one of those poor lobotomized bitches too.

For I, like them, have been given a clinical diagnosis of mental illness, and I, like them, have laughed and cried too loudly, danced unhinged, screamed in desperation and ecstasy, not been able to sleep, slept too much, taken the name of god in vain, been a nuisance, inconvenience, and danger to myself and others. I have tried to destroy myself, I have been desperate. Also, like them, I earn my own money, got a divorce, have sex, am gay, cavort with other gays, can read, enjoy singing to myself, dress how I want (sometimes like a man), drink, smoke, curse, stay out late, am childless, like being alone, am ambitious and want a career, insist that my work is important, and don't want to clean the house nor cook.

And I, like those poor lobotomized bitches, have been obstreperous and protective about my bodily sovereignty, and I am not docile or obsequious toward men. I have said no to men, argued with men, told men their opinions are wrong, and those men have been my father, my grandfather, my professors, my bosses, my doctors, my husbands, my lovers, my enemies. I have spit in the faces of men, struck men, pushed men, thrown things at men. I have been dominated and harmed and controlled by men; I've been belittled and disrespected by men, harassed by men; I've tried to run away from men who wouldn't let me leave; I've been threatened, slapped, restrained, assaulted, abused, and violated by men; I've had a man call the cops on me because I was "hysterical"; I've had policemen put me in handcuffs and take me against my will to the psych ward; and I have fled from and divorced an abusive man who later partnered with someone forty years younger than him.

I believe I have reacted proportionally to the conditions in this last paragraph, but this starts the whole ouroboros over—take it from the top of the second paragraph—and here I am again crying, furious, screaming, tearing my hair from my head, causing a scene, out of control, too much, uh-oh, this bitch is psycho, better lock her up. If this were any time in history, a meager selection of the above behaviors, let alone the comprehensive list, would have been enough to have me forcibly committed to an insane asylum for life. Indeed, just a couple from that list were enough to forcibly commit me in the twenty-first century, but thankfully only for seventy-two hours.

Although I am not a cis woman, I look like and was socialized as one. So, when I'm doing the more expressive shit from the list above, I pretty much fit the role, for all intents and purposes, of a "psychotic woman."

One of the only modes of resistance available to those of us who reside in the undercommons is hermeneutical. It's not the same as actual political power—it does not restructure the mechanisms of oppression in society so that they oppress us less, and it does not give us more material resources—but it's not nothing. Hermeneutical power is the power to disagree with what those in actual power and their institutions say is true about you. It's the insistence on a different truth, which is to say it's the power of meaning, which means it's the power to unmake meaning, to trouble the normative kind, and make it anew. It's the simple statement: "What you say I am is not what I am. What you say is true is not." It's refusal, it's ungovernability. It's fun, it makes fun of. It's laughing at that which you are not allowed to laugh. It deflates what is supposed to be impervious. It's the slipperiness, tricksterism, pluralism, multiplicity inherent in all meaning, all language, but especially the kind of language that has been turned into a weapon, language that is used to surveil, dominate, police. It's the slipping out of reach of that language, wriggling out of its bonds. Again, this is not the same as actual political power, but, again, it is not nothing to spit back.

Hermeneutical power is essentially and always a punk impulse to say *fuck you* to whoever's in charge—whether that be a government or an ideology, or your parents or boss or a shitty man. It can be pranky and stupid because sometimes that's the most appropriate gesture, I think of the hacker group LulzSec hacking the CBS news home page to say that Tupac was alive. As much as it can be adolescent and puerile, it can also be a forceful, eloquent mode of protest. The history of oppressed peoples is a history of hermeneutical power—hermeneutical refusal, hermeneutical tricksterism—being exercised over and over and over again. I think of Fred Moten's first line to *In the Break: The Aesthetics of the Black Radical Tradition*: "The history of blackness is testament to the fact that objects can and do resist." I think of how the term "queer"—once a slur that, if fastened onto you, got you assaulted, fired, arrested, incarcerated—has been reclaimed in pride and celebration. "Crip" is similar—a slur from "cripple" that disabled people have taken up with a kind of strategic relish, forming the politics of disability justice, which demands more rights and access, while at the same time not interested in hiding or erasing any element of our deviant non-normative bodies.

I hope "psycho" gets a similar treatment soon. Where is the bumper sticker, the Target T-shirt, the option on social media profiles that says: *I identify as psycho*. As someone clinically diagnosed as a psycho cunt, I'm doing my best to reclaim it, because, let me tell you, being psycho is fun as hell. (On my Feeld profile I say: *Any femininity I bring is akin to Isabelle Adjani in the subway scene of* Possession. You can imagine the weirdos that brings to the yard.)

I would suggest that being psycho is the ideological opposite of heteropessimism, which is the recent trend-theory where straight women feel bad about themselves for liking men, the humiliation and abjection of being attracted to that which oppresses you. While there might be a worthwhile inquiry here about the mess of desire converging with politics, more often, heteropessimism goes the way of something inane like, *Oh no, I like sucking dick I must not be a feminist*, etc., ignoring decades of queer and trans theory—let alone all of us perverts, kink freaks, and sluts in practice—that have shown how bottoming is the most powerful position there is. Heteropessimists seem to have missed the many documents, records, testimonies, examples, and works of art that have done this hermeneutical-fucking-with-the-theme-of-abjection, in favor of a kind of grim tantrum of entitlement that whines, "You mean I can't have my cake (suck dick) and eat it too?" A psycho, no doubt, would say, "Yes, bitch, you *totally* can! Suck it, then chew it, and swallow it whole."

The question of psychosis is always the question of why someone is that way. As someone who has had this question asked about themself, I have found that it splinters and proliferates into answers that are at once thorny and slippery. One image that flashes in my mind when I try to reach into that question is of a witch piercing a piece of rotting fruit with pins and needles, but the pins and needles are socioeconomic, historical, and political forces, and the witch is not the kind of witch we root for but a conservative and powerful white man and all that he ideologically represents. It's an image that bears resemblance to the sacred heart because it is drenched in a suffering that has a tinge of the holy to it—for what madness is not mystical?—but it's also wan and sad in its domestication. How many images of the sacred heart are printed cheaply on a laminated index card and tacked to a corkboard in a kitchen? The question of why someone is psychotic is never only a question of one individual's mental state or psychological interior, but how that interiority is sliced into and impaled by the external world. Which means it's a question of power, which means it's a question of who does not have power, and why not, and what they do in the face of such conditions. It's an interrogation into how external forces of political and ideological power have infested a person's body and mind, and I use the word "infest" on purpose, for it's an invasion, a molestation, an assailing. The specific question of how a psychotic woman got that way is a larger, indexical question of how any of us is occupied by a social condition that makes us crazy, makes us sick. How do we understand trauma and abjection and the pathologies that come from them as one individual's condition when we live in the kind of society we do? What power might be possible from the bottom? What can be said when there's a dick in your mouth?

Strategies for survival of all kinds have been invented. I do not believe that artistic strategies are frivolous, that in despairing times art is a luxury (the logical conclusion of which is that art only belongs to, is for, ought to be made by those for whom despair does not exist. Who is that?). What do we have if we do not have art? When trauma assails us from the very world we live in, the only way I can see to approach such an abject condition is the hermeneutically promiscuous way that asks in what possible ways such terror and difficulty might be metabolized, expressed, processed in forms that are, I don't know, interesting, illuminating, surprising, creative, inspiring, entertaining, maybe pleasurable, even—*gasp*—fun?

Kier-La Janisse's *House of Psychotic Women: An Autobiographical Topography of Female Neurosis in Horror and Exploitation Films* attempts to answer that thorny, slippery wreck of questions about why a bitch is crazy and succeeds with vivid gusto in a colossal survey of depictions of women losing their minds in horror movies since the beginning of cinema. *House of Psychotic Women* is a stunning accomplishment: a multivalent, encyclopedic film history project, begun in 2012, of research, criticism, and memoir that manifests as a book citing nearly two hundred films; a DVD box set of four films with thirteen hours of bonus material; a curated collection of three dozen films on Shudder; and years of lectures, screenings, and events. It has inspired new scholarship, art, and criticism across a wide variety of fields and brought dozens of neglected and overlooked films into context, mapping a genre, territory, and canon that both critically engages with them as well as enjoys them because they're enjoyable.

Janisse, a cult icon among those of us who feel represented by Isabelle Adjani's *Possession* subway scene, is a polymathic mind whose work as a feminist writer, producer, critic, and scholar of genre cinema has mostly functioned para-institutionally (she adjuncts here and there), despite effectively being an entire film studies department on her own. (She's also the founder of The Miskatonic Institute of Horror Studies, which offers film classes online and in person around the world.) This lack of institutional canonization only substantiates the fact that both the body of work that Janisse has brought to light, its historical merit and contemporary significance, as well as her own scholarship, are about subjects and topics still seen as belonging to the margins by those who decide where such lines are drawn.

Aside from its underground status and subversive relationship to the academy, what's so radical in political and aesthetic terms about Janisse's project is that she allows for a seemingly mutually exclusive duality to be the heart and guts of her inquiry, and she gives neither more hierarchical importance than the other. On the one hand, she shows how insanity is the only sane reaction to the conditions of patriarchy, misogyny, and sexism, and, with great care, by presenting hundreds of films in which such conditions and their reactions are depicted on-screen. On the other hand, Janisse makes ample space for psychosis in women and femmes to simply exist on its own terms, unto itself, ex nihilo—because sometimes a bitch *is* just crazy, violent, evil, maybe she's a homicidal maniac just because it feels good— and isn't that fun to watch in movies, especially ones with lots of fake blood?

Each chapter of Janisse's book investigates a theme through dozens of films that orbit it—there's a chapter on rape-revenge, the double, misandrist vigilantism, et al. The book is gorgeously printed, on glossy paper, with black-and-white film stills on every page, of women covered in blood, sweat, tears, and other bodily fluids; faces moved by rage and pleasure, stunned confusion, and murderous determination. Knives quiver in fists above heads, viscera pours from bellies, legs are spread, tongues are out and dripping, and there's also a lovely clutch at the center of thirty-three pages printed in color, full-bleed (lol), of movie posters and other promotional materials. It struck me more than once, as I lugged this coffee-table monograph of splatter and gore around in my bag on my book tour, from hotel to hotel, airport to airport, that it was heavy enough to wield as a weapon should I have the need to brain someone (always a possibility). The sensuality of its carnage is extraordinary. The appendix, "A Compendium of Female Neurosis," which takes up half of the book and consists of 192 films, is according to Janisse, "by no means comprehensive." (On MUBI.com Dana Reinoos has compiled a list that I urge you to bookmark.)

There is something basically exhilarating for the project of feminism to hold in one's hand so many, many images of women behaving how they're not supposed to. This might be a low-hanging political, but in a world where women are still not seen as people who ought to have agency, rights, or financial or bodily self-determination, who are seen as lacking both the capacity to think and to murder someone, I will admit to a small thrill at how great it looked, felt, to hold.

The other radical flame in Janisse's project is that thrumming through each chapter is her autobiography, the events in her own life that illustrate the theme of each chapter. And, yow, wow, do they illustrate. We begin with her first memory ever:

> ... Of waking up in a dark apartment at night with a start, after hearing a strange noise. I get up to investigate, but I'm locked in my room from the outside. . . . Next there's a flurry of shadows and distorted noises and a distinct feeling of fear. My mother sweeps me up in her arms and we sit on my windowsill while she tells me everything is going to be okay, but her voice is shaking and I don't quite feel comforted.

Janisse later learns that the noise that awoke her was the sound of her mother being raped. What follows is chapter upon chapter of episodes from Janisse's life, painted in strokes brutal and fragile.

There is her abusive childhood, her methods of coping through self-harm and addiction, her stints in foster care, her running away, doing crime; here she is screaming, crying, tearing her hair from her head, being violent, ungovernable, furious, psycho. The men in her life as father figures suck, and she still longs for their attention and approval. Her mother looms large, as a monster and as a woman trying her best. Janisse shows us that sometimes a woman goes crazy because she's had horrible things done to her, and sometimes this makes her do horrible things unto others, and then there's that ouroboros again. This interplay of trauma and harm, how it is played out in relationships, intergenerationally and socially, is the bloody bowel tying Janisse's book together.

Autobiography structuring—corroborating—scholarship is still, in the face of a patriarchy that dismisses and invalidates the experiences of anyone who's not a cis man, an exercise in the sort of feminism to which I feel most allegiance. It's the kind that insists on another meaning than the one the hegemony says is true, the kind that laughs and spits back in the face of those with power over us. Traditional forms of academic scholarship have doubted and outright banished subjectivities that are seen as lying outside the universal, especially when such subjectivities purport to speak from, and about, their specific, othered embodiments. It was not long ago that the academy started to let these voices, bodies, and minds into its canon under the condition that their otherness be loudly pronounced. I wonder if a Film Studies 101 syllabus would be approved by department heads from the 1950s, let alone even ten years ago, if it was comprised of films made only by women or Black people or filmmakers from the Global South, and not noted as such—simply presented as Film Studies 101.

There are ample depictions of male psychosis in film, and they are rarely relegated to the B-movie genre territory of horror and exploitation films. They are among the dignified and lauded hallmarks of the cinematic canon. Think of *Taxi Driver*, *Fight Club*, *Apocalypse Now*, *The Aviator*, *On the Waterfront*, each one of which features a male lead who's lost his mind, but—as is typical to anything that depicts a man's interior state—these examples show a valiant, virtuous man fighting a good, if doomed, fight. He's up against history, society, machinations of unethical power. He is propelled by his potent ambition, will, and drive. He is not undone by something as unstable as his own psyche, but in glorious conflict with the obstacles of the world. He is doing great battle. That thorny, slippery question of how the external world has sliced into us and infested our minds is—when it comes to men—never seen as something the man should be faulted for.

One of my favorite examples of male psychosis in film of the last few years that troubles this valor is *Once Upon a Time in Hollywood*. I can think of no other film that disturbs the standard heteronormative read of it, offers that hermeneutical mischief I am so pleased by. To me, this film is one of the best ever made about queer care. It revels in the melodrama and neurosis of needy, nagging characters, but with a sweetness, a tenderness, that neither Tarantino, nor many others before him, have ever shown before. Leonardo DiCaprio gives the campiest performance of his career as Rick Dalton, a bloated, broken-down, has-been diva who's well past her prime. It's Leo's Norma Desmond, and he does it deliciously; it made me respect him again. In interviews, Tarantino has said the character has bipolar disorder but doesn't know it, which is, in my opinion, one of the most dramatic scenarios to start with: Does a crazy bitch know she's crazy? Tarantino and Leo let Rick Dalton's face be red, puffy, and tearstained, and he plunges it into a bowl of ice to try to reduce the swelling. Throughout the film, Rick whines and whimpers and tantrums and gives up; his ego is broken, like the TV antenna on his roof. He is sentimental, weepy. When an eight-year-old child actor tells him he's just done some of the best acting she's ever seen, his face opens in a grin, tears in his eyes, and he cocks his fake gun and says his own name out loud. He can't drive himself nor remember his lines, he has a stutter when he's nervous, and he drinks too much. And Brad Pitt is there for him, to drive him around, fix his broken antenna, wipe his tears (or, in the man version of this, give him back his aviator sunglasses and say, "Don't cry in front of Mexicans").

Why is a man losing his mind and caterwauling with need so much more sympathetic than a woman losing hers? Is it that a man's self-destruction is something we feel moved to prevent, while a woman's feels inevitable, so why bother to try to stop it?

In the 1974 film *Identikit*, Elizabeth Taylor plays Lise, a middle-aged woman who goes to Rome to find a man to murder her. She is unwavering and focused in her search, sizing men up in ways that the film teases as romantic, as if she's searching for the perfect partner. "You're not my type," she tells several, including Andy Warhol. She speaks with a misty voice of a boyfriend who's waiting for her. The men she encounters assume she wants sex; one tries to rape her and she must run down the road in high heels to get away from him. One man proclaims he must orgasm once a day as part of his diet, which summons one of Taylor's most iconic lines: "When I diet, I diet. When I orgasm, I orgasm. I don't mix the two."

The film dresses Taylor in garish colors, rat-nests her hair, gives us a grotesque close-up of her applying yet more eyeliner to her wild eyes. She is incomprehensible not because she's crazy, but because Taylor plays her with a conviction that feels magisterial in its purpose. The most devastating scene is when she goes shopping and upbraids the salesgirl for bringing her a dress made of stain-resistant fabric, attacking the assumption that she'd ever spill something on herself. Later, when we learn she wants to be stabbed to death, this scene returns to sing.

I would advise against reading any reviews of this film, especially those written by men, because they mostly talk about how bewildering Lise is, and how ugly Taylor has become at age forty-two. For example, writing in *Slant Magazine* in 2013, the critic David Ehrenstein says: "Taylor shows off very little of her (at this point, rather massive) body, outside of a scene where she fingers her breasts through her see-through bra. It's a long way from her decorous semi-nude scenes in *Cleopatra*, and thanks to her ever-expanding avoirdupois, hardly a memorable moment in cinematic eroticism."

When I say that hermeneutical power is all that those of us in the undercommons have, you can see why it still falls maddeningly short from actual power. Here, I can say to David Ehrenstein that he is a small-minded nitwit who subtracts from the sum of human knowledge when he puts his thoughts on paper, but I'm on the bottom saying this. Let me put it this way: If David Ehrenstein and I walk into a room, what will be determined about us simply by the bodies we've been born into? Who will have more power in that room, no matter what kind of room it is? If David Ehrenstein and I were in a public place, and we both started tearing at our hair, crying out, screaming, cackling, which one of us would be taken away in handcuffs and which one of us would be spoken to, treated like a human being, and asked what he needed to feel better?

Sometimes I feel as if there are no possibilities in this wasteland. Janisse's project, though, reminds me that, at least when alchemized through the vehicle of art, the possibilities are myriad, the representations abundant. There's the blood-slicked smile of a homicidal maniac, the fierce eyes of a telekinetic sorceress. There are severed limbs, decapitated heads. Daggers. Grins. There's Elizabeth Taylor's eyes radiant in their lunatic resolve. There's Sissy Spacek in *Carrie*, aflame in vermillion blood, achieving a god-like wrath. There's Tippi Hedren in *Marnie* dressed in a velvet blazer, ascot, and riding gloves, pointing a gun. There's a moment in *Daddy*, of Niki de Saint Phalle standing regally over one of her sculptures, a body-sized penis in a coffin. She has a hand on one hip, a smile kinking the side of her mouth. She stares confidently into the camera. She looks like she's having fun.

She, Et Cetera

On Susan Sontag
and the Mythology of Illness

*"I'm always trying not to position the
dead in service to our romances."*

SAIDIYA HARTMAN

Every brainy queer of my generation, especially those born under the sign of Saturn, went through a phase where Susan Sontag was their Daddy. She schooled you on everything: what to read, what to watch, who was important, why you should know about it, and, most importantly, that you find the most iconic look for your hair. She was how to pay attention to everything and why you should. She was why seriousness was cool, why being a snob was sexy. She was the singular archetype of the twentieth-century American public intellectual. She was New York City, Paris, Beijing, Sarajevo. She was Artaud, Bresson, Sebald, Cioran, Canetti, and Weil. She was smoking in bars with your friends, talking until dawn. She was slow, black-and-white, foreign-language films that you watched with the person you were dating and, when they fell asleep during them, it gave you a reason why things wouldn't work out between you. She was an informed, sophisticated opinion that you could bring out at parties to impress everyone. And she was an opinion about almost everything: how camp puts quotation marks around all it touches (one of her most famous sentences: "not a lamp but a 'lamp,' not a woman but a 'woman'"), how the erotics of art are what we need, how the language around illness is often a lie.

I found her as a teenager, in the late 1990s, though I can't remember which of her books I first read. She always existed as more than her books. My initial encounter with her, as I'm sure is true for many, was with the image of her, which matched the voice in her essays: forbidding, glamorous, sovereign. The streak of white in her hair, those big, intrepid black eyes, that imperious, authorial gaze, not suffering fools. My bookshelves at the time held the standard role models if you were an adolescent girl who wanted to be a writer: Virginia Woolf, Sylvia Plath, Joan Didion. These were the writers available to me in a family that did not read, the ones on the shelves in chain bookstores, within reach. All of these women existed beyond their books, and I adored the images of them as much as I did their actual writing—all the legendary photographs: Didion in her long slinky nightgown, creeping next to her Corvette, Plath's face creased by a smile that looks like a gash, Woolf's faraway look at once blurred by its intelligence as it was refined by it. If you were, like me, a queer child who wanted to be a writer but started to realize you didn't identify as a girl, Sontag emerged from that group as the gatekeeper to a different kind of gate—a secret one you hoped existed but couldn't find on your own. You had to be taken there by someone who knew the way.

When you are trying to get somewhere that is not where you come from, from where you are starting, you need a compass. When lost in the woods, look to the North Star. In many ways, a Daddy is a guide, a leader; follow the one who knows the way, or at least, acts like he does. For many of us, especially when we're young, when we're queer, when we're weird, we need to see theory meet practice, see how misfitted, wayward dreams might arrive on Earth and walk upon the ground: *that's* how you pop your collar; *that's* how you order a martini; *that's* how you enter a room. For those of us who want to be artists, it's things like, *that's* how you persevere with your work; *that's* how you let it be important.

Sontag was my Daddy for a number of years when I was a brainy queer, touched by Saturn, from a working-class family in Southern California, and my ache to learn about culture, in the hope of one day producing it, felt like it was the only thing that could take me somewhere different than where I came from. My ambition was not a matter of ego but my ticket out—not unlike Sontag, a Jewish girl born in 1933 to an uncultured, uneducated middle-class family, who went to North Hollywood High School and ached to belong to the European intellectual elite. Hearing the story of Sontag discovering the Modern Library series at the back of a stationery store in Tucson as a child—devotedly reading its entire catalog and checking titles off the list on the back cover—showed me that it was possible, purely through sheer force of appetite, to become who you wanted to be rather than what you'd been born into. In "Pilgrimage," she writes about finding "a real bookstore, the first of my bookstore-besotted life," in Hollywood: "I went every few days after school to read on my feet through some more of world literature—buying when I could, stealing when I dared. . . . I had to acquire them, see them in rows along a wall of my tiny bedroom. My household deities. My spaceships." As a book- and bookstore-besotted teenager myself, I followed her lead and read and read and read because books were food. When I was living on my own, paycheck to paycheck by age sixteen, I often bought them instead of food. There was a solitary evening, $15 to my name, when I brought a $14.99 bilingual edition of César Vallejo's poetry to the cashier and told him I could not afford the tax. "So, you get the 10 percent discount because you're a member, right?" he said mercifully. I felt Sontag would have approved of my cunning, my priorities.

Of course, like any Daddy, as we brainy queers grew into ourselves, she began to lose her necessity. (I've noticed that people just a couple of years younger than me have different Daddies; born in 1984, I am likely in the last generation fathered by her). As the twenty-first century barreled along into post-2008 precarity and social-media time spans and climate catastrophe, we learned that Cioran and Canetti didn't really matter anymore. The moral quest for the perfect soul—a classical standard to which Sontag held both herself and the second half of the twentieth century—was not only impossible and perhaps misguided, but irrelevant. Does having a perfect soul matter if the world is ending? Who decides what's perfect?

Still, the queer elder is a godsend. Even though we who are fathered by Sontag outgrow her at some point, she was the first to help us grow, and for this she marks us deeply. I had others after Sontag, but her intellectual patronage shaded the tenor of all of them, making me most teachable by those who were defiant, declarative outsiders. On a momentous day in 2002, when I was eighteen, I was in Borders, where I'd often spend hours, browsing all sections, like Sontag did in Hollywood. My favorite was to go into the basement's fiction section and start at the first book in the A section, on the upper left corner of the top shelf, and work my way through the alphabet. Just to read the titles, see the spines, pull the books out and hold them, to learn, to start to know. On that day, the first book in the A section was the recently published Grove anthology of Kathy Acker's writing. It had a fluorescent magenta cover with a black-and-white image of Acker staring into the camera, right at me. I took it off the shelf and opened it to a page with a line drawing of a cock and balls. The first paragraph I read absconded with the top of my head: something about a girl fucking her own father, cunt this, cock that, fuck suck lick. I stared at the page. You could write like this? You could *be* like this? I still have that book, slotted into the row along the wall of my room. One of my spaceships.

My first queer elder who was a real person whom I knew and could speak to was my design professor at UCLA, Willem Henri Lucas. He was the only non-white, not-straight professor in the department, and he came and got me. Henri taught me the most necessary, crucial things: how to look ravishingly bored when a straight person is gushing about how cool you look, how to hold a cigarette, how to build a bookshelf. *Never* let a straight man think he's better than you. *Never* wear ugly shoes. And he taught me to make my work, to insist on my art, no matter what. His advice to me when I was in my twenties:

You have to be willing to be poor and invisible until you're forty, and during that time, you only make the work you want to make, only take the jobs that give you the most creative freedom. You say no to everything else. You do not compromise yourself. Least of all for something as stupid as money. If you do this, by the time you're forty, you will have a body of work that is absolutely who you are. And you will start to be recognized for it. It will pay off. It will be worth it.

I followed his advice. And he was right.

Negative examples help too—they show you what not to do, what not to be like, what you don't have to accept, what you can refuse. Although both my mother and my father were creative, sensitive, loved to dance and sing in the house, longing to be artists, he a musician, she a painter and textile artist, much about their lives functioned in this negative capacity. I did not want to inherit their dejection, their poverty, their cramped lives of foiled ambitions, insecurities, and self-doubt, spending what little was left over from the paycheck on drugs for the weekend, a brief cloud of escape before clocking into reality the next Monday morning. Each of their parents' lives were not what I wanted either, so restricted by what was available to them as working-class people who never went to college, had nothing in front of them but the task of trying to survive: my father's mother coming from Korea at age twenty-eight to work double shifts as a janitor in a hospital for her entire life, shaving her head and wearing a wig because she couldn't afford shampoo; my mother's mother, who, by marrying a man from a lower-middle-class family in Los Angeles, achieved a little upward mobility after being the oldest of six children who did not always have enough to eat, growing up on an Oklahoma farm during the Great Depression. My maternal grandmother was brought into suburbia, grateful, cooked three meals a day for her husband and their daughters, the husband suffering silently with PTSD from World War II, the daughters neurodivergent but never diagnosed, one of whom would die from her addiction, and for her entire life my grandmother's stomach was anxious, her uterus miscarrying and sprouting cysts that put her to bed every month for a week of white-hot pain, a lifetime of her mouth folded in on itself.

I remember having a conversation with her when I was a teenager. We were talking about how I was already writing poetry and stories, writing songs, recording albums, reaching for the sun. "I'm not like you. My generation isn't like yours," my grandmother said. "All this"—she waved a hand as if shooing away a mosquito—"expressing yourself."

"But what do you *do* with your thoughts? Your feelings?" I said. "How do you deal with how difficult it is to be alive? What gives you a way out of your own mind?" I was practically begging.

She gave a little shrug. "I iron." Pause. A sad, meek nod. "I like to iron."

Sometimes I think of this moment when I'm ironing, which I rarely do. I try to feel the tumult of my inner life getting smoothed out in the steam and heavy metal. I imagine a lifetime of that, feeling the weight of it in my hand.

Soon after that conversation, I would leave home at age sixteen, graduate high school two years early, get a full-time job and, by the time I was eighteen, a room of my own. I left a few days after my mother had punched me in the head. My dad noticed the bruise the next day and, in his typical manner of not really being a father, suggested that I be the one to leave. The places where I would stay in those first few weeks became incrementally less and less familiar: first a boyfriend, then a friend, then a friend of a friend, then a bed in a dirty squat with used condoms buried in the sheets. Thank god for the twenty-four-hour coffee shop by the beach—I could always go there, stay up all night with the other runaway goths and punks, playing cards. Those initial days of homeless freedom were exhilarating as fuck. I will never forget standing on a street corner at nine p.m., not knowing where I was going to sleep that night, with maybe five bucks in my pocket, thinking to myself that I wanted an ice cream. It hit me, then, that I could just walk into a store and buy one and eat it and there was no one to tell me no, no adult to shout at me, to make me do something I didn't want to do, that I could make my own life exactly how I want from now on.

I like this anecdote as part of my origin story, my mythology. The young person on a street corner waking up to themselves and their desire, their hunger, to their determination that their own choices are important even, or perhaps especially, if they are frivolous like ice cream.

The opera director Peter Sellars paraphrasing Bill Viola said, "Myth is the form you fill in at the DMV. It's *your* name, *your* address. Myth exists because it's *not* someone else's story. It's about you." But in order to tell your own story, you first need a form to fill it into. None of us start with a blank page.

❋

Sontag was one of the most inimitable myths of the twentieth century, a feat she seemingly engineered through her own nerve, her relish for life. "I *love* being alive," she said in the interview that opens the documentary *Regarding Susan Sontag*, "I wake up every morning very grateful that I'm alive. It's *more* than enjoyment." She had the sort of passionate shrewdness and dedication to the invention of her own story that comes to those for whom a story can offer rescue, for those who understand how totally a story can save you when you find it in the back of a stationery store in Tucson or on a shelf in a bookstore.

Elizabeth Hardwick writes: "I remember when she first *appeared*, appearance signifying in this case not a mere social presence but the offering of intense literary work in an arresting combination with the person, the one writing. Of course, it was immediately clear that she was a romantic. . . . Scarcely anyone is more alive to the *interesting*." (These italics are Hardwick's own.)

Sontag was worlds cooler and more cosmopolitan than the other standard female writer icons—Didion, Woolf, or Plath—but what she shares with them is the juggernaut of a legacy that eclipses the books they wrote. The iconic photos, the Twitter bots, the famous quotations, the memed interview clips, the biographical industry bustling around each. I know more about Sontag's life—who she was friends with, who her lovers were, the unforgettable things she said—than I do about her actual writing, although I've read almost all of it. Reading her can feel prescriptive, like eating something that doesn't taste great but is supposed to be good for you. Telling stories about her is much more fun. The myths that helicopter around her never stop gleaming.

The official biography of her, *Sontag: Her Life and Work*, by Benjamin Moser, released in 2019 (which I tore to shreds in my review, published in *The White Review*, mostly because Moser writes like a twerp and lines his pockets with the intellectual labor of women scholars without giving them due credit), dazzles with stories like these, adding to the chorus that's been purring for years. I love the one where she's in a relationship with Jasper Johns and, in the wake of their breakup, he gives her his apartment, whose walls are covered with sketches for his paintings, and Susan has them all painted over. How about the one where, sitting in her teenage bedroom at age fifteen, she adumbrates Kant's *Critique of Pure Reason* for her classmate? In addition to Johns, she'd been lovers with Lucinda Childs and Annie Leibovitz, and, as reported in *Come Back in September*, the fabulously gossipy memoir by Darryl Pinckney of the New York intellectual scene of the 1970s, she'd danced in gay bars with Fran Lebowitz (my other Daddy).

Even before *Sontag: Her Life and Work* came out, the mythology of Sontag was its own industry, and because of the brimming dynamism of it all, ranging from scuttlebutt and hearsay to lofty tomes analyzing Sontag's importance, I sort of felt like I'd been waiting to read this biography—the authorized, definitive one—my entire life. When Sontag's journals were published (in 2008 and 2012), their revelations were fulsome: there were her endless lists and outlines for what would become her most famous essays, alongside awkward missives about her heartbreaks and eviscerating self-doubt. They sparked yet another round of think pieces about her legacy and extended her influence. Soon, younger writers (including myself) were publishing essays as numbered lists, a form Sontag, if not invented, canonized.

Some of the most enthralling topics revealed in Sontag's journals, and in the official biography, show how Sontag's spirited propensity for life was often propelled by her need for a guide to show her the way out of where she came from, or had ended up. Her exemplary life of multiple reinventions (she wrote essays *and* novels, directed films *and* plays) was stoked by a reproachful dissatisfaction smoldering beneath the blazing ardor in her excited eyes. Many of her relationships, even if they began in passion, functioned in this negative capacity of comparison, critique, and ultimate rejection. She had anguished relationships to her mother, her childhood, her Jewishness, her queerness, her body, and her gender. She was married at seventeen and in a bitter divorce by twenty-six. She was torturously, punishingly disappointed in herself, but also her friends and colleagues, the world. "I *like* being an adversary," she once said in an interview.

Like any good Daddy, before she stepped into those shoes herself, she needed Daddy after Daddy of her own. I don't think I'll forget the image of Sontag kneeling at the feet of her lover, Anna Carlotta del Pezzo, a duchess who is not on "first-name terms with reality" (one compliment I can give: when Moser throws shade, he kills). A friend says that, "Susan literally sat at the feet of only two people. If she came into a room and saw either of these two people she'd sit right here on the floor: Hannah Arendt and Carlotta." What a picture: Susan Sontag kneeling at the feet of Arendt and a duchess who, the biography claims, "had probably never read a book in her entire life."

Despite being a writer synonymous with an almost ascetic devotion for her subjects, Sontag as a person was scrutinous, egomaniacal, arrogant, and demanding. She famously acted like a man: in *Regarding Susan Sontag*, we are told that she broke the custom at her publisher's dinner parties, where the men, after dinner, went to one room to have conversation while the women went to another. Sontag, without ceremony, joined the men, and the custom was ended forever. One of the most vivid pieces on her is Joan Acocella's 2000 profile for the *New Yorker*, "The Hunger Artist," where we are given the indelible image of Sontag, in glee and enthusiasm, with wide eyes and flapping arms, "talking for six hours, no problem." Another image that won't leave my mind is from Sigrid Nunez's 2011 memoir *Sempre Susan*, where we are told that, as an anemic child who suffered migraines, Sontag would drink daily glasses of blood that her mother brought home from the butcher. "When she was unhappy with the world, she lashed out; she wanted to hurt someone," Nunez writes. "At the worst of such times, I'd flash on the image of her as a girl drinking those glasses of blood." (A part of me—the part whose political imagination is assembled by the necessity of a blood-soaked pit—stirred when I read this.)

Moser's *Sontag* is rife with accounts of her withering scrutiny, and the most visceral, painful to read, are when she inflicts them on herself. This is how Daddies work, how patriarchal conditioning is passed down. Saturn devoured each of his children because he'd castrated his own father to assume the throne of Heaven—he did not want the same fate to happen to him—so, in effect, he is the inventor of patriarchy in Western myth, instantiating the law of the father as the most dominant, conclusive law. Among other things, in astrology, Saturn rules how we discipline and punish ourselves, how we toil and labor and hold ourselves to an exacting standard, and the only standard Saturn cares about is what will have lasting consequence in our lives for decades to come. Saturn rules what we make of ourselves, what we do with what we've been given, how much purchase we can get out of it. He is not concerned with what we *wish* were real—he cares only about what is actually real, which is why he's constantly disappointed. With Saturn, it's never good enough. There's always more work to do.

Upon finishing *On Photography*, Sontag, with four planets in Saturn-ruled signs, threw herself on the bed and bemoaned that it wasn't as good as Walter Benjamin. She was dismayed when J. M.

Coetzee won the Nobel Prize in Literature in 2003, because it meant that she, then aged seventy, as another writer in English, would never win it. When she has her first orgasm with a man, in her twenties, she says, "Oh shit, now I'm just like everybody else." In her journals she crucifies herself in nearly every other entry. About her writing: "A problem: the *thinness* of my writing—it's meager, sentence by sentence—too architectural, discursive." Coming to a conclusion after meditating on Simone Weil: "My problem (and perhaps the most profound source of my mediocrity): I wanted to be both pure and wise." From 1957 (age twenty-four), a list of her faults: "Never on time / Lying, talking too much / Laziness / No volition for refusal." To put together this short list of examples, I merely opened her journals at random. Part of what's so fascinating about Sontag is to know her CV against her lists of all the ways she found herself to be mediocre; to read her excoriate herself for laziness, only to turn the page to find lists of books she'd recently *re*-read (Gertrude Stein, Kafka, Gide), films she'd seen, ideas for stories, and sketches for arguments citing Descartes, Victor Hugo, and St. Theresa. Her quest to attain unattainable standards of purity, wisdom, and success feels religious, equal parts savior and martyr, something for which her very longing deserves punishment, and, smarting from the self-inflicted wounds of this punishment, she can spur herself further on.

She inflicts plenty of punishment on others too. More than one person calls her a monster in the biography. Acocella says that interviewing her "was like being in a cave with a dragon." The poet Brenda Shaughnessy goes into therapy to heal from the abusive relationship she had with Sontag. Some of the most repulsive passages describe Sontag's dynamic with her long-term partner Annie Leibovitz, who was with her from the late 1980s until she died (and who notoriously photographed her corpse). Susan, both in private and in public, "violently repudiated" their relationship every chance she got. Sontag belittles and berates Annie in public, calling her stupid for not having read Balzac, being "so surprised!" to realize that Annie, one of the most successful photographers in the world, "really has an eye." They break up and get back together regularly, in a cycle of harm and penance. Their friends recoil, stop going to dinner with them, we've all known couples like this.

Annie, interviewed by Moser, maintains that Sontag was merely pushing her to be better, Sontag's standards being so legendarily high, and that she was happy, even honored to provide Susan with emotional and financial support, especially when Sontag was ill. Beneath that tribute, though, comes one of the most scintillating revelations of the book. Moser interviews Susan's accountant, who attests that, over the course of their relationship, through lavish purchases of apartments, gifts of first-class trips around the world, and a regular allowance, Annie gave Susan a cumulative total of *eight million dollars*. Daddy much?

Here's the tea of the century: in 1975, when she got diagnosed with the first of her three cancers—already "Susan Sontag," a name synonymous with high culture and intellectual success, author of by then four books, two of which were bestsellers, sitting on the jury of the Cannes Film Festival—Susan Sontag didn't have health insurance. Her treatment cost $150,000, which is at least $700,000 in today's money. She was able to pay it only by picking up the phone and asking her friends to chip in: a proto-GoFundMe. When I read this, I sat back in defeat. If *Susan Sontag* didn't have health insurance when *she* got sick, what about the rest of us? (Much of her later cancer treatment was paid for by Leibovitz.)

Sontag is a hard read, hardest when it covers her illnesses. Despite the position she takes in *Illness as Metaphor*, criticizing our tendency to think a sick person's illness is their own fault, Sontag held herself to the other side of that ableist idea, which is that a person can, and should, think their way out of their illness. When it came to herself, she believed that if she was not healed, even completely cured, she had failed. As Moser points out, "To deny the body is also to deny death with a doggedness that made Sontag's own end unnecessarily ghastly. She believed—literally believed—that an applied mind could, eventually, triumph over death." Here, I thought of the "Bi's Progress," an account in her journal of a similarly misguided endeavor to try to think her way out of her queer body, as she would try to outwit her illnesses. Although she did a lot to undo the prejudices against illness in her writing, ultimately I see Susan Sontag as someone who further entrenched the destructive ideology of ableism in how she lived her life, because we all know that, for better or worse, it's by living them, day in and day out, that ideologies become entrenched at all.

That she could write an entire book on illness without once mentioning that she was writing it while she had cancer is—odd. It seems beyond an anxiety to trust the first-person "I" when writing a philosophical essay. This continued a decade later when she wrote a book about AIDS without claiming her own queerness. The agon of the biography, and indeed Sontag's life, is that she stayed in the closet, despite all her friends knowing about her queerness. Many of them, by the end of her life, were exasperated at her refusal to come out, since it was so clear already. (Though, I think of Wayne Koestenbaum, in *Regarding Susan Sontag*, saying, "Does the author of 'Notes on Camp' *have* to come out?")

It still smarts that such an icon to the queer community never publicly allied herself with it, and this is the one topic in the biography where we start to hear Moser's own desires for and disappointments in his subject. He rightly takes her to task for the marmoreal and abstruse language of *AIDS and Its Metaphors*, which appeared in 1989, at the height of the AIDS crisis. Moser writes, "A refusal of names—'the body' rather than 'my body'—provided false comfort, and added to the gauzy atmosphere of silence and shame." Moser uncovers notes in her archive that reveal an early title for "Notes on Camp" to be "Notes on Homosexuality." The *Regarding Susan Sontag* documentary pushes the narrative thread of her queerness front and center, in a not-so-subtle attempt at revealing this fact to any last holdouts that might not know about it. Acocella's *New Yorker* profile was partially meant to be an opportunity for Sontag to come out on the record, while she was alive, but instead Sontag bristled, relenting only, "That I have had girlfriends as well as boyfriends is what? Is something I guess I never thought I was supposed to have to say, since it seems to me the most natural thing in the world." Moser quotes Acocella describing the transcriber of that interview, "a completely out gay guy," bursting into tears upon hearing this.

It's hard not to read Sontag's internalized ableism as an extension of the disavowal she felt for her body, coming from the same place as her internalized homophobia and misogyny—which all, it seems to me, originate from her foundational dissatisfaction in herself, the severe, saturnine nature that defines her. Even with the most compassion, these passages read like tragedy. In the last hundred pages of my reading copy of *Sontag: Her Life and Work*, the thing I drew more and more in the margins was a sad face.

I don't fault a sick person, a disabled person, for never climbing out from under the ableism they've internalized. The sad face I was drawing in the margins was a mark of recognition—*oooh bitch, have I been there too*. It is difficult enough to disentangle the ways in which we are imbricated with ideologies that shape our identities while alive. Posthumously, it becomes even more nettlesome. How do we retroactively understand a queer person's queerness if she never claimed it? How do we understand a person's illness if she wrote around it but never disclosed it as being part of her own body?

One can feel Sontag's apprehension as motivated by her not wanting to be reducible to her body, and, in many ways, she had good reason for this. The illnesses and madnesses and disabilities that swarm around so many writers and artists—especially the women and queers and non-white—become a kind of perfume to their legacies. With a Sick Woman, we smell this legacy first before we've actually met her; for the most famous of them, the smell is an entire stratosphere. She's both romanticized and pathologized by her body and mind's condition. Her work is read through it, determined by it, and this gives her a gravity that cuts both ways, keeping her earthbound as much as it's made her grave.

There are the suicides in the river and the oven of Woolf and Plath, the cancers of Sontag and Acker, the MS diagnosis of Didion, the stroke and aphasia of Bowles. The rambling and digressive indulgences of Sontag's last novels are explained via the fact that she was on heavy painkillers for her last cancer, writing in a narcotic fog. Didion's penetrating gaze and furrowed brow reveal not only the project at the heart of her writing that contends with disorder, but her nervous, migraine-y, breakdown-prone constitution. Plath's immense fame cannot be separated from knowing that her best work was produced in the blackness of a suicidal depression, the telos of *Ariel* driving us headfirst into the oven. As I got older, returning to these role models every few years, rereading their work and reading the biographies, letters, and journals that have been published, snacking on the gossip told about them by others, the weight of these legacies started to feel heavy with dread and pathos. Each is fogged in by hagiographies that practically worship suffering, render it otherworldly, not the stuff of anyone's regular life but the crucible through which our sick, mad geniuses have been formed and then undone. I remember the torture of reading the biography of Jane

Bowles, *A Little Original Sin*, because it described the many botched attempts to care for her, by her husband and friends, in the aftermath of a stroke that left her unable to read or write. Rather than see her despair at her aphasia as reasonable, they thought she was hysterical; they frequently threw up their hands. It took me ten years to finish reading that book because I had to keep putting it down—the ableism and anguish were too great.

It feels singular to our mythologizing of women writers, artists, thinkers, and creatives that we not only account for their genius via their illness, but we also punish them for it. A counterexample: Tony Iommi, the guitarist of Black Sabbath, plays with a maimed hand. The tips of his middle and ring fingers were cut off in an accident when he worked at a sheet metal factory at age seventeen, and this is his right hand—and since he plays left-handed, this is his fretboard hand; for a guitarist, the important one. He devised various DIY prosthetics, including plastic bottle tops and pieces from a cut-up leather jacket, and relearned how to play. In his mythology, this disability and how it affected his technique (he had to tune his guitar down so the strings would be easier to bend, for instance) forced him down a path wherein, it is said with reverence, he invented the singular sound of heavy metal. That Iommi himself gently refuted this— "It's just something I've had to learn to live with"—does not gleam with the same luster as a momentous cultural discovery found in the wreckage of pain.

A certain detached, indifferent acceptance of one's suffering is categorical to Daddies. Daddies have no time for wimps or whining. Toughen up, get through it, don't be a pussy. Patriarchy admires sick people most when they appear unbothered by their sickness—similarly to how it rewards women who "act like men." This is one of those contradictory tautologies that are foundational to the values of patriarchy: that it would first define you, reduce you, to your othered body—indeed, going so far as to conflate such otherness with suffering itself—and then reward you when you behave, act, and live as though your body, this othered, suffering identity, is actually not important to who you are. It reduces you, then celebrates you when you "overcome" the reduction.

When I got sick and started to read and write my story according to this new identity of the Sick Woman, the De-Person, the Psycho, finding myself lost in the woods of ableism and searching for a North Star, this paradoxical negation was everywhere. I became anxious that I'd be reduced by the very thing that doled out the reducibility. I noticed that there are few female Daddies who were stoic and even silent about their illness, other than Sontag, who are also as famous as she. I wondered if her fame got as big as it did because she was so fierce about refuting such categories as sick, queer, and woman to be attached to her—as if that is a choice—or is it that her anxiety at this mythologizing has become the very thing that animates her legacy? Are these the only options? To be a Daddy or a Sick Woman? A patriarch or a De-Person? A *Malerschwein* or a Psycho? Is the best you can hope for to be defined by how you buck against these?

There is no shortage of Sick Women and Psychos among the women writers and artists who had their own illnesses, breakdowns, hospitalizations, infirmity, disability, addictions, depressions, anxieties, hallucinations: Frida Kahlo, Audre Lorde, Flannery O'Connor, Unica Zürn, Billie Holiday, Leonora Carrington, Jean Rhys, Shirley Jackson, Tove Ditlevsen, Simone Weil, Katherine Mansfield, Yayoi Kusama, Sarah Kane, Hannah Wilke, Barbara Hammer, Catherine Lord, Zelda Fitzgerald, Emily Dickinson, Charlotte Perkins Gilman, Anne Sexton, Sarah Manguso, Hilary Mantel, Kay Sage, Bette Howland, Gayl Jones, Violette Leduc, Camille Claudel, Séraphine Louis, Marina Tsvetaeva, Alejandra Pizarnik, Agnes Martin, Valerie Solanas, Janet Frame, Shulamith Firestone—the list goes on and on and *on*. Each of these women documented— some explicitly, some obliquely, often a swirl of both—her own life and what she went through, what she wanted and reached for, and how at times she fell out of the sky. All of them were the authors of their own stories. But these stories have become cud chewed by the literary-biography-industrial complex. Their struggles have been capitalized upon, commercialized, rendered symbolic rather than real, images without depth, icons without clay feet. There is the "Sylvia Plath Effect," the armchair theory that poets and writers are more prone to have mental illness; there are pop psychology books like *Touched with Fire: Manic-Depressive Illness and the Artistic Temperament* that ratify this with statistics. In 2013, *Vice* magazine published a fashion spread of reenactments of the more famous suicides of women writers, where we get to see a model as Iris Chang bringing a revolver up to her open mouth. There are the Hollywood biopics: Gwyneth as Sylvia talking to herself in a halo of light from a pallid bulb in a hallway, hours away from her death; Nicole Kidman with an Oscar-winning prosthetic nose wading into the river with rocks in her pockets. We don't need to go on. The unabridged version is unnecessary. We all know how the story goes because it's more than a story by now—here we are again with the stuff of myth.

The mythology of illness is a sort of lubricant for pathos, poignancy, and meaning, as is death. As Walter Benjamin said, "Death is the sanction of everything that the storyteller can tell. He has borrowed his authority from death." I have felt this get close to me, the suffocating wetness, almost like being covered in a dank, putrid film. Will my story be eaten by the mythologizing machine of illness? Will I be mostly known, not for my talent, my craft, my ambition, but the fact that I suffered and wrote about it? That my body fought me, that death fought me, and even though I fought back; that I lost?

When I've been hospitalized, one of the thoughts that crowds my mind is what will happen to my work, my story, when I die. I've kept a regular journal since I was a child, and I keep all my drafts, sometimes written and all edited by hand. My partner cannot read my handwriting, not one word of it. We laugh at this, but sometimes I think it might determine more about my fate than anything else— that I'll leave behind a pile of paper covered in chicken scratch, my life's work, that no one can read. I think of the artist Sara Kathryn Arledge, hospitalized four times for schizophrenia by her husband, who died in obscurity and whose work was rescued from the garbage by her neighbor after her family threw it out. In a museum in Vienna, I marveled at the letters encased in vitrines written by Klimt and Schiele, in microscopic, hieroglyphic script, scratched onto scraps of torn paper. Whose bits of writing receive such care? One of Sontag's good fortunes seems to be that her son, David Rieff, has been a good boy to his Daddy and painstakingly maintained her estate, commissioning Moser for the official biography, and editing and publishing her journals (although, the fact that we are still waiting for the third volume of her journals, more than a decade after the second volume was published, seems to imply the sedulousness required to be a good son to Sontag).

Morbidly, bombastically, in the hospital, when I have been unsure if I would live or die, I fret over the fact that I have no children I can task with maintaining my legacy. I've worried that what might happen to my papers is what happened to Arledge's work, or worse, to Plath's. Although Plath was recently acrimoniously separated from her husband, Ted Hughes, they were still married at the time of her death, so he became the executor of her literary estate. With this authority, he destroyed some of her diaries, rearranged and edited her work into a shape different than how she'd left it, and refused biographers and editors to have access to her papers. Finally, in the 1970s, feeling overwhelmed by the demands of the Plath-industrial complex, he hired his sister Olwyn to take over the executor position. Olwyn was not a writer, and she didn't like Plath even when Plath was alive. Janet Malcolm's book *The Silent Woman* details the soap-opera saga of Olwyn's continued resentment of Plath after she died, resulting in her many attempts to stymie and refuse the Plath myth to be told in any way other than the one Olwyn wanted. Olwyn paid for a biography that she insisted tell the "honest" story, so it included an account by a former friend of Plath's, about when Plath was staying at their house and ate all the food in the refrigerator so there was nothing left for dinner. Malcolm notes that the inclusion of accounts like this does less to add to the Plath story and more to the myth of Olwyn herself, but where and how exactly are these differentiated?

In my low moments, I obsess over the chance that my partner's brother might come to be the executor of my papers, my Olwyn. My brother-in-law is an oil and gas executive, a straight white abled man who wears a lot of navy and has Ayn Rand on his shelf. In our first conversation, he told me he didn't like art. I asked, "But haven't you ever seen a film, or a painting, or heard a song, or read a book that made you feel something?" He answered no.

A psychiatrist might see this as evidence of my grandiosity. That I would even think about this as a possibility, let alone worry that it might come true and make plans to thwart it. But it's real. The story written about me after my death might include testimony from, say, a person who is no longer a friend, recalling that I'd summoned him to the hospital and given him a stack of loose paper covered in illegible scribble, demanding that he make copies of it for posterity. (He did not.) It might include comments from the opera set designer I'd worked for—the one who'd supported my 5150—saying it was like watching a train wreck after I'd miscarried. It might consist of journalists attempting to explain my political activism as a result of my illness, as the German media did to Ulrike Meinhof, saying she turned to terrorism because she'd had a (benign) brain tumor removed a decade before. It might quote from my doctor's notes—as the biography of Anne Sexton did, where her psychiatrist gave the biographer the entire file, including the transcripts of each of her

sessions, which were reprinted at length; as the biographies of
Virginia Woolf have, which also included her husband's copious and
meticulous diaries of each of her breakdowns. It might include
friends recounting how much they disagreed with the choices I've
made about my own body, refusing to take certain medications,
going to shamans and psychics and witches instead, like Kathy
Acker's biography did. If I become famous enough, it might include
family members writing their own memoirs about knowing me, like
the one Virginia Woolf's nephew wrote where he dismisses her claims
that she'd been molested by a relative as a child, a trauma that dev-
astated her life and was not believed by anyone close to her. I can
only pray I never reach the kind of fame that has produced the
Joan-Didion-hagiographical complex, with pieces in the *New Yorker*
about the posthumous auctioning of my trash can for $5,500. And
if a biography is ever to be written about me, I beseech the gods to
please give me a sympathetic writer—someone crip, someone queer,
someone who gets it. Unlike James Baldwin, all of whose biographies
have been written by white men, who at some point become exasperated with their subject's insistence to keep making everything about
race. Or Simone Weil's biographer, Francine du Plessix Gray, finding
Weil's anorexia tiresome—*Why doesn't she just eat something
already?*

In 2008, Sontag's son, David Rieff, published an extraordinary memoir called *Swimming in a Sea of Death*, which details the torment of
her death. Rieff describes Susan's belief in her own exceptionalism, a
belief substantiated by actual evidence throughout her life—not only
that she was an exceptional person because of her intellect and her
tenacity, but also because she'd beat her two previous cancers, against
all odds. She was so certain that she would beat the third cancer

(which was caused by treatment she'd received for the second cancer)
that when it became clear she wouldn't, she refused to believe it. She
couldn't die, she insisted, because she had so much yet to do. (Near
the end of her life, she renounced her early work to write novels:
"Essays! Pooh! Forget essays! From now on, I'm writing fiction. I
have a whole new life. It's going to be terrific.") Rieff's slender book,
under two hundred pages, is some of the best writing on Sontag there
is. He clarifies her in a way that no other has. When Moser's sentences started to feel like a slog, I'd return to my dog-eared copy of
Rieff. "For someone in love with the past," Rieff writes, "or, more
exactly, who identified with the great achievements of the past and
their architects—in a sense, she was her admirations—my mother
was surprisingly untroubled by nostalgia." That clause between the
em dashes—that she was her admirations—is one of the most eloquent about her ever written. A good son.

Rieff's portrayal of himself and his mother during the time she
was dying (in agony, from blood cancer), when they colluded together
in a grotesque, yet completely understandable, denial, is one of the
most haunting things I've read, and of the most powerful on how
ableism protects, coddles, even helps us to cope with realities that are
unendurable. Rieff wonders if, by trying to participate in her despondent search for hope, he made her suffering worse. He asks if guilt is
the only thing survivors can feel, wishes he could have died in her
place, and castigates himself for letting her hope at all. Knowing that
Sontag's relationship with her only child was invasive and overpow-
ering (she writes, "I identify myself too much with him, him too
much with myself") makes the memoir that much more agonizing, as
we see the strains of self-punishment continue, the saturnine family
legacy.

I often return to this sentence in Rieff's memoir: "I very much
doubt that 'hope' . . . offers much to someone trying to organize
his or her thoughts and feelings in the shadow of extinction." For

someone whose life was powered both by an unending wonder and a terrifying fear of being ordinary, the concept of extinction, to which we all must go, was anathema to Susan Sontag. Rieff writes, "She had the death that somewhere she must have come to believe that *other* people had from cancer—the death where knowledge meant nothing, the will to fight meant nothing." One of the most heartbreaking scenes comes at the end: "Shortly before she died, she turned to one of the nurses' aides—a superb woman who cared for her like her own daughter—and said, 'I'm going to die,' and then began to weep." Her last words are to David, an unfinished sentence: "I want to tell you . . ."

Over the years of writing this book, my reading has been saturated with stories of Sick Women, and for a long time I thought my own book would be a sort of survey of the ones who had most guided me, the Daddies and the godmothers. As much as I wanted to analyze and pick it apart, I also wanted to participate in the mythmaking, fill in that form at the DMV. I wanted to show how such role models have come to live in my own story, how they helped make that story alive in the first place. It was to be an act of gratitude, homage, tribute. I wanted to be a dutiful daughter, a good son.

I envisioned a long piece on Plath, how for a decade I reread her every October, following the darkening of the season into the darkening of her mood, until it ultimately darkens her life. I wanted to write about the moments in James Baldwin's life that he described as "collapses," where friends had to swarm in and nurse him for months, how I started to use this word to describe mine too, yet another of his elegances that has given me so much. There was to be a piece on David Wojnarowicz and Félix González-Torres, reassessing their work through the lens of disability. I wanted to examine the hallucinations of Toni Morrison—how she describes *Beloved* originating from when she watched a woman in a hat walk out of the river in front of her house, how she atmospheres her characters with hallucinations, visions, of their own. Around when I first read Kathy Acker, I read Toni Morrison's *Beloved* and spent years being haunted by it; whole scenes, images, paragraphs, still sing in my memory now, twenty years later. My paperback copy got exposed to rain, grew mildew, its pages rippled and mottled, so I bought a new copy, and then another one, I think by now I'm on my fifth. I wanted to be the one to bring Unica Zürn to an English-speaking audience; to write about Rosalind Belben's forgotten novel, *The Limit*, one of the funniest, most grotesque accounts of illness I've ever read that is also one of the sweetest. I wanted to write about Frida Kahlo, the patron saint of queer disabled women. The essay would begin with the tattoo I got in her handwriting of the last thing she wrote in her journal: "I hope the exit is joyful and I hope never to return." These unwritten essays were some of my ambitions. I am already disappointed by what I've failed to accomplish with this book. Who knows, maybe I'll still get to some of them—in one version of my story, I have a good fifty years of life left. But in another version of this story, there just isn't enough time to write all the things I want to write. Being touched by Saturn, I know the difference between what I wish were real and what actually is. Perhaps more than anything else, this is what Sontag passed down to me: the dread of having the kind of death which I am inconsolable in the face of because I feel there is more work to do.

Capitalism is an evil genius.
It has succeeded in making us think there's
a difference between our needs and our desires—
but it makes us pay for both.

Notes on Ambition
(aka Notes on Survival)

I want to write about ambition. It is the engine driving me forward, has made me into one of the most diligent people I know, one of the most prolific—although that makes me think of a favorite tweet, by Lara Mimosa Montes, that said: "Not prolific. Just afraid of dying." The story of my life could be told as one dominated by ambition, that nothing else has more authority over any of my given days. Ambition for what exactly? Everything! I have ambitions to reach certain career achievements; ambitions about my ethics and activism and political dreams; ambitions for what hangs in my closet, furnishes my living room, houses me and my loved ones; most of all, ambitions about my craft, for what I can make my art do. I place goals in front of myself that hone the direction of each day, and the aim of them that guides me is engine, yes, but also escape, giving me something to focus on so that I might tune out not only distractions or detours but all that is difficult—for there is a lot—about the mechanical clicking-forward of life. I like that the aim of these ambitions can organize my life. Rather than the others vying for this role, I prefer to let them be my taskmasters, managers of my time and labor. Without them I don't know how I'd live through what I've got to live through.

Where does ambition come from? Do we reach for something that we want or that we must have? Is it propelled by desire or need? As an instigator to ambition, need feels different than desire. Need seems to cheapen ambition, dirty it, make it heavy with the earthly concern of trying to survive; and at the same time, desire can always be rendered excessive, laughed at, diminished. We all want something that we don't, perhaps cannot, have, and it's easy to stand outside of that burning and say that desire is the root of all suffering, why don't you just chill out? Perhaps we could say that one kind of ambition is an aim toward a requirement and another is an aim toward abundance, but how are these individuated? When does it happen that we cross over from needing a meal, a home, a job to pay the bills, to wanting a marker of prestige, evidence of plenitude, to following a dream beyond scarcity, yearning toward a life that might give us something more?

Another way to ask this question: Is ambition that's propelled by a need to survive somehow not ambition? Or is it—under capitalism—the only kind?

I wrote a novel reinterpreting the Icarus myth, so I've spent a lot of time thinking about the word "hubris," which to the ancient Greeks meant to disobey the gods, to go against the fate they have planned for you, but now represents a kind of fearless courage to believe in yourself when others do not. These days, Icarus, who flew too close to the sun on wings of feathers and wax made for him by his father, has become a symbol for many who fancy themselves to have outsized ambition, to do what they are told they shouldn't or can't, to be

reaching too far. To be moving too fast and breaking stuff. His plunge
into the sea—seen as his failure—has been leveraged to demonstrate
that neoliberal capitalist belief which cannibalizes failure into the
narrative trajectory of success. Icarus has become synonymous with
both the dangers of ambition and the glory of it, showing that what
someone is willing to risk, just how far past the limit they are willing
to push, proves their worth. He's become the role model, the mascot,
for fuckers like Mark Zuckerberg and Elon Musk and those who
hold them as guides.

We forget that Icarus was a slave, the child of slaves. His father
Daedalus, an architect and craftsman, was enslaved by King Minos,
forced to build anything at the king's command, and then imprisoned to keep his masterwork, the labyrinth, a secret. As a reward for
his labor, the king gave Daedalus not his freedom but a slave named
Naucrate to be his wife. She appears fleetingly in the literature and
nowhere on the Icarus Wikipedia page. Icarus and Daedalus, son and
father, are well-worn in the myth, but, while researching my novel, I
had to Google, "Who was Icarus's mother?" (Related searches:
"What happened to Naucrate?" "How did Naucrate die?")

Icarus was not moving too fast and breaking things, in the way of
the twenty-first-century disrupter, the white boy with a laptop and a
plan for a start-up that will exploit labor. Icarus flew too close to the
sun because he was trying to flee the conditions he was born into. His
father's warning not to fly too close to the sun was not, as it is now
said to be, an admonishment to keep Icarus in his place, proof that
Daedalus did not support his son's ambition. The father was trying
to help his son—he'd made the wings after all—by offering advice to
ensure his son could escape their family's enslavement and be free.

While writing my Icarus novel, I came up with the phrase "decol-
onize ambition" as what I was trying to write into. I'd never heard
anyone say that before. I was curious what it would entail. At the
time, I'd started to notice that ambition was a trait said to belong to

a certain kind of person—the Zuckerbergs and Musks. They are reaching for the sun. They want to thrive. But what about a fugitive slave? Does he have ambition? In what conditions would we understand a fugitive slave's attempt to escape as being propelled by a desire to thrive rather than a need to survive?

Is it that Zuckerberg and Musk *want* to thrive but a fugitive slave *needs* to?

While writing this essay, I was reading *Strangers to Ourselves* by Rachel Aviv. The most tragic figure in a book full of tragic figures is Hava, a girl whom the author meets as a child in the hospital, where they are both being treated for anorexia, Aviv at the age of six and Hava a few years older. Aviv sees herself in Hava, feels like they could be sisters. Hava is vivid, gentle, loving. In the epilogue of the book, Aviv, as an adult several decades on, tries to retrace her childhood experience, the youngest person to be diagnosed with anorexia in America, meeting with the doctors who treated her, interviewing them, comparing notes. During this—I hesitate on what to call it, pilgrimage?—Aviv discovers that Hava has died only ten weeks earlier. Although Hava's life was one spent in and out of hospitals and institutions, struggling to live with her mental illness, she did not die of suicide. After decades of living with an eating disorder, first anorexia as a youth, then bulimia as an adult, Hava's esophagus muscles adapted and did independently what she had for so long forced them to do. She vomited in her sleep and was asphyxiated. Her partner found her the next morning after making coffee and getting ready for work: "As was his routine, [he] came back to bed to kiss Hava goodbye. She didn't respond." I started crying in this paragraph. The weight of the news heavies because Hava had been doing so well recently. "She was thriving," someone remarks, and the pathos blooms. I am struck by this emotional moment. To point out that Hava was thriving when she died, happier than she'd ever been, makes it all the more tragic. I cannot help but wonder if the force of this would land in the story the same way if she'd died in the hospital, by her own hand, after weeks of not getting out of bed. Rather than newly in love and finally hopeful about the future, if she'd been struggling to survive and simply not succeeded, would we mourn the tragedy in the same way?

Often, I hear activists for all kinds of movements on the left demand better treatment, more rights, less violence, so that we might "thrive" instead of merely "trying to survive." To move from a need to survive to a capacity to thrive is understood as the trajectory that everyone wants, should have, and deserves. We nod. We feel it in our gut. Yes, we want to thrive! After all this fighting to survive, after all these years of struggle, to enjoy a place in the sun? We deserve it!

I am troubled by this as an aim. Not because I don't believe there's a significant difference between the struggle to survive and the condition of thriving, because I definitely do. But I am unsettled by the fact that longing for it in such a homogenous way shores up a structure, a belief system, a value judgment, a trajectory, that ought not to be reified. There are many suns—not only one—to reach for. There are many ways one's wings can be melted and destroyed. There is an ocean all of us fall into in defeat, but it is not necessarily the same ocean. As Natalie Diaz said in an interview, "Allness doesn't have to mean sameness."

I know very well the difference between struggling to survive and thriving. It's a difference I can smell in my hair, skin, and clothes, when they are unwashed and neglected, versus when I have the energy and money to make them laundered and perfumed. I know the difference in my face between pain knotting my eyebrows and depression sagging my mouth, versus how big my smile can get, how loud my laughter, how alive my eyes. I know it in my body, my posture, my silhouette, my gait. I can also see the difference on the faces, in the bodies, of those who are watching me, my friends and family and lovers, as well as those with the power to decide my fate, the ones in positions to be the judge of what I deserve.

A proposal: Perhaps the word "deserve" is the problem—that we formulate our demands for thriving as what we "deserve." When used in the context of what life ought to be like, what political conditions we should have, what is accessible to us, is the verb that indicates what one is entitled to, worthy of, really helpful? Do people *deserve* rights, *deserve* a quality of life, *deserve* freedom, *deserve* not to be starving, suffering, dying?

One of my favorite questions to ask someone is, What do you want? What's next? Where are you hoping to go? I've noticed that my sick and disabled friends, my mentally ill friends, my Black and Brown and Asian friends, my poor friends, my trans friends, my Autistic friends, have the most ambitious and often best-organized plans—this grant, this certificate, this position. They are shrewd and strategic about the hustle. They are clear-eyed about the time frame: if I do *x*, then next year I'll be eligible for *y*, and in five more years, I'll be promoted to *z*. When one of them gets a coveted position, we all applaud, even if it's with some of the worst institutions in the land. During the pandemic, a friend got into a graduate school that did not allow remote learning, and we all congratulated them, even though the possibility that it would kill them or their partner—both severely immunocompromised—was very real. But they would have health insurance. They would have a steady income, some cultural capital. So, we congratulated them. My friends are realistic about their chances, clever about their methods, they make color-coordinated charts and spreadsheets, their days are time-managed down to the minute. They do not suffer from torpor. Yes, they struggle to get out of bed, they lose focus and capacity by the afternoon, they've lost months and years of their lives to despair and limitation and pain and will keep losing. Every day they face colossal social inequality, microaggressions, discrimination, and they do not have such fierce ambitions *in spite of* these facts. No, they keep their ambitions close *because of* and *alongside*.

Obviously, they have to be this way. Their lives—both their survival and their thriving—are considered not worth living, and the world is structured around this belief, keeping their resources and opportunities limited, even foreclosed. The other truth is that all of my disabled friends are poor (I have friends who live on $400 per month), and it has struck me over the years that the few who do manage to get a chunk of money, a big grant, tenure, maybe a little upward mobility, a place with a guest room, share the wealth with the rest of us. They open their homes, refrigerators, PayPals, Venmos, stipends. The one or two that come from money use it to sustain entire friend groups, social circles. They buy everyone dinner, they host the gatherings and meetings, and they pay for the rideshares or drive everyone around in their own cars.

Crips understand that life is fleeting, health is fleeting, and tomorrow is a long time, so we carve out a little space for ourselves in a world hostile to our flourishing and decorate it. We prioritize beauty and pleasure and joy because no one else is going to do that for us. I know that our abundance and decadence and fun are things the abled world sees as us "just trying to survive"—that our acts of creative expression, dance, music, art, poetry, fashion, comfort, our laughter, our moments of stillness, daydreaming, contemplation, our chilling on back porches and front stoops with wine and conversation, our seeing and discussing of films, our tending to gardens, our getting dressed up, our cooking together, are rarely understood as expressions of our desires, ambitions, talents and vision and curiosity.

I remember a friend who went back to school in her forties, her back injury aggravated by the cheap plastic chairs in the classrooms, so she started to bring lumbar pillows and cushions and shawls with her to school. "Let's turn this piece-of-shit chair around!" I can still hear her saying. The mascs I know save up money to buy a custom-tailored suit. The femmes, even (or especially) on high-pain days when they cannot get out of bed, paint their nails, put glitter around their eyes. I will always keep close how a crip friend said that glamour was one of the most important things in their life, their identity, their soul. *Same.*

One night, my friend Neve Mazique-Bianco and I were getting ready to go onstage for a disability symposium. Neve was in front of the mirror putting on lipstick.

A stagehand came by to give us the countdown. "Fifteen minutes till places! Ten! Five!"

"Thank you fifteen. Thank you ten. Thank you five!" we chimed.

When the stagehand returned and we were almost but still not ready, Neve said, "Listen. I'm femme *and* I'm disabled. Which means I'm gonna be late."

I am aware that much of my disability justice activism, in a certain light, can read as if I'm appealing for a sort of bourgeois lifestyle. My Disability Access Rider, which requires accommodations, travel, and the logistics of the event to be accessible to me and my disabled audience—requirements like my own room to sleep in, chairs for everyone to sit in—can seem like I'm asking for luxuries, requiring the organizations hosting me to be replete with resources. Sometimes, when I arrive at the event and I am able to walk without my cane, when I seem energetic rather than worn down by pain, my hosts have looked confused. Why did they have to arrange and fund such things as a business-class flight, a taxi to pick me up at the airport, when I seem so not disabled? Let me say that, when access is there, I am usually pretty okay. In the instances where there *hasn't* been access, I am acutely disabled. Long economy flights with several changes of plane, walking through the airport dragging luggage rather than using wheelchair service, needing to climb onto and off the bus, carrying my bags upstairs where I'm staying, no available food where I'll be staying—my symptoms flare, the pain goes off the charts, I become debilitated to the extent that doing the actual work is impossible.

I was reminded of this when I was asked to teach for a week at an art school in a smallish European city, not long ago. It was a new department, not even two years old, about half an hour outside the city, in the woods. The organizers had no money, and they were people I was friendly with, so I didn't bother sending my Access Rider. I figured they knew me well enough, and I also worried I'd burden them and their shoestring budget to make a fuss about access. When I arrived to find that I needed to pay for my own transportation from the hotel to the school, twenty minutes one way, or take a bus whose stop was a fifteen-minute walk away, and that the room where I was to teach was unheated in wintertime, with only a bare wooden chair, and that the food available was gray slop from the cafeteria, only served until two p.m., that I would have to pay for, with no food in the hotel and no per diem for food at all, I was reminded why I need disability access. The above conditions were fine, if a little uncomfortable, a little annoying, for the abled people there. They muscled through them—they could choose to muscle through if they needed to. I could not. By day three, I could barely get out of bed. At the end of the second day, as if I were an addict trying to score, I asked the students if they knew of a chair, a couch, anything soft, anywhere in the school, where I could sit down and rest. One student slipped me the information that they'd heard there was a couch in the office of the department head. Turns out it wasn't a couch but a rectangular object that was somewhat soft. The department head told me he hoped to find money in the budget next year to buy a pillow. He advised me against turning on the lights because they were reminiscent of *The Lives of Others*: DDR fluorescents. I lay there in the cold dark on this rectangle and faced the wall. Later, I hobbled out to the street to wait for the taxi I'd called to come, and it just didn't. I stood on a lonely road in the dark German forest at night for half an hour before realizing I'd been forsaken. When I said I'd need to do my last day of meetings in the bar of the hotel (which had heating and a cushioned chair), the head of the department balked.

"If I'd known you'd be doing meetings from the hotel, I wouldn't have invited you," he said.

"If *I* had known you wouldn't support my disability during this job, I wouldn't have said yes."

We got into it—the thing I heard over and over was that there wasn't enough money for the things I was asking for. To someone born in a Soviet bloc country, as he was, I know I seemed tediously, irritatingly American, demanding convenience and comfort from a place where such things were barely possible even for those who lived and worked there all the time. It's true that when I've tried to use my Access Rider in countries and contexts that are poor, that are scraping by, that are doing the best they can with barely anything at all, it can seem like a gross misjudgment, oblivious and ignorant. I know I sound like a diva. Why should I—the visitor—be granted things like better food, more convenient transportation, a heater, when the ones who are there every day don't have them?

What I would say to that is everyone, not just me, should have this—and my Access Rider is a way to measure how some, but not all, already do. Specifically, I'm pointing out how impactful it is for the disabled to have them, which should draw attention to the fact of what happens to us when we don't. This insistence on material support and comfort does not discredit my disability justice activism but bolsters its central argument: having enough money and support—and, crucially, having the freedom to make a choice in how our money and energy and time are spent—is the very thing that guarantees thriving at all. That it would be so powerful to the disabled community to have what we *need* to survive, and therefore be able to do what we *want*, only demonstrates how hardly any of us have this yet. Shouldn't everyone have this?

At some point, I started talking about "crip diva solidarity," the activism that works toward supporting each other to be divas. Girl, tell them what you need—don't ask, state. You need more time, a bigger room, a higher fee. You need a care person to accompany you, you need a deadline that is not ridiculous, you need better working conditions. This is what you need—period. Don't feel shame about it. Now, what would happen if we reached for the future where we say what we *want*?

Bitch, get into it.

Hedva's Disability
Access Rider

As I've received invitations to speak and/or perform at arts, culture, and literary institutions and universities (often internationally), I've learned a lot about my own capacity and how working with institutions tends to go. So that we can work together better, now, when I am invited somewhere, the first thing I do in response is send my Disability Access Rider.

Accessibility is still taking root in how institutions understand and work with disabled artists and communities. They've often never heard of "access intimacy" before, or if they have, they don't know what it means in actual practice. I've found that my access rider is often the first of its kind that they've seen.

In 2019, I made my Access Rider public because many people have asked to see it, and I've heard from a range of folks—from other crip artists to abled curators and organizers and hosts who want to work with us—that this document has been a useful model for them.

I welcome anyone who wants to use this as a template for your own rider, or to share with institutions who invite you to do stuff. And I invite anyone working within the institution to use it too.

Thank you for inviting me to contribute to your event. I am disabled, so for me to participate, I need support from my hosts. I also require the events I'm part of to be accessible to the disabled community. What's cool about this is that more people can come, and we'll all feel better when we're there.

This means that we're going to have to embark on access intimacy together (if you don't know what that is, please read the online article by Mia Mingus called "Access Intimacy: The Missing Link"). Before I can commit to that process with you—and honey, it is a pro*cess*!—please take a moment to read the below, and let me know how you can support each item. If you need more specifics about any component, ask me. I'm happy to clarify and assist where I can. If you can't provide something on this list, let's have a conversation about it. I am more interested in accessibility as something for which we work together rather than a punitive standard I measure you against.

0.

Money—

Access should not be funded solely by me, the disabled individual (e.g., taken out of my fee or production/materials/travel budget), but shared with the institution, and/or city, state, and/or federal funding. The fact that it is often funded by me, in more ways than just financial, signals how inaccessible the world is. Please join me in carrying this weight.

1.

Time—

Accessibility takes a really long time, and it's messy af! I will not be able—literally *will not be able*—to work with you if we let the demands of capitalist time run our lives. I require the timeline of our work, including expected response times and deadlines for the project/event itself, as well as the accessibility elements, to be as un-stressful (for everyone involved) as possible.

I've found that it works best to have all the below confirmed and agreed upon by contract at least three weeks before the event takes place. Trust me, the more time there is to work out all the logistics, the better.

I cannot travel the day of the event.

2.

For the entirety of the trip—

I require a care person to assist me. I cannot travel alone. I prefer to bring a care person with me, because we will already have a relationship and they will know what is needed. Their travel, lodging, food, and transportation must be paid for by the host, as mine are. If this cannot be supported, please make available someone within the institution who can lend a hand while I'm there.

3.

For air travel—

The flight cannot depart before 14:00. The airport cannot be more than one hour away from my house or where I'm staying. Nonstop is preferred. If a layover must happen, it cannot be longer than two hours. I need to be picked up from, and taken to, the airport. I must have an aisle seat on the flight because I use a cane. This has to be booked in advance. On flights longer than six hours, I require a business-class seat. Depending on my health, sometimes I require wheelchair assistance at the airport. Please check with me about this before booking flights.

4.

For lodging—

I require my own room, bed, and private bathroom in a nonsmoking room that has a window. There needs to be access to food *at* the place I'm staying; hotels must have room service. The lodging has to be a reasonable distance from where the event will take place. I require an elevator if there are more than two flights of stairs. I require all meals for the duration of my stay to be paid for by my host. My food allergies/intolerances are: no nuts, seeds, shellfish, cephalopods.

5.

For the event itself—

I cannot participate in anything before 16:00. I, and my audience, cannot sit for longer than ninety minutes without a fifteen-minute break. I require a dressing room/backstage area, and would not be bothered if fresh flowers appeared there. On the stage, I require a cushioned chair with a back for the event; I cannot stand.

6.

For the accessibility of the event—

I require that the event take place in a wheelchair-accessible space—no exceptions. I require every effort be made to provide both CART and sign language interpretation for the event; at least one of these has to happen. I require all-gender restrooms at the space. I require spaces to be as scent-free as possible. I require masks. If someone makes an access request, I require that the hosts make every effort to provide it.

If you can't provide what's been requested, tell me with enough time before the event so we can find a solution.

7.

For the publicity of the event—

I require that the accessibility information of the event be posted with all materials that include my name. This includes information about parking, elevators, wheelchair- and all-gender-accessible restrooms, CART, and ASL interpretation during the event. Best practice is to be transparent and as detailed as possible about how the event is, and is not, accessible.

For example, if there is one step, anywhere in the space, say so and where it is and if there are any additional routes. For example, if only CART is being provided and not ASL, say so. For example, if the parking is a five-minute walk, or a fifteen-minute walk, from the space, say so. For example, if the space must be kept at a noticeably cold temperature, as it is in most archives, say so (in this case, I've seen an institution provide blankets—a good idea!).

A contact email and/or phone number must be posted with all materials that include my name, in order for people to request specific access items.

A sentence I've found works well: "If you have an access requirement, please contact us at [X] by [date], and we will make every effort to provide it."

8.

For the documentation of the event—

I require open/closed captioning of all video documentation. I require textual image descriptions (alt text) for all photos posted online. I reserve the right to approve all final language published that includes my name. NOTE: I use they/them/their pronouns.

9.

In case—

Because I have chronic illnesses, I may have to cancel the trip at the last moment if I have a flare. This doesn't happen often, but it has happened. If there's a way that I am able to participate remotely, I will.

10.

For the future—

It would be so cool, and you'd make me and my friends and many others very happy, and you'd increase the attendance of your events by a lot, and you'd become a working part of building the kind of world that needs to be built, if you would follow this document not just for me, but for all your work in the future.

"The earth wants you."

MY HERBALIST

explaining gravity to me

Room Day

*"It fled / from the one who was dead /
and hid in you."*

SASKIA HAMILTON

MAY 2, 2018, BERLIN

I woke up today and something was wrong. Johannes was there,
opening the window and tucking me in. There was a text from Rhia:
Hey call me once you're awake and the heart emoji. I asked Johannes
why he was home, and he said because he felt sick. I knew he was
lying, he was home for me. I thought of who had died—I thought of
Grandma, Dad, Auntie.

But it was Mom.

They found her on Tuesday, May 1. She was alone in her room, on
the floor. She'd died Monday, April 30, sometime in the night, our
wedding anniversary, six days before my birthday, I guess she wanted
to make sure I'd never forget. She'd complained of chest pains for a
few days, her roommates told the sheriff. But her door was locked.
On Sunday she didn't answer the phone when Rhia called, which was
unlike her, Rhia said. She died alone, but how long was she on the
floor? The sheriff said she was yellow, which means she had cirrhosis,

but she died of a heart attack. They had to climb in the window to get her.

Yesterday our kitchen window banged open, and a suncatcher flew off and landed on the floor by my feet. I'd hung the suncatchers recently, they make me think of her. The cat went to inspect it, and I put it on my altar. I think I knew.

The last few days I've felt strange, like I can't wake up, like I'm in a dream, it's felt like something was pulling behind my eyes, I couldn't keep them open, a darkening. I now know this was when she was dying. She'd been dying for a while. On Monday I woke up with a full-blown shingles eruption, sick, so much pain. Today I feel clear—the dream fog has lifted, the death complete—I feel strangely calm. It was like I'd expected it, and my body had already started to feel it. It knew too.

I lit the Holy Death candle, I sent emails to friends, spoke to Rhia and Auntie, and booked the ticket to LA.

I keep thinking of the card I sent her for her birthday. The lunar moth on it, the first time I'd communicated in I don't know how long. I haven't seen her in seven years. On Friday I got her card for my birthday, sent on April 20. She died ten days later.

Rhia said they spoke when Mom got my card, and that she'd been so happy to get it. Rhia remembers saying, "Hanna loves you" to Mom and Mom saying, "I know."

I didn't get to tell her I forgive her—Mom, I forgive you. I'm sorry we haven't spoken in so very long, I'm sorry I have not been able to—but I do feel we were always communicating. I feel you speak to me in my body, in how I hurt, but also the beauty of the things you taught me to notice, suncatchers, animals, the ocean, waves, stars. Please know that I love you and I'll miss you. And how much I think of you, how often I tell your story. I'll be the keeper of your story, as you were the keeper of my life.

I sent Joey a text with your chart. I apologized if it was morbid to send such a thing, and they said, "It's not morbid—it's her life." A few months before, I had been looking at the astrology for the year, trying to note how the transits would hit me, and I saw Saturn and Jupiter and the moon and the south node, and there was a zap that said, *Someone in your family will die.* I pushed it out of mind immediately. I told myself I didn't know enough to see that, wasn't a good enough astrologer, astrology couldn't show such a thing. I was being superstitious. *Don't be silly. Don't worry.*

Then this happened. Part of the guilt and regret that swarms me is at my fear to investigate this knowledge. Perhaps if I had been braver, known more, wanted to know more, I would have seen, perhaps I could have warned you, told you to go to the doctor and get your heart checked, I could have reached out, I could have said I love you, I need you, I forgive you, while you were alive.

It was your life, Mom. It was a hard one, and I want to say a beautiful one.

I'm sorry you were alone. I tried to get to you. I could feel you. It was you pulling on my eyes. I'm sorry I couldn't be there. I hope Grandma came to be with you. I hope Mosaic was there too. I love you.

MAY 4, LA, HOME

That first night, I kept waking up with visions of her dead body, alone in her room. The room is light blue, and I keep trying to make it like the one from childhood, but it's also not. I wonder if she's face down or not, sometimes she is. She wears the Moose N' Crew sweatshirt, because that's what she wears in three out of four pictures that I have of her, so frayed, skin-thin.

The feelings are still subdued. I keep thinking, *I've spent so long already mourning my mother. So many years grieving for what never was or could be, grieving for what was inevitable.*

On the flight I spoke to someone, which I never do, and it was lovely and enjoyable—we talked for five hours—and I found myself saying I was excited to come home, and he said, "It'll be good to see your family," and I said, "yes it will," and at first I thought I was lying or forcing the words out to be polite, but as I said it, I realized it was true. The man—his name was Damian, he was from Detroit but had lived in LA for a year, he had taken his first trip abroad and gone to Iceland for three days, born August 3, 1989, in the morning, he said he wants to start his own fashion line, also that he doesn't stress about things, likes music, he was gentle and thoughtful—he seemed like an angel. At some point while we spoke I had the image of Mom watching us, listening, and chatting too.

Being home—all the smells are the same, the muscle memory, I reach for the mugs without thinking, know how hard to turn the taps in the bathroom. It feels so alive here—Auntie, her house, our shared memories, already laughing in the car, knowing to take the 105 to the 110 to the 5 to the 2 to get home. For the first time in my life, I've put a photo of Mom by my bed.

MAY 6, 10:06 P.M.,
BEST WESTERN INN, CARPINTERIA

Mom's room smelled like incense (sandalwood and frankincense) and cheap scented candles, it made us sick, and was mostly blue. Many images of the ocean, waves, sea turtles under water, surfers, and sunsets over the sea were taped to the walls. She never threw anything out, but she was also meticulous, kept files of everything—her applications to the housing authority, her social security checks, her food stamps, her court dates and fines, the DMV letters suspending her license, I found the little calendar she'd kept in jail, counting the days, and notes on tide calendars about what happened that day, who called or texted, and how she replied. Often she wrote one word about how she felt—"good," "bad," "sad." So many of the objects in that room I remembered—they were from our house on Jacaranda Way—the flatware, the mugs and plastic cups, some of the images, her sewing machines, all the furniture. She slept on Rhia's childhood bed—the twin—we'd had no money to buy a new one—which was broken and shredded. Her roommates said she never showered in the communal bathroom in the two years she lived there. She must have taken sponge baths in the sink in her room. Ashamed. None of the lamps worked—just a strand of Christmas lights. And a TV. She meticulously kept track of her favorite shows and sports scores. Her roommates said she drank two to three half gallons of whiskey a week but never drank with them. If they were all hanging out back or on the front porch, she'd retreat to her room, then return drunker— even though all of them seem to be alcoholics themselves, yellow, deteriorating skin—she tried to keep it secret.

We started with the papers on one part of the desk. We went through them one by one, and so many things made us cry. She kept everything, like a person who's been homeless has learned to do. Batteries, junk mail, plastic spoons, packets of salt and pepper, newspapers—but also notes written on old documents taped into a handmade notebook of lined pages held together by masking tape. We looked at some of her jewelry and clothes, but it was too much. She had little altars everywhere, photos of us and family and Mosaic and some prayer cards. I kept the coaster with the drops of her blood—three drops. I could not bear to throw away any part of what was left of her body. She'd fallen and hit her head a few days before April 30. The roommates cleaned up the blood from the floor before we came—good of them. My birthday card to her was on the middle of a shelf, in pride of place. I was struck by the blues, the smell, so like her—and in the disarray and the dust and the junk, how aesthetic it all was, how designed and collected and cared for and needed. That's how it all felt—as though she really, really needed every piece of paper, note, picture of a wave, object of her past, even if it was faded, cheap, and broken. The room had good light and a nice view onto the backyard. In the window hung many suncatchers and pieces of blue glass, one in the shape of a heart, one of a crescent moon. When I found her cane, I started crying. That she needed it, that I need it too. There are a few things I'd really like to have—one of her paintings, a piece of jewelry, a piece of clothing. I remember all the jewelry, I remember all the paintings. Some things came swimming out of my memory in full force when I saw them today, I thought they'd been gone forever. But they were still here.

MAY 7, 9:54 P.M.,
BEST WESTERN

Read her journal this morning, the one she kept up until the day she died. So many days marked "Room Day." I felt that in my bones, my inheritance. And each day is documented. When she woke up, took naps, went to bed, woke up in the night, and what she ate, watched. Who she called and what they said, if she left a message, if there was no answer. She wrote her bank balance every day. Her handwriting starts to get bad in the last days. She writes of chest pain on April 20, swollen ankles on April 23. She falls and hits her head, "blood everywhere," a few days before the thirtieth. There is an earlier day where she falls too. I read it on the balcony and cried. We did so much today. We chose the outfit for her to be cremated in: her Carpinteria Bluffs T-shirt, ancient by now as I remember it from childhood, and so very soft, pants she made for herself with fish on them, and her bathing suit instead of underwear, so—I sob—she can swim. We selected things to be burned with her—I printed her chart and put in the birthday card I'd sent her and gave her twenty dollars for the ferryman. Rhia put some moss from New Orleans. We found some shells in her jewelry box, little ones, a clamshell, a piece of abalone. Auntie put rosemary. We figured out the service, called around. Drove to Ventura to the crematorium to drop off the stuff and sign the forms. Then Rhia and I had about an hour in her room, just us, throwing away trash, trying not to get sucked in to the emotional stuff, as if that's possible. I found an old yellow Japanese teapot with two of my grade-school pictures inside and some coins, a little spell. I must keep it intact, keep the magic she was working. The trash was hard—lots of strange relics—homelessness logic—napkins, plastic bags, empty liquid soap dispensers covered in dust. Then there was the sheet on the bed that smelled like death—we staggered backward and held our breath and I felt sick and exhausted and Rhia retched. There was so much dust on everything, and I kept thinking of how much of it was her skin. The dust was flaky, chunky, alive. I felt myself breathing it in, getting it on my hands.

We went to dinner with Dad and then talked in his van in the hotel parking lot about what money Mom had and how we're going to pay for anything. We'd gone to the bank to close her account, and when we asked how much was in the account, the teller said she couldn't tell us that, privacy reasons, and Rhia asked with big eyes, "Is it minus?" The teller said no and we sighed audibly with relief. I felt the teller's pity.

Rhia and I walked from the hotel to the house in the late afternoon light and picked flowers from people's front yards—hummingbird sage, cosmos, jasmine, lavender, poppy, and gave some to Mom's roommate, Sue, who lived across the hall. We put the lavender and jasmine in Mom's room. My body's on fire, mind in a pain fog, and yet somehow I am not depleted. Death has made me gentle. I saw my name in her journal, when she received my cards—next to it, she'd written: "WOW." In more than a decade, that's all I sent her; that's all I could bear. How rarely I returned her texts. Every voice message she ever left, she was sobbing and I deleted them one by one. We set up a little shrine to her in the hotel room. I pulled three cards for each of us. Me: Knight of Disks, Five of Cups, Page of Cups. Rhia: Death, Six of Wands, Six of Cups.

Room Day. And always "Bed Prayers" at the end of each, which both Rhia and I instantly started reciting from memory. "Dear Lord, bless my family and my friends, and thank you for all that I have, amen." We will print it on the funeral cards.

The pen is in her notebook, in the last page. She wrote only "Fog" on the last day—at least we think that's what it says—then called Bank of America to check her balance.

MAY 8, 9:40 P.M.,
DAD'S HOUSE

Today she was cremated. At 7:45 p.m. at a facility in Ventura. We went to 4th Street Beach in Carpinteria, sat on a log, and watched the waves and the immense blue sky. The light was dancing. We cried and held each other. Auntie read a poem from a Native American cere-mony book about the spirit not being tempted to linger because of the earth's pleasures, nor being hindered by its burdens. She read it twice. The sun set and the dusk came in and the clouds became pink, then pale soft purple. The ocean was glowing with the blue of the sky. At some point it became peaceful, and we walked back to the car to come here.

This morning I wrote her obituary—I'm glad I could do that for her. I've been feeling ruined by how few memories I have of her in the last decade, and how so many of them are painful. I was eighteen when I drew my hard boundary, I needed it to survive, how old am I now? Rhia has a lot of memories, and I feel jealous, envious. I wrote her a good obituary. We chose a photo taken at my eighth grade graduation—we photoshopped Grandma and I out. She looks sweet and happy.

We cleared out her clothes. We found her purse, buried in the closet, zipped into a backpack, hidden. Her ID card made us break. Her red eyes and puffy, swollen face—how she looks as if she's about to cry, which is always what her smile verged on. The ID was taken in 2013—it expires next year on her birthday. She'll never get it renewed. This is what makes it final, what makes her dead. Her wallet had her bus pass, twenty dollars, her library card, her disability pass. We kept sobbing and saying, "Her little life. Her little life." How hard she tried.

She had nail files and eye drops and scrap pieces of paper in her purse. Where did she go? We found an older wallet—in it were ancient photos of Mosaic, Topaz, and a school picture each of Rhia and me. This feeling will crack me open, I will not recover. But then I think of how I've been in pieces this whole time. My little life— there *is* nothing to recover.

We found a lot of weed and pills in a drawer. We keep leaving messages on her best friend's answering machine, telling him about the death, the funeral. He never calls us back. We never see him again. He was her dealer for thirty years.

We threw out so many T-shirts with holes, stains. I kept think- ing of her homeless, afraid, sad, lost, the years when I refused to speak to her until she went to rehab. I kept saying, "I'll be there for you. I'll stay with you. The minute you decide to go to rehab, to a meeting, I'll be there, I'll go with you," and how she never, ever went. Instead she called to tell me she'd been beaten, she'd been raped, always she needed money, and I didn't—couldn't—believe her. She'd call to tell me the cat had cancer and she needed money for medicine, and I was hard, unflinching, no. She will use it for drugs, I explained. For years, I explained this. Now I am putting twenty dollars in with her corpse.

Rhia told me a story of when Mom had had a room in the back of a man's house at the end of the street near 4th Street Beach. The man had been a hoarder, the bathroom didn't work, Mom had hated living there, been afraid of the man. Rhia had given Mom information and contacts for homeless shelters, and Mom had responded by spitting on Rhia. Rhia said, "It didn't make me mad, just sad." We reminisced about the time Mom had chased our neighbor down the street with a kitchen knife. We laughed.

MAY 10, 11:17 A.M.,
BEST WESTERN, CARPINTERIA

Yesterday was the first day since I found out that I didn't cry. Rhia said that was true for them too. We planned the service, invited people, took things to the dumpster and to donate, twice. On our second trip to the thrift store, there was an old scraggly-looking man, probably a volunteer, looking through the things we'd brought and carrying them inside. He looked like a servant to the underworld. We ate dinner just the two of us at a restaurant in Carpinteria and talked about what we want to happen when we die, what to do if the other is suddenly gone. Rhia and I are fitting together, with ease and love and gladness. It feels like all these years of tension and distance are gone in an instant, and the only thing between us now is recognition. We're sharing memories of childhood, Mom and Dad, each other. Rhia told me yesterday, when we were alone in Mom's room with our gloves and black trash bags, that the only thing that had pulled at them when they were in the Church was their love for me—Rhia said they didn't think they could do what the Church kept asking them to do because they loved me so much, and that contradicted what the Church people were telling them was okay. In the room, at this, I crumpled. I crumple now.

While sitting in Mom's chair, cleaning out the closet, something mean bit the back of my left thigh and I cried out, and now I have three red welts the size of a hand that ache and throb and itch. I took some Benadryl last night and slept a full eleven hours, and I'm grateful.

We contacted some people for the funeral. I'm looking forward to seeing them. It's strange how death brings people together, reminds the living of what they share.

MONDAY, MAY 14, 9:49 P.M.,
AUNTIE'S

Today we finished the room. We left it empty, save for some pieces of broken furniture that the landlady wanted inexplicably. Rhia and I stood in the room, taking it in. We said we feel we've erased her. We talked about how it was the perfect place for her to die; even if she had been alone, at least she was surrounded by her things, in the one place she could feel safest. If she'd have been in a hospital, if somehow we'd gotten there in time, she'd have hated it, dying in the hospital, surrounded by ugly colors.

The funeral was on Saturday—the days have bled together. I am exhausted and can't remember things. Today I couldn't cry but was overcome with death anxiety, a pernicious and stubborn attack, I've been having this more and more. The thought that now my mother has ceased to exist on her own, independent of us and what we may feel about her, our selective memories, our projections—this feels excruciating. Some large black void now exists behind me—where I come from. I feel like a vital cord has been cut, the primary thing that connected me to this life—what gave me life—now that it's gone—she's gone—I feel tenuous, as though my own existence has been compromised.

We dropped the box of her ashes into the sea, and it sank into the dark blue. The day was perfect, warm, clear sky, and I got a terrible sunburn from the boat trip and then the service. So many people came—we counted thirty attendees—more than we thought. I feel guilty that I thought this at all. I didn't know she knew so many people. Everyone told us that it was a beautiful service, that we, Rhia and I, were beautiful, and the day was too. When I think of it now, I feel empty. I hope I don't forget these days. Seeing all these people— so many of them, like Mom, have lived here their whole lives, in a town just over ten thousand people, and I've spent my whole life trying to get away from it—older and fatter and with worse skin and thinner hair, the entire thing is so, so sad. But it also feels like home. It is home. She was home. I had so believed that if I could stay away from California for three full years, I could be free of it. But it didn't happen that way, and now that I am here, it feels like I never left, that Berlin will be just a phase, that I must return here eventually. I'm gripped by the feeling that I can't die anywhere else—that my ashes too must be dropped into the Pacific—all the Johannas and Hedvas from her side that I'm named after are buried in Forest Lawn Cemetery, a few miles from Auntie's house.

What I will never forgive myself for is how close I was coming to forgiving her, how I was almost there, but not yet. I wanted to try. I wanted to stop being so ungentle. I wanted to arrive at the place where I could tell her I'd be okay if she kept using—Rhia says, if Mom could have stopped, she would have—that I wanted us as an us. I wanted us to have the future. I thought I had more time. That didn't happen. Mom called me home, both of us alone, and I came.

Soft Until It Gets Hard

*"There are moments when the ooze of the flesh of
the world is swept into structure, howsoever that may
happen: molecules congealing, language making,
labor into wages, any kind of naming."*

HARRY DODGE

◆

"Sometimes to be known is tender, abundant hurt."

JUSTIN PHILLIP REED

We were going through the park on scooters, in the long blue evening of Berlin summer, giggling. I was singing, my scooter went twice as fast as theirs, they called after me, and then I smashed into the dirt. Took a turn too sharp. It didn't hurt at all. "They're a faller," they said about me and we laughed. There was a wound the size of a quarter on the heel of my hand. I watched the blood stop itself by thickening, which is a perfect metaphor—to watch something stop because it got too thick. During everything that happened next, the wound on my hand slowly scabbed over, and watching the progress of the scab was a kind of clock. Time was sneaky and refused to be grasped, hours would vanish mischievously, we got lost in each other, slipped through a gate to somewhere not here, so a wound on my hand that moved at a terrestrial pace but nevertheless transformed completely felt apt. My own little clock, near where a watch would be, that counted out what I couldn't hold and what, despite trying to let go, I was.

It was July. I'd met this person in April, online. They looked like Caravaggio's *Lute Player*. The texting, their words, brazen in abundant perversity, was the best I'd ever had. There were a few dates in May that rearranged what I thought was possible between two people, in ways that hurt because it went so deep so fast and ways that dilated because I became weightless, I could fly, everything got rearranged.

In June, I petitioned Zeus to bring them across an ocean to me, for a short tour I had through Eastern Europe. The plan was for them to play in my band, be my care person on the road, and fall in love with me. When I asked if they wanted to do this, they said YES YES YES. We had a few minor deities on our side, the tricksters, the satyrs, the muses, but there were a lot of earthly inconveniences stacked against us (expired passports, money, my health), so I petitioned Zeus because I wanted help that was big and hard. I wanted power enough to move cosmic realms to accommodate whatever we wanted and right now. I asked my classics professor friend for the right Orphic hymn, and she suggested the one that asks Zeus, the king of Heaven who'd shape-shifted his body in order to rape, to be fair and temperate. Twenty minutes after my petition, the sky split open with thunder, lightning, and lashing rain, and these flamboyances from the god of thunderbolts did not abate for the rest of the summer. My tarot cards were good ones, but they were all reversed; my astrology was the kind that prophesied transformation, but also where a world or two might have to get broken in the process. Still, I worked my magic, made my request: Please bring my love to me. I need them next to me, right here, right now.

The original ancient Greek definition of "hubris" means to disobey the gods. I am good at disobeying authority. So I seem to never
quite get away from suffering the fates that some of the most malicious, authoritarian gods have in store for me. Or, that's one way of
telling it. I like the ancient Greek framework that sees each god as
having a different fate for you, and, since the gods are capricious,
selfish, absorbed in their own machinations and dramas, making
deals with each other, this means that one's fate not only can change
but that it does all the time. This is why thinking of hubris as disobeying the gods can feel emancipatory. When the god of suffering
and misery has a fate they want to impose on you, what happens
when you try to negotiate with them, trick them, make a deal with
another god to double-cross them, tell them to fuck off?

Around day three or four after the fall, my scab started to hurt
more than the wound ever had (another metaphor?). Day five
brought the itching. The colors were like an O'Keeffe landscape:
dark pink, dirty orange, the green of dry sage. For the first few days,
the scab wasn't yet a scab but that slimy surface which is not all the
way solid. That was when the green was the most luminescent; it
seemed to glow.

One week before, my love and I had met in Ljubljana. My flight
was delayed because of Zeus's thunderstorms, and I almost missed
my connection. When I landed, the wheelchair-service person told
me I'd already missed my flight, but I checked the internet and said,
no, I think we can make it if you go fast. So they sped me through the
Munich airport, honking at people to get out of the way, and, against
all odds, I made it. Was that Zeus? Disguised as the tenacious
wheelchair-service employee? My love and I tangled the hotel bed's
sheets, loped around a Slovenian castle built into a mountain, and
swam in the Mediterranean Sea. We never stopped laughing, they
never stopped saying how happy they were. They'd get on their knees
and service me with their mouth and hands, feeding me, one night

they put me into a state where my orgasm lasted forty-five minutes and I became pure light, and this, this, was exactly right. We went to Berlin and started rehearsing music every day together. I learned they were a genius. I learned they were a mess. They carried me up the stairs when I couldn't walk. There were all the wounds and all the joys. We were honing bliss.

One night in Berlin, they went out to buy drugs, then came home at six a.m., blacked out, eyes skidding back and forth in their sockets. They said, on repeat, "I'm not okay." They'd been high and drunk for days, weeks, months. Yeah, years. I hadn't noticed at first, even though I was raised by an addict. Addicts are good at hiding how bad it is. Addicts are the supreme shape-shifters. There is the wonderful, beautiful, brilliant, sweet person that I love, and the drunk and high version. That early morning, in the dark of my bedroom, that other version reached for me, used their body weight to pin me down, grabbed and held onto my neck. It was terrifying, but it was not malicious. It was a desperate reaching, like they were drowning and trying to hang on to something. I said, "Stop, honey, stop. Please stop." They let go and sobbed themself to sleep while I told them everything was going to be okay.

A week later we were on a train to Prague, to play at a music festival. They were drunk on five splits of wine, high on MDMA and four Klonopin taken that day so far. They were the person I was falling in love with, and they reached for my throat again. When I lurched backward, I watched shame cloud their eyes. They looked like how my mother had looked in the moments when she'd realize what she was doing.

My love's face was angry and lost and confused. I have been on the other side of a face like theirs before. I have thrashed, flailed, needed earplugs, shouted, cackled, screamed, thrown punches, reached for someone while saying *I'm not okay*. Never with drugs or alcohol, but in dissociative panic attacks, autistic meltdowns, psychotic episodes, trauma flashbacks. I often don't remember what happens during them; if I do, it's prismatic, flashing, a jar of broken things being shaken, and the jar is my head. There have been friends, family, lovers who've watched this happen to me, been on the other side of my head when it looks like that, and afterward, some of them, most, left forever. I can only assume that what those people saw in me then was enough to make them never want to see any other version of me again.

There have also been friends, family, and lovers who stayed. Put earplugs in my ears. Said, "Everything is going to be okay." Ran after me when I flung myself out of rooms, moving cars. Grabbed me before I went out of a window on the second floor. Forgave me. Tried to hold me when I pushed them away. Reached after I'd thrown punches and then reached again.

I am alive today because, in 2013, I met a man who loved me more than I'd ever been loved before, more than he'd ever loved before. We are still loving each other now; we have the same name. He is not in this book because this is a book about pain, and he has given me none. What sort of law of physics can account for that?

During everything that happens next in this essay, I would ask myself what he would do.

Care is a lemniscate of taking and giving. It's not a transaction of plus and minus but a continuous moving, like a roller coaster, a lot of ups and a lot of downs. Repeat. It can scare you, like a roller coaster, show you viscerally how the law of gravity feels, and it can teach you, let you know briefly, what it feels like to escape gravity.

Maybe what I mean is that pain—sharing it with someone, giving and taking it, agreeing to hold it for and with each other—can feel like an infinity symbol too. In the place where we'd expect pain to cut and rupture, instead there is torque, centripetal and centrifugal motion, orbit. I am trying to say something about how care and pain make paths for each other to move along.

I wondered how we would make it through the two more hours until we were to arrive in Prague. It had already been three hours on the train from Berlin. They sobbed for most of the train trip. Or cackled. Or shouted. Or stumbled and fell and pushed and fought. There was a man in a nearby seat who wasn't looking at us, and they shouted at him, "Are you looking at me?" They tried to fight the man, then tried to fight me when I pulled them into the vestibule near the water closet, between the cars.

The train pulled into a deserted station somewhere in the Czech countryside. I thought we could stand there in that little pocket of space and everything would be okay. I reached for them and said, to both of us, "Everything is going to be okay." They pushed me. I reached. They pushed me again, and I reached again. They pushed me harder, I fell backward, and then they turned, and I watched them push the button to open the train doors, and then I watched them throw themself out of the train.

They had opened the doors on the opposite side of the platform. There was no platform, no stairs down. They fell five, six feet onto the tracks. I watched them clamber across the rails and rocks to a short concrete wall on the other side. I shouted their name three times. Then I watched them jump over the wall and disappear. I could not see what was on the other side of the wall, but the station was raised, the street far below, twenty feet at least.

I thought, *I just watched my love die.*

The train started to move. The doors closed. It took all but five seconds, and I know this because that's how long it takes to shout their name three times. Two syllables, three times, five seconds: they jumped from the train, they went behind the wall, down, below, gone, and then the train was going faster. Trauma did that thing where it made me calm by taking me out of my body. I couldn't move. I stood there. The image replayed in my mind—them going over the wall, them being gone—it's never stopped playing in my mind.

It was when I took out my phone in the next moment to call them that I saw I was in my body because it was shaking. I did not stop shaking for twenty-four hours, for the next week, months. I called and called. I wondered how I would live with this hard, bright, unbearable reality in which they had disappeared behind a wall.

Then they answered.

"You're alive?" My voice was small.

"I'm where you left me." Their voice was smaller. I pictured them lying in a crumpled pile in the street.

"The train is moving. I can't come get you," I said.

"Then I'll find my own way home," they said and hung up.

I called fifty times, but they didn't answer. I didn't hear from them again for fifteen hours, and during those hours, I did not know if they were alive or dying.

Later, I would try to understand the fate of this encounter. We'd met online, a portal had opened, and now we were in hell. Why? Was there a reason? Was it easier if there was a reason, or did that make it feel worse? It was separate hells, each of us in our own. Which realm—earthly, chthonic, divine—might be ours? I tried to see the story from their perspective. Why had *I* happened to *them*? I would tell myself that this episode, for them, was a proportional confrontation with the ways in which the coping mechanisms they'd relied on to survive their past traumas were causing harm, to themself and others. But that story only worked if they agreed with it.

I wanted to understand because I believe in fate, because I am by definition a fatalist. But it's not that I believe in fate because believing in it makes me feel better. God, I wish. "Everything happens for a reason" is a phrase I balk at—a woo-woo sham that insists on the affirmative at the expense of anything useful or nuanced. It's not very helpful for me to rely on there being "a" reason that "everything" happened. I need to know exactly what that reason might be, and then reach my mind into all the other possible ones. What about the ones that don't make sense of anything? What about the reasons that are intolerable, absurd, arbitrary? In the same way that I understand "everything" and the many reasons for it, I think of fate as multiplicitous—the *fates*, plural. Fate, as a singular entity, can feel like it's got you by the scruff of the neck, a trajectory that you have no choice but to be moved by. The fates, plural, are as tricky and treacherous as they are vehicles upon which wisdom and growth might arrive, and often there are several at play at any given time, as much trick as wisdom, and I guess I find solace in the fact that if there are more than one there's room to negotiate. I want to think of fate as a raw material that can be crafted. If it's a material to be crafted, one can approach it like any other craft: with discipline, skill, curiosity. Shape it, make it, feel it form as you work it in your hands.

My love was stranded, alone, drunk, high, fucked up, blacked out, in the middle of nowhere in the Czech countryside, two hours outside Prague. They had nothing but a fanny pack with their wallet and drugs. They had their phone when they jumped from the train, but when they hung up on me, they would lose it; maybe a satyr hid it from them. All I knew was there was a likelihood they were dead. If they were alive, it was an alive that was nothing but hurt. All their stuff was in a suitcase on the train with me—passport, laptop, phone charger, cameras, music gear, clothes. That, plus two guitars, a backpack, two tote bags, and a case with an electronic sampler in it that weighed fifteen pounds on its own. I could not lift the backpack, let alone the suitcase, they were so heavy. I paid a stranger ten euros to carry the bags down the steps of the train car. I called my friend in Prague and asked her to meet me on the platform. I said my care person had gotten sick on the train and had to get off. This was not a lie.

It took an entire hour for my friend and I to carry the bags from the train platform, down the ramp (the platform elevators were broken, but we only learned that after walking the fifty meters to each one; I joked that my disabled friends and I like to say, "Everything is great—except ableism!"), through the station, into the elevator, out of the elevator, across the street, and into the parking lot where the taxi was. We had to stop every few steps and rest. Repeat. Crip time.

A version of this story is a comedy. In Prague I was attending a residency hosted by an artist-led project called the Institute of Anxiety. Through the Institute of Anxiety, I was to stay in an apartment that looked like a wellness spa, serene open spaces hiding all accoutrements of living. You had to feel along the wall for secret handles to secret cabinets where toilet paper was concealed. The woman who owned the flat greeted me. She had just come from yoga. She told me, "I always feel so proud of myself when I can do a full headstand." When she said this, I still didn't know if my love was alive or dead, which parts of their body were broken. For the days I stayed there, my sobs filled the fair and temperate rooms of the Institute of Anxiety.

This is not the first time I have been in love with an addict. My mother began that story. My first memory ever is at night, my mother peering down into my crib. I am three years old. She is saying that she has to leave to have spinal surgery and might die, but that's okay because I don't love her as much as I love Dad. For years, she'd threaten to kill herself because, she'd say, I didn't love her enough. Throughout my childhood, a kind of clock, she would come into my room in the middle of the night. Sometimes she'd trash it. Sometimes she'd shake me awake sobbing. Sometimes she'd punch me in the head. The Buddhists call addicts "hungry ghosts." Hungry ghosts have a stomach the size of a mountain and a throat the size of a needle's eye. I am often able to forgive desperation.

It's terrifying to watch someone bash into their own mind as it disobeys them, that hubris, to witness them tear at their body as if it were a concrete wall enclosed around them. To watch someone want to jump over that wall and disappear. Did I watch my love's fate take them over that wall, or was it their will that took them, or is the difference between these two irrelevant? Is wanting to know the difference a kind of empathy I am trying to extend?

When humans invented gods, we also invented the concept, the possibility, of disobeying them. For the Greeks, hubris leads to "nemesis," which means destruction, and this destruction is the gods' punishment on those mortals who'd be so arrogant as to defy them. Etymologically, "nemesis" means to distribute, to allot; it's a kind of measurement of what is due. Nemesis is also a goddess, symbolized by a sword and a lash. She is goddess of divine revenge and retribution, outright indignation at when humans fuck up. The *Dictionary of Greek and Roman Biography and Mythology* explains her:

> Nemesis is a kind of fatal divinity, for she directs human affairs in such a manner as to restore the right proportions or equilibrium wherever it has been disturbed; she measures out happiness and unhappiness, and he who is blessed with too many or too frequent gifts of fortune, is visited by her with losses and sufferings, in order that he may become humble, and feel that there are bounds beyond which human happiness cannot proceed with safety.

It makes sense to me that humans want and need to find ways to personify, articulate, and orient ourselves around how destruction happens to us—not only to give it a name but to try to account for why—because this feels a little better than not. Animating the functions of the world as acts of the gods (plural) feels more alive, more dramatic; it situates us as players on their stage. To claim our own disobedience as the cause for what would otherwise be random, meaningless destruction, returns a little agency back to us. I think what I mean is that it's simply a way to work with our lots—what's been doled out to us—as material. To see ourselves as authors of our own stories, even if there are other authors vying for space on the page. When something bad happens, we often cry out in bewilderment: *Why did this happen? Why must I suffer?* There is always the question of whether we caused it—if our wills are gods in themselves, or if it was out of our control, a function of fate, the fates, our gods.

The gods as I have known them speak cryptically, sure, but they are also pretty blunt. They do seem to enjoy turning the world in a cosmic enforcement of unforgiving symmetry, that lemniscate of taking and giving a kind of rope around all of our necks. Yet, I've also found that the gods will break the sky open to send a deity on wings to help you—maybe not to save you but at least to deliver a message—but only sometimes, and sometimes this deity wears a face that changes. Sometimes the gods make the world's engine churn with mercy and patience and small moments of ease and joy. Sometimes I think I had to witness my love throwing themself off a train so I'd understand why people from my past have abandoned me during my own crises. I had to feel my love's hands on my shoulders violently pushing me away so I'd know how hard it is to keep reaching after someone does that to you—hard, but not impossible. What makes it possible? Which one of us is the winged one in this story?

Is this me trying to find a reason that everything happened? Does Nemesis have me by the neck, or is this me wriggling free from her ruthless hand? Someone once told me that what's cool about spirituality is that you can choose what to believe in. When they said that, I realized I've never felt that I've had a choice. Is it that I *choose* to believe "that there are bounds beyond which human happiness cannot proceed with safety"? Do I *choose* to brace myself for the worst? Nemesis has often saw fit to make me humble; she has visited me with loss and sufferings that seem to exceed the amount I ought to be allotted. How can I unknow what that has felt like, what that has taught me?

Deborah Levy has said that the things we don't want to know are the things we already do. Simone Weil wrote: "We possess nothing in the world—a mere chance can strip us of everything—except the power to say 'I.' That is what we have to give to God—in other words, to destroy."

I lay awake in the Institute of Anxiety, my face elasticized by sobs, and became suffused with dread, thinking the unbearable, wondering what was happening to my love, to me, what kind of story we were in. I was not interested only in how different my version of this story was from the version my love was telling. It's that I wanted to know all the versions, especially the ones I didn't want to know. What about the versions that made no sense, that were out of my hands? What if my love continued to use drugs after this? (They did.) What if something even worse happens? (With addicts, it often does.) What if my love lets their addiction kill them, like it did my mother? There must be a knowledge that is different than dread, of knowing in my bones and fascia that deep pain will always be present in sites that also excavate love. But what will be left of me when I have become full of the kind of love that also empties me completely?

Perhaps I am writing about empathy. I wonder if empathy is something that Nemesis includes in what she doles out, or is empathy, like disobedience, like hubris, a human invention.

The trouble with empathy is that asking someone to have it for an experience they haven't yet felt in their body is futile. Empathy can only be engendered when it's embodied, when it moves in your own body, gives your own trajectory a shape. Until then, you will only be able to map yourself on top of the other to be moved to care for them. The golden rule—"Do unto others as you would have them do unto you"—still places the emphasis, the action, not in the hands of the others, but the you. Saidiya Hartman's world-changing book from 1997, *Scenes of Subjection*, is about this: why white people think racism and white supremacy is not something that affects them at all, is not their problem but a problem for Black people both to suffer and to solve. When white people *can* be moved to care, as Hartman elucidates using abolition narratives as examples, it's often because they have superimposed themselves onto the scene, imagining their wife, daughter, self, etc., in the place of the slave. They cannot be moved to join the cause because they've watched countless others suffer; they need to feel it impact them. They choose to know only one version of the story—the one where they are the protagonist, even, or perhaps especially, in scenes where they are the antagonist. The limits of their empathy are a function of their inability to know, or want to know, another version of the story. In another example, the critic Jessa Crispin put it perfectly in terms of how certain it is that men have not yet encountered feminism: "Don't you think we'd know it if they had?"

For years, I've been furious that people don't seem to have any time for disability until it happens close to them—they get sick, someone they love gets sick. *What about all of us who've already been here?* I want to shout. But this can be forgiven, I guess, because another way of saying it is that there is a limit to what one can understand in abstraction. At some point, the knowledge needs to move into your body for it to be fully known; it needs to go from unformed to formed, soft to hard.

Empathy is not the softness nor the hardness, but the movement, the transformation between the two. Soft into hard and back to soft. Repeat. Which is to say that empathy is not knowledge but the curiosity to know.

Fate at its worst can feel like the impossibility of empathy toward life itself.

In ancient Athens, the god who had the most shrines built in their honor was not Zeus, the chief of gods, but Hermes. There would have been a shrine to Hermes in every home and on every street corner. Hermes is the god of language, meaning, and messages being conveyed, which means he's the god of deception, trickery, and messages being lost. This gave him more power over our daily lives than any other god. He was the only one able to move between all the worlds: the mortal, the divine, and the one underneath. If you needed to get a message to anyone—another creature, dead or alive, or a god—you asked Hermes for help. If you needed to decode a message you received, you asked him, praying he would not to take too much poetic license. As the ruler of meaning, he was also the ruler of the way meaning can shape-shift. Ruth Padel writes, "He is god of the possibility that my meaning may not be your meaning, though the words sound the same." She goes on, "The streets must have bristled. . . . People spoke to him. He spoke back. . . . Relationship with Hermes was one of dialogue. In sacrificing, one offered him the tongue."

Sometimes I wonder what I've sacrificed, what I've offered, without knowing. I wonder what Hermes has not let me know, the messages he didn't let me receive, that he saw fit to encrypt. My tarot cards reversed, my stars full of dread, the thunder cracking outside my window, the gods I disobeyed, the fate(s) I tried to craft in my own hands.

My Caravaggio, I learned later, would break their ankle in three places and collapse in the street. They'd call for help, and the first two people who came by and stared would not help. The third would. At the hospital, the overhead lighting would scare them, the nurses would be mean, yelling at my love in Czech. They'd check themselves out against the doctor's orders that they have surgery immediately. They'd go back to the train station looking for their phone so they could call me and would reach their hand into the bushes, right into a pile of human shit. They wouldn't be able to wash their hands for hours. They'd find a jacket with shit on it and wear it anyway because they had nothing and they were cold. They'd call me at five a.m. and we'd sob into the phone. *You're alive you're alive you're alive.* I'd text them the train timetable. They'd take the next train to Prague. I would not tell them where I was. I was still shaking. The ghost of my mother gripped my neck. They'd find a cheap hotel and not leave the room for sixteen days except to go to the hospital, where they would be told their ankle was now too inflamed to be operated on, and they'd need to inject themselves with anticoagulants for ten days. They had no insurance. They'd call the front desk of their hotel to ask for ice and put it in dry cleaning bags that would break and leak onto their cast. They'd piss in the bucket the ice was brought in because they couldn't always make it to the toilet on their crutches. I'd speak with them on the phone every day, until I couldn't. I'd text their mom and oldest friend every day, until I couldn't. Then I would again. Every fourth or fifth text, their mom would apologize, embarrassed, for her child's behavior. I would want to write back, *You should be embarrassed if you own stocks or if you're a landlord or voted for a cop, not because your child needs help*, but I didn't. I would say, "I will help in every way I can," and I did.

I wanted to learn to speak the languages of will and fate with equal fluency. I wanted to haul Nemesis off her throne. I thought of the line from the Rosalind Belben novel, *The Limit*: "Everything a human body can in tenderness do, I do." I would do my best to get close to that. My own body would collapse in an immune flare from the stress. The lemniscate of care, a lot of ups and a lot of downs. I wouldn't be able to get out of bed, couldn't walk more than a few steps without my joints screaming, and I'd get shingles. I would order ibuprofen through an app to be delivered to my love's room. A week into taking it every day, they noticed they were jittery, anxious, and couldn't sleep and would realize that I'd mistakenly ordered them ibuprofen with caffeine in it. When they tell their version of this story, this is the element that ratchets up the comedy, but I will never not carry the guilt of my error. I'd Uber over there and leave my own bottle of (caffeine-less) ibuprofen at the front desk. I'd shake for that whole errand, terrified I'd see them at the hotel. If I had seen them, I would have turned and run. Would they have run after me?

One kind of knowledge that my own suffering has brought to me is that suffering is brought to all of us. Some of us call it in, accidentally or knowingly. Some of us are surprised by it, petulant that it arrives at all. Some of us can only understand ourselves through it, can only feel at home there. Some of us had parents who could not, for whatever reason, protect us enough from their own suffering, and we follow in that lineage. Some of us were born when the gods were at war with each other. Some of us have made shitty deals with the wrong god at the wrong time. Some of us have turned our backs on the gods who might help us. Some of us have not understood the language in which these potentially helpful gods spoke to us, so it's sounded silent, empty, when we cry out. Fate is all these things all at once.

Amidst these, the one certainty is that suffering will come. If there are so many reasons that this might be, pulling the potential meaning, the possible reasons, this way and that, I think the one thing that centers the storm is how we meet this certainty of suffering—which is another way of saying that kindness is a form of magic we can choose to know how to do. What matters is to attend to suffering, no matter why it's there.

We might not know how magic works, but we can want to know.

Some people have the privilege of not believing in magic. When I've told the story of what happened to my love on the train, the responses, even from friends who are active in disability justice and understand how ableism works, shocked me. The tone was punitive, judgmental, moralizing. More than one friend disapproved that I'd even continue a relationship with this person at all. Because my love's injury happened while they were drunk and high, the attitude seemed to be that they deserved what they got, that they'd made their own bed and now had to suffer the consequences. It was an appraisal both of Nemesis doling out what was right and that for which my love had only themselves to blame. What exactly should they be blamed for? That they've been turned hard by trauma and don't know how to get soft again? That they've reached for something to ease their pain? That they've been desperate, thrashing, confused, afraid?

There is knowledge that we should be curious to know: Why is care so hard to do? Why does it take more than we have to give? If care fails, is it someone's fault? What if it fails a lot? Does that failure mean something, not about what we as individuals can or cannot do, but what we as a society have taught ourselves is important to know? What have we built our world to hold? What have we not built enough space for? If something stops because it gets too thick, if the soft parts of ourselves get too hard, if our curiosity to know hits a wall, how do we make room for this to change?

Getting sick together, sharing care together, helping each other through the blast radius of disability, can be one of the ways to most deeply bond with someone. It can be like a trauma bond, with as much damage, but the difference is that you can both choose to hold the damage rather than punish it, feed on it, or recoil from it. Many of us punish and recoil from it, enforce a narrative in service to ableism rather than the reality of our soft little bodies and what they need, and many of us feed on the grim fatedness that says we deserve this, should be blamed for it, we brought it on ourselves. I have found that folding damage, grief, and pain into the story will mean there will be too much to hold sometimes, so many things we do not want to know. The trick is to know that these big hard parts are important to the story—and in some versions, they are the entire story—and it's okay to take breaks, feel furious, sob for hours. The grief never stops. Neither does care, if you let it.

What surprised me most in those days I spent at the Institute of Anxiety was not only how familiar the grief which bore down upon me felt, but also how different I felt about how to meet it. There was a little more space than there had been before between the trauma and what I could decide to do about it. I looked at the scene and wanted to know all the possible versions. What I mean is: I was surprised to learn how much I loved them, which made me know how much I loved my mother, and how much I loved myself. Sometimes I think all we can hope for is to let the story surprise us.

My love's hands would blister from the crutches. They would fall in the shower, in their room, in the hospital. They'd hit their head.

They'd lie down in the street because they couldn't move anymore, then they'd get back up and keep going. They'd tell me about it and do the thing they were better at than anyone—make me laugh. I'd say over and over that laughing in the face of disaster is all we have. We'd joke that, on the trip where they were supposed to be my care person, they were getting a personal, pun-intended, crash course in crip life, that they were in the blast radius of disability. I would send them my essays. They'd read what they could, through the pain fog, and text me their favorite lines. They were ashamed, embarrassed, crying during every phone call. They remembered nothing on the train, in the bed, were horrified to learn what they'd done. They'd apologize and apologize and apologize. They'd thank and thank and thank me. They'd regret their "missteps," and I'd say, "Funny you call them that, as if you'd simply stepped on your foot wrong."

I'm trying to tell you what I've learned about how care and pain shape each other without limit, which is to say that I am living this knowledge, that I have been curious to know it, and still am. For what is knowledge but the writing into being of that which wasn't yet articulated? And what is writing but language given shape, space, and time in a body? It doesn't have to be words on a page. It can be messages never sent, screaming in a room, dragging a hand through water. It can be a hand on my neck that had, the day before, helped carry me up the stairs. Our bodies hold many meanings, knowledges, tricks, truths. If there isn't enough space to hold them all yet, we can trust that the gods will break us open to make more. I tell my astrology clients that there are many kinds of knowledges that can arrive for us throughout life. The way to know which is wisdom is that it's the kind that hurts.

We can be soft until we get hard, then soft again. Repeat. We can speak to our gods with fate and will—perhaps fate and will are simply the most sacred languages of all, the ones that, when we speak them, our gods can understand. We can tell Nemesis to fuck off. We can let our hubris be a form of magic.

Care is a Möbius strip where one side is pain but also, somehow, the same side as care.

A Möbius strip is the tricky kind of lemniscate. My favorites are things that can be more than one thing.

I wrote the first paragraph of this piece, about the scab, in the first thirty minutes on the train. I read it out loud to my love. They'd only had one Klonopin and two splits of wine by then. We laughed at my trying to make a scab sound like a potboiler. I said I was trying to get the right sentence to describe how a scab changes from slime to crust. They nodded and their brilliance set to work. Helping me make a metaphor, giving me the language I needed, reaching toward the knowledge I was trying to know, and so they tried to know it too. They gave it to me: they said, "Soft until it gets hard. I got you."

Why It's
Taking So Long

1.

In January 2016, "Sick Woman Theory" was published online and, within a few weeks, went viral. The illnesses and injury that precipitated my writing it were a bewildering, totalizing transformation of everything I'd known to be true about me and the world, but this was even more destabilizing. Not only was it my first attempt at thinking through the politics of chronic illness and disability, it was my first-ever attempt at writing an essay. I called it "Sick Woman Theory" because I realized that, despite not identifying as a woman, and before any of my other identities or occupations, and no matter what I said, did, produced, or defined myself as, that's how I was now seen—a sick woman. This was a raw fucking deal.

In the years since "Sick Woman Theory" landed, my visibility—how I'm seen—by literary organizations, publishing houses, and art institutions has expanded from "the sick woman," to now a sort of representative spokesperson for the disabled and chronically ill community. Within a week of its publication, I started to receive invitations to speak and write on the topics of care, illness, disability, and ableism, even though none of my work, besides "SWT," was about this. I remember being invited to give a reading in Oakland, and when I said I'd like to read some of my poetry, the organizers shouted into the Skype call, "No! We want you to read 'Sick Woman Theory'!" Editors from publishing houses, large and small, asked me if they could buy the Sick Woman Theory book. I said I hadn't written it yet, but I did have two finished novels, a collection of poetry and essays, and another novel in the works. I asked if they would be interested in those, and of course, they were not. It was here that I learned the first of many lessons about exactly how the insidious twins of visibility and cultural capital work.

It was not lost on me that I—who pass as abled, white, and cis— was being invited into places where other disabled artists and activists—who do not pass—were not. I had written the kind of theory-heavy text that is somehow democratically palatable, and its reach shocked me at first. Suddenly my audience included people I would never have before imagined writing to, for, or with. The places to which I was being invited felt exotic and foreign, and not a little hostile. I laughed that I was dressed for the underground kink party in the dungeon but was finding myself at dinner parties with stiff white tablecloths and respectability politics. For instance, I noticed that on panels about disability hosted by more mainstream organizations, programmed next to, say, a successful white woman who wrote about her migraines, I'd often be the only person who publicly identified as disabled, the token activist to round out the cast, albeit with my disabilities appearing to be manageably contained. Once a white woman in the audience at an event asked me what was the one thing I wanted abled people to know about disabled people. I said I would want them to know more than one thing. I found myself giving Ableism 101 lectures over and over, and it made me want to scream. At some point months into the COVID pandemic, as I received what felt like the hundredth invitation to talk about why care is important, I cried out to no one, "What else do you need to see to make it clear?"

This blade of attention cut both ways. Once, onstage in conversation, my interlocutor used the word "crippling" to describe anxiety— which is an obfuscation of the word that is considered mildly ableist by the disabled community—and many months later, during another event's Q&A, a person in the audience demanded to know why I hadn't more sternly corrected the interlocutor for their trespass, as if I'd failed to successfully police that moment on behalf of anti-ableism. Once, I was one of the few white-passing people on a panel, and a white man in the audience asked me what I thought of "Angela Davis's concept of intersectionality."

"Angela Davis's concept?" I repeated the error while it sank in that he was asking me, and not the others, because he felt more comfortable speaking to a face that resembled his own. "Um," I said, as I glanced down the row at my friend, a Black artist and activist who's a dear, savagely sarcastic friend. They were looking at me with a glint in their eye, and I passed them the microphone so they could correct him, which they did with as gentle a smirk as possible. We still laugh about this today.

I felt like an underground band who has an unexpected hit on the radio. I'd been working as an artist for over a decade at that point and publishing my writing since 2001, when I was seventeen. For the majority of my career, I'd enjoyed a small amount of attention from an even smaller audience, but they were devoted, as I was to them, and they loved me for my strangeness, my profligacy with genre, everything about me that did not fit into any category. Now, I was enjoying what felt like a huge amount of attention from a much larger audience who had only read this one text. I became legible as one thing. Squirming in that shining, singular spotlight, I tried to suggest that I had other songs, even whole albums, that might be worth listening to, but mostly the crowd just wanted me to play my one hit. A precious few seemed to want to listen to the other stuff.

In the wake of my viral moment, several editors got in touch to buy the book that was at that point only twenty pages. I knew I wanted to write the book someday, but first I wanted to finish the novel I was working on, and I needed to figure out what the Sick Woman Theory book should, and could, be. "I think I need five more years before I can even know what it is," I told my agent. She advised me to do what was best for the book, what was best for me, and for this, I will trust her forever. We turned down the editors, some of whom worked for presses I had long dreamed of being published by.

That was a turning point. In 2016, I made $9,255. And I wanted to be published *so badly*, I thought I would have done anything. The editors in my inbox didn't say any numbers outright, but it was implied that I could sell the Sick Woman Theory book for what would be called "a nice deal" in the publishing trades, and I would be set up for six months, maybe even a whole year to write my book. Money like that, security like that, a life like that, was something my ancestors and I could only dream of. It was a fairy tale. But when you've been poor your whole life, and are descended from generations marked by it, you become street smart. You know a scam when you see one because the whole world has been scamming you since birth. You've perpetrated plenty of little ones yourself.

So, when these editors sidled up to me, a line of heat shot up my spine, and I knew it wasn't what they were telling me it was. When it was offered to me, I saw only the strings attached, the price. I saw that they would want an illness memoir and not what I wanted to write, which was an analysis of ableism fractured through different literary forms that refused to be contained in a traditional genre. I saw that they'd want me to write a book with more answers than questions, which was the opposite of what I had. I saw that they'd want a *ka-ching* memoir to lead the parade of chronic illness to the peak of its trending topic, which, at that time, was just starting its ascent in the mainstream. I saw that they saw only my hit, my one piece that went viral, not my body of work, nor the range of subjects I was inquisitive about, nor the genre-fuckery I felt the most allegiance to, nor the long and varied career I was aiming for. In short, they saw the Sick Woman—not me. Since I'd never had, nor hoped to have, any money, it cost me nothing to keep that part of me—the poor part—intact for the sake of another part that felt infinitely more valuable.

If nothing else, my career has been a demonstration of the kind of time that is propelled, not by money or fame or capitalist production, but by the conditions a body needs to be supported, the kind that divorces itself from the spurious capitalist conflation with money, the kind that demands rest, detour, refusal, long queer days and nights, and also insists on what it needs to be sustained, to stay interested and maintained and devoted.

I put an auto-reply on my email for two years that said, "I may never reply to you." I turned down every invitation that came in about illness and instead wrote about many other topics—Nine Inch Nails, the mysticism of mosh pits, Sunn O))), astrology, hair— reminding myself that promiscuity and curiosity, rather than expertise, are the primary functions of the mind's reach that feel sustainable to me. After taking a decade-long hiatus from music, I returned to it in my thirties, and this required a changing of direction not unlike the moving of a planet into a new orbit. When invitations came in to speak at a conference about care, or participate in a group exhibition about illness, I'd say that what I had to offer was a live doom-metal performance, take it or leave it. Many did not take it.

It became easier and easier to accept these rejections. In fact, they started to feel fortifying, vindicating, of what is important about who I am. Alongside the greedy appetite of my mind, I am an all-in or all-out kind of bitch in terms of heart and body. I'm only interested in relationships that can have big things built upon them, and something easily forgotten about a career that persists is that it is a machine sustained through relationships like this. To me, what those relationships are, and how they feel, and if they can hang for the long haul, if they can carry the heaviest of weight, is what matters. I don't want to do meaningful work with editors, curators, agents, or organizers whom I wouldn't also want to have a long dinner with, go dancing and get sweaty with, talk about heartbreak, desire, and ambition with. If it's just a job or a gig or a little hoisting up, it's fine—I'll forget their name afterward and they can forget mine too. But if it's a book that I'm going to spend a decade pouring the blood of my mind into, that I'm going to push against the skin of my insides until everything breaks, I need to trust these bitches with my life, because that's what's at stake. Trust takes time. Bodies, of any kind, but certainly the ones that we endeavor to build around our creative projects, are fragile as fuck. There's a little flame and a long black storm, and I know I will walk through most of it alone, but it would be nice to have company for the part where the light comes.

Most of my friends were puzzled as to why I complained about the success of "Sick Woman Theory" so much. One of them said, "You just made a really big rainstorm and a lot of bitches got wet. What's the problem?" Some wondered why I didn't cash in on my tiny moment. Even a small book deal would have been twice what I made in a year. And wasn't this what every writer hopes for? To write a piece that lands with people, that, if only a little, changes the public conversation?

The only way I can explain my disquiet is to say that what changed was not what needed to change. When I wrote "Sick Woman Theory," I was writing into the gargantuan climate of ableism, which, at best, renders invisible anyone who deviates from its invented norm, and, at worst, kills them outright. I was writing into the institutional practices of gaslighting, discrimination, incarceration, brutality, and eugenics. I was broiling with rage. I wanted scorched earth. When I say I wrote "into," rather than "about," I mean that I couldn't see another way to make my case but to go deep into the shit so I could report back on its exact and specific qualities, which means I got covered in shit. I summoned a voice—zealous, galvanized, grandiose—that was not how my own sounded at the time, and I did this because I needed a voice like that, to rally, to cut a path through, to shout, "Is anyone there?" into the lonesome dark and maybe hear back a "Here we are!" I needed to bellow "Follow me!" just to give myself a direction, somewhere to go that was not where I was. But when the shit started getting into the water supply, I saw that this voice was its own cruel optimism, a promise that could never deliver. What I had conjured up was a Sick Woman that seemed empowering and righteous and who promised a community—but what I quickly learned is that no promise of community can hold, and all promises of solidarity fail. Anyone who's worked in activism for longer than five minutes knows this. Because the promise is not enough. If there is not actual, material change that comes with it, a promise is just hot air. And worse, it's hot air that puffs up around an individual, a heroic leader, leaving everyone else in the dust.

What I mean is, what I wanted "Sick Woman Theory" to change was the world, but it only ended up changing me.

Here's another way I can explain it: One morning in 2019, I opened my Instagram to see that I'd been tagged in a photo by someone I didn't know. The photo was from a tattoo account, the torso of someone, head cut off, with a large fresh tattoo on their upper arm and shoulder. The tattoo was an illustration of a person in a frame, like a tarot card. I frowned and squinted, not seeing why I'd be tagged in this. I had to stare at it for a minute before I saw that it was an illustration of me, based on one of the portraits by Pamila Payne that accompanied the "Sick Woman Theory" text, where I'm lying in bed

with my hair fanned out on the pillow like the ink cloud of a frightened octopus. The second I recognized myself tattooed on this
stranger's arm, my nose exploded with blood and wouldn't stop for
forty-five minutes.

I know I am being contradictory and asking for too much: I both
wanted "Sick Woman Theory" to change the world, and I'd prefer it
not make such a fuss about its author. I wanted to articulate my
experiences with chronic pain and poverty, the medical-industrial
complex, the gaslighting from doctors, but I did not want to be cast
in a romantic face-off with my tragic lot, my "fate worse than death."
I wanted to describe the figure of the Sick Woman so I could then
explain in detail why she shouldn't exist, but I also wanted those
who would identify with her not to feel that their suffering was
unseen and worthless. I wanted to write a manifesto, but I quickly
learned that a manifesto is only ever a document that reaches too
far, that speculates too impossibly, and that the only use a manifesto
can have is to lay bare why it cannot be manifested, to open itself to
all the ways its un-manifestation shapes the world and is its very
foundation.

2.

About six months into the Sick Woman storm, as my inbox swelled
with invitations to speak, I started making a list of accessibility
requirements that I would need if I were going to work with institutions, so they could host my disabled ass and make the event accessible for the audience. The document began as a necessity—I had to
put into emails that, if I were to stay overnight for the event, I'd need
to sleep in my own bed in an actual room, and not on an air mattress
in an unheated hallway, because bitches tried it. I had to write that

the venue hosting the disability conference had to be wheelchair accessible because bitches, so many, tried it.

Within a few days of publishing my Disability Access Rider on Tumblr, I saw some tweets go around that said, essentially, "If I used a document like this, I'd never get invited anywhere." I lol'd. Bitch, same! It seems that some are under the impression that I send that document and it just . . . *works*?

As soon as it was born, my Disability Access Rider became a document of failure. I learned that institutions had often never seen a document like this before, nor had they given much thought to access at all. Because of this, I decided to "grade on improvement," rather than using my rider punitively. In response to any invitation, I send it and ask if we can have a conversation about how they can or cannot support each item. I say that I hope this document can open space for us to work on access together. Which means that it's an itemized list of all the things I'm going to have to pour uncompensated educational labor into and, more often than not, be told that the institution cannot support them, even though the institution has far more resources and power than I do, and if they're not using that to support access, what exactly are they doing? The reasons they cannot support them are myriad: I've heard everything from the more understandable (though still not great), "We don't have a budget for that," to the less, "But I find sign language distracting."

I'm not sure if my policy of grading on improvement has been a good idea. I did it because it was more realistic than expecting accessibility to be there already, but in reality it's meant that I spend most of my time not on my actual work, but writing emails that explain, say, why live captioning or ASL are important to have at lectures, or an all-gender restroom is preferred, or the building needs to have a ramp and an elevator, and then getting into email fights about it. It's meant that I enter into a relationship that is by default unequal in terms of the time and energy I must make available to an entity that is making itself far less available to me. It's meant that I try very hard to see the person that I'm speaking with not only within their institutional context, but as an individual with whom I might collaborate, find convergences of interest and values with, maybe build something together with, even though this sets me up to be exploited, because the institution is never out of the context—it is always there. In fact, it is the premise of our entire relationship, and it consumes without compunction the resources it requires to survive, even if those resources are me. It's meant that I have to point out this power dynamic frequently, which is fucking tiring. It's meant that when I point it out, I'm told I'm wrong, or there's nothing that can be done, or more often, I just don't receive a reply. It's meant that, sometimes years after working in some of the most exploitative and ableist conditions of my career, the institution will include me on BCC in an email asking to give them feedback on my experience by filling out a Google form; and if I agree to Skype with them about it, they'll give me a hundred dollars. It's meant that curators regularly send me long texts they've written about "radical interdependency" and "care, repair, and healing," conceptual frameworks for exhibitions they want me to participate in, and then I won't hear from them for months when I ask how much I'll be paid. It's meant that I cannot just say, "I need an aisle seat on the flight," but "I need an aisle seat on the flight because I use a cane." And even if I do bring my cane into the discussion, I've often boarded flights and found myself booked in a middle or window seat, and when I alert the institution to this, they tell me that, at the airport, they "are sure you can advocate for yourself." *But*—I want to say—*I thought I already did.*

Grading on improvement has meant that the costs of the institution's "improvements" have been borne by me, for free. At best, it has meant that I've served as a learning experience I did not particularly want, nor was I paid, to be. Worse, I've been ignored, argued with, chastised for being difficult, and disinvited because of that document. And if the organizers are white women—fuck me. There will be obsequious apologies, testimonies of guilt, lots of emails about how they are so very overworked and trying so very hard, and, of course, tears. (Recently I made a rule for myself: if an invitation comes in for anything about "care" and it's organized by only white women, it's an automatic *no*. Also, recently, I read this text aloud for an event with machine-generated live captioning, and the AI transcribed white women as "right women.") It says something that any event you've seen me participate in since 2016 was one where the access conditions were tolerable—and nearly all of these events were inaccessible in some way. The first one who had secured and budgeted for comprehensive accessibility *before* inviting me came five years after "SWT" was published.

Getting into email fights about disability access is the only part of my public role as the Sick Woman that feels like it is worth anything, because it takes this condition of "being seen as" by something external and returns a small amount of agency to me in terms of what I can do with it. It's not some chip I can cash in for my ego, but something that might make meaningful change and bring actual support to the disabled community. It is not performative—and it is often the only thing that feels that way. Institutions love to perform themselves, flaunt their mission statements, their "ethics," their "values," and the main way they do this is by shoving their fists up the asses of puppets like me. That I would be leveraged as a performative virtue signal the institution can hold up to make itself look good is the game being played and, for better or worse, I choose to play it. I try to insist on my own terms for playing it, even though I know I can't win, but it seems better than not playing at all.

So, although I have less and less patience with the rules of the game, I know that I must play it, at least for a little while longer. While I'm here and I have the energy, I can try to do what I can to be helpful for others. That I am being invited instead of other disability activists, who've been doing the work decades longer than I have, is enraging, and the only way I can mitigate my rage is to try to leave something that might be useful for those who come in after. If I think a friend would find the invite advantageous, I ask if it's okay that I suggest their name; I tend to decline by offering lists of others that could be invited instead. However, this still requires that I engage, which makes me seem available. I remember once being invited to contribute to a magazine whose issue's theme was "on violence," and out of twenty-five invited artists, fewer than five were not white. I pointed this out as the reason I declined ("I would implore you to ask yourself what exactly a publication featuring a masthead and table of contents dominated by whiteness could say, directly or indirectly, about violence"). Sometime later, the same editor invited me to a new issue, this one "on care," and apologized if my seeing their name in my inbox would be triggering. When I declined, they wrote back to tell me that if I ever needed anyone to edit my work, they would be happy to provide this service. As I say, I have less and less patience.

I've found that, as my cultural capital increases, if I insist on certain accessibility requirements, not in the name of the audience who might need them but for myself, I am more likely to get them. This is because riders are traditionally used by divas and rock stars, and this is an economy that institutions understand—the economy of idiosyncratic spectacle, of throwing one's weight around, of power. A crip friend put it well: "They seem to think access is the same as wanting my name in lowercase letters." I have adapted to this, joking with friends that access is crip diva solidarity—but this is limited comfort. If access is seen as one individual's "special needs" or "accommodations," that access can then be separated from the structural inaccessibility of the world that necessitates it. It scales disability down to the quirk of a single person's body, an extravagance to be indulged, an inconvenience to be controlled. I know that most venues I've worked with only ever made events accessible because of me, and that the moment my rider was taken off the table, the moment I wasn't there to make my demands, everything went back to how it had been before. I'm not sure what to do with the disappointment, the failure of this. Is it mine to bear? I know it shouldn't be. But then why am I the one who carries it?

One response I've gotten to my Access Rider is that the institution did not budget for accessibility, but one or a few of the organizers who care enough will personally try to make it work, putting in extra hours of their own unpaid labor. For one music festival I performed at, the person who took my rider seriously was the only woman of color on staff. She said she understood why disability access was important but said to me that it felt like I "was dumping all this extra work on her." I nodded. "That's exactly what this document is about," I said. My Disability Access Rider is not a list of things we can "achieve" together if we just put our minds to it. If only! I'm not asking the staff of an institution to be more overworked, stressed out, and underpaid in working against ableism. I'm trying to point out that they already are—overworked, stressed out, and underpaid, that is—and it's *because of* ableism. I'm trying to point out that the most fucked-up conditions of capitalism exist *because of* ableism— because ableism demands that the staff work for ableism only, making the possibility of wear, depletion, fatigue, and illness, chronic or not, impossible under the relentless conditions of capitalism—*and so*, we should help each other deal with this nonsense together. My rider is a way to acknowledge that structural inequality and discrimination exist, that ableism infects all ideologies of oppression, that capitalism cannot work without it—*and so*, we can't fight it alone.

Making events accessible takes an impossible amount of labor, money, and time; it is not something to which the word "achieved" can even be applied; and ultimately, perfect access is not accessible to us. It does not exist. In practice it's a goddamn mess. Hiring signers for an event of two hours costs hundreds of dollars, live captioners are booked out months in advance because they're so scarce, and so many buildings have fucking stairs. The world is inaccessible, the ideology of ableism is everywhere, in everything, from urban planning to legal policy, to wealth inequality, to the super-cripple myth, to the word "lame" being used in casual conversation about things that suck. And this is why I'm asking that we bear it together.

I tried to explain to this woman that my rider is a way of taking seriously the fact that, even if we are told we have to, we cannot do this alone. Care is *always* a deficit, access is *always* insolvent—and that's the point. This is because the body, by definition, is a thing that needs support—it needs food, rest, sleep, shelter, care. I like to truncate this definition, to make the body simply a thing that needs, period, because what else would support be—but needed? The body's dependency *is* its ontology: it cannot survive alone unto itself, even if it wanted to. Yet we've been taught that such dependencies, such needs, are abnormal, disgraceful, an index of one's inadequacy, and to support them is indulgent.

Capitalism and its attendant ideologies have used powerful magic to make us believe the opposite of what is true. They have persuaded us that the most important force on Earth is one's individual will and the ability to manifest it, regardless of what that would require in terms of material resources. They have convinced us that any one person's success is the simple result of a decision they made to thrive, and not because of the support any individual requires to do anything, on any scale, always. They have induced us to think that the failure to lead a life of wealth, ease, comfort, and privilege is because that person just couldn't get it together, couldn't pull themselves up by their bootstraps, wasn't willing to put in the work. This is a mighty myth—one that is vaunted as universal, and it is the vehicle for that most romantic and nonexistent of subjects: the man who makes new worlds simply because he wants to, who shapes his destiny of his own accord. His body cuts through the void without history or politics or needs of any kind, no tether to anyone or anything else. He is not us, because he is impossible—but we all wish he was us. We all throw ourselves at his feet, try to make ourselves in his image. What is required to sustain this myth? Who hoists him up? Who is that behind him, in the background, helping him get there, defining him as what she is not—but the Sick Woman?

The reason why disability access takes so long, so many resources, so much energy and labor, and why, of course, it can never be perfect is because it foregrounds the Sick Woman and gives her center stage. It does not make her into a hero, rather it explodes the concept of the hero at all, asking not what she needs to be heroic but what she needs just to live. The magic trick capitalism has managed to pull off is not only to make us believe that we *do not* need, but that we *should not*—and disability access is a long needle piercing the bubble of this magic trick. Without this magic, without this myth, we are left with the truth: The body is never going to be solvent; it's always going to need too much, be too expensive, not do everything we want it to, hurt more than we can bear, and then deteriorate until it can no longer move. Disability access is about orienting time to a scale that prioritizes this truth, prioritizes what we need and whom we support, which is in direct opposition to the capitalist order of time that ignores and devalues such things. My Access Rider is not about sharing the load so that we can suddenly be in the black—it's about redefining what being in the red means, what being insolvent to each other does, and it's about acknowledging that we will *always* be there, covered, totally, in red.

And yet we've built our world as if this fact deviates us from where we should be. We've framed care within the context of debt—where my "giving" care to you means I'm depleting my own stash, and your "taking" from me means that now you owe me—and although we've made debt into an index of our deficiency, we've also made it the only possible condition of life under capitalism. To be alive in capitalism is by definition to live in debt, and yet we've defined debt not as a kind of radical interdependency, as the ontological mutuality of being alive together on this planet—which it is—but as all that reveals our worst, what happens when we fail, a moral flaw that ought to be temporary and expunged. By doing this, the omnipresence of our need is framed as a kind of weird bankruptcy that happens only to the weak—which is a fucking canard. The logic of capitalism states that the person who needs support from society is a burden on that society, but this logic can only work when the premise holds that our natural state is one of surplus—and it is not. Yes, it might be nice to labor without limits, survive without support, live without loss, decline, and fatigue, but that's not how it is. If we should have learned anything from the COVID pandemic, it's that, for better and most certainly for worse, we're in this together.

Obviously, I'd prefer the conversation about access to be about real shit like universal health care, a living wage, and abolishing the police and prison-industrial complex, but I have to start where I am, with what is within reach, so for now, all-gender bathrooms and ramps and alt text will have to do. But what I'm trying to smuggle in with my gentle but determined requests is the more revolutionary proposal of all-out institutional change, a restructuring on a systemic level of our values and the resources we allot to them, the power imbalance scrutinized and remade. I want accessibility to be seen as the political movement it is, advocating for the rights of a group that hardly has any and needs them the most. I want ableism understood as the most integral component of all oppressive ideologies—capitalism, white supremacy, sexism and misogyny, homo- and transphobia, classism, imperial- and settler-colonialism— that these all feed off each other, that they need each other to work, and what they need most of all is ableism, because it's the ideology that most sweepingly invents the false hierarchy of that which can be deemed normal, which is to say, *who* can be deemed *not* normal. I don't want accessibility because the disabled community "deserves" it, because we've proven ourselves "worthy," allowed into the category of the good and legitimate human by those who decide and define it. I don't want accessibility because someone is being "generous" in giving it to me, nor do I want the labor I have committed to accessibility to be framed in terms of my own generosity, that I'm insisting we have a bench to sit on in the museum out of the goodness of my heart. I'm not talking about trying to feel good—I'm talking about trying to survive.

I know that, to some, I probably sound bitter and cranky, but what else should I be? Fucking grateful for the opportunity? Focusing on the silver lining? Appreciative of all that I've learned from the pain of the struggle? Should I be watching my tone?

Hands down, the best thing that happened to me because of "Sick Woman Theory" was that other crips read it and came and got me. When I'd shouted, "Is anyone there?" into that lonesome dark, they replied, "Yes, bitch, and we're waiting for you!" Because of that text, I am now part of an actual crip fam, friends who have my back as I have theirs, friends who get it, who are just as tired as I am, who know that, yes, we are fighting for our very lives, and it's going to take all we have, so let's make a plan for the long haul, build something to carry the heaviest weight, and find a way. For we will find it. We're not going anywhere. If the future is anything, it's disabled—and that is true for everyone.

If you don't believe me, just wait.

3.

In November 2021, I read a draft of this text at my first IRL reading in more than two years. It was to a sold-out, socially distanced crowd in the atrium of the Gropius Bau in Berlin. Reading something in public and not to a Zoom screen, where I'd done the book tour for my second book, *Minerva the Miscarriage of the Brain*, during the pandemic, was weird. I got my hair done. I wore a Britney mic. The chair I was sitting in dipped low, so it was hard to get breath. When I got to that last paragraph about finding my crip fam because of "Sick Woman Theory," my voice caught. I felt tears start to come. My mouth was dry. I apologized to the crowd. I tried to explain that I was crying because, when I think of what my life was like before I found my people—and even that sentence I couldn't get out.

A crip friend was in the crowd, and we spoke for a long time afterward while the atrium emptied around us and all the chairs were put away. We were the only ones left in the huge room of the museum. They had their cane leaning against them. They had a question for me, which they hadn't asked during the Q&A, because they said it was just for us. With their voice measured and slow, as if they were asking themselves too, they said, "If you didn't have to do all this work about access, all this labor, send all these emails, get into all these fights, what would you do? Like, if you were just— welcomed. Supported. What would you make? What is your *actual* work?"

I cried again. The word "you" in their question could have been the word "we," and the meaning wouldn't change.

Some might assume that the great tragedy of my life is my illness. But in my opinion, the far greater tragedy is that I can, for whatever reason, write about it pretty well. I once went to an astrologer who pointed a long finger at my chart and said, "Your illness is more dig-nified than your life."

"I fucking *knew* it," I said. In astrology, the word "dignified" means that a planet is supported to do what it wants to do, but the connotations of an elegant seriousness also apply. I can see my illness, out in front, distinguished, noble, and me and my little life behind it. That external condition that erases the internal one. That conundrum of how I am seen eclipsing what I know myself to be, all the many possible words, versions of the story, the knowledges that are there mantled into one kind of narrative. I can see my other works, my other passions, reduced to hobbies—or worse, things I do to "cope." I can see my craft bent in service to this one subject—that I am not seen as a writer whose subject is, sometimes, illness, but that I am seen as a sick person who is always writing about their sickness, even when they're not. I can see my work flattened by ableism and the machinations of capitalism, letting me "self-actualize" only if the story conforms to the legible story of what I overcame, the battles I fought, how hard it is for me, and all that I accomplished despite my wretched condition. I don't know if I—my body, my self, my life, my work—can ever be as dignified as my illness. I see that I will never fit into that mythical universal subject of the man who shapes his own destiny unburdened by anything but his own will. The other side of that truth is that I don't think the world will ever let me be something other than the Sick Woman. The only consolation, at this point, is to make space for that paradox, that capacity for shape-shifting. It's that I'm both, all, and none of it. It's that I know this will change, and I know at the same time that if it stays the same, even if it gets worse, I'll be nimble enough to hold that too.

I know that my illness is part of who I am, as are my wit, my ambition, my diva-ness, my penchant for kink, my love of perfume and leather, my preference that every meal I eat be delicious, my tendency to collect guitar pedals and complicated words, my love of movies and freaks and fine whiskey, but I also know that I didn't choose to be ill, and that I chose and chose and keep choosing many other things to be true about me, to be included in my life, and this distinction feels important. I want a life capacious enough to contain what I choose to be true about myself and that which I did not but have nevertheless learned to work with, to use, to wield. I know that there is a place in me where things from the outside meet the things from the inside and that, even if this place won't stop moving with pain, my body has enough room to carry both. I know that I prefer to fight and bite rather than acquiesce and let go. I know I never roll over unless I'm being told to by a good service-top and the sheets beneath me are five-hundred-thread count. I know that my rage heats and leads me, and that I have never gotten over anything. I know that care is not a virtue signal, accessibility is not performative, and my disability cannot be mined as an abstract concept. I know that my body cannot be separated from my work. I know that I will survive, even though I'm not supposed to. I know that I know how to live, and will.

And I know how this fight goes. I know that this fight is about the negotiation between complacencies and fury, about what one can and cannot afford to lose. I know that I cannot afford to step out of the ring, to stop playing the game, at least not yet. I know that I am fighting for my life, my worth, and the fact that I am dimensional— and my opponent is the institutionality that insists on flattening me. I know that this opponent is fucked-up and much bigger than me and sure as shit fights dirty and, of course, will win. But I am getting better at this fight. I've been in it for years now. I go to my corner, blood and water pouring from all the holes in my head. I joke with those in my corner about how much time I've spent getting into fights and losing. That I will not surrender, but I guess I'll just keep losing? They laugh with me, "Oh no, you're winning, haha—but maybe there's no prize."

My editor asked me, now that this book is finally going to be done, if things might feel differently, if I might want to make a note here that marks this change. I had to think about it for months.

All I can say is that I have realized this book is not for me. I have come to understand that many aspects of my life and work, the purpose they might have, are not for me. I did not write this, did not do this work, did not spend all these years reaching, to care for and heal myself.

No. This has not been for me. This won't *be* for me.

This has been, and will continue to be, for whatever "us" it might assemble, for whomever might not have recognized themselves in its first pages, but by now, is right here.

The Hag in Charge

For thirty-six years I was poor. Now, as a freelance artist who's lost income because of COVID-19, the German government just gave me five thousand euro. Three days after filling out an online form, the money appeared in my bank account. I cannot believe it. It is not a student loan disbursement, nor a loan at all. It does not need to be paid back. It is mine. This is the first time in my life I do not get down to pennies in my bank account. It changes everything.

FEBRUARY 2021

I win an award and sell my novel. The award is for ten thousand pounds—more than a third of my annual income, and it will come in chunks throughout the year. The first check that will arrive for the novel, the first of three of the advance, is for $4,250, which will be the second largest amount I've ever received in my life after the German COVID money last year.

JULY 2021

The check clears. I have been locked down for seventeen months in a one-bedroom apartment where my partner and I both worked from home, and we have not gone anywhere except sad little walks in the park, and I need to get out of here, need a change of air and scenery, and now I have enough money that I can do something about it. As soon as the immunity window of my second vaccine dose closed, and there is somewhat of a lull between COVID surges, I book a trip to Greece for ten days by myself. It is the first time in eighteen years that I will travel alone for pleasure. The last time I'd been nineteen, on a train with a backpack and a blue cowboy hat, eating trail mix, reading Sartre (lol, I know), trying to make it on five dollars a day. This time I can afford the extra airline fees to bring a checked bag in addition to my carry-on. I pack three kimonos, thirty books, and a big black sun hat. I feel like a queen.

APRIL 2011

When I say I was poor for thirty-six years, I mean poor like this: One day, while at UCLA finishing my bachelor's degree in design, I have three dollars and seventeen cents to my name. Three dollars in my savings account and seventeen cents in my checking account. This is not the first time, nor the last, that I live like this. It happens every week or two. Alongside my full course load, I have a part-time job as the studio assistant for one of my professors. He is an opera set designer who lives in a big house in the hills of Brentwood, near where Joan Didion had lived with her family. He's done many of Philip Glass's operas. Chuck Close painted his portrait, and a print of it hangs in the foyer. Taped above his desk is a scrap of paper where, years ago, Susan Sontag had written out her address for him, and I look at it sometimes, her handwriting. The phone rings, and it is this famous artist, that director of a museum. He wears Yohji Yamamoto and pays me fifteen dollars an hour to putz around his studio with him. On this day in April, after work, I have to drive across town to Pasadena to visit my grandmother in the hospital. The gas tank meter in my car is below E. It's about twenty-five miles from Brentwood to Pasadena, and I am leaving at rush hour, so it will likely take me two hours to get there. The traffic on Sunset to get onto the 405 (then the 10 to the 110) is stuck in long ribbons of red and white lights. From the car, I call my bank. A helpful woman does what I ask: she transfers two dollars from my savings account to my checking account. I have too much to worry about, no time, to feel shame. I stop at a gas station and get $1.75 worth of gas, which makes the gas tank meter move not at all. I get back in my car and keep going. I listen to Kanye West and roll all the windows down as I inch across Los Angeles in the dusk. *What if my car dies on the freeway?* I think. Then I think, *Well, what?*

At the hospital, my grandmother is happy to see me, and I am happy to see her. She has been there for some time and will stay longer still. I try to visit her every day, as do my aunt and sibling. We eat dinner together, hospital food or sometimes In-N-Out sneaked in at my grandmother's request. I will hold her hand, lying beside her in a bed in that hospital, when she dies in August the next year. But on this night in April, I have a date, and she is glad when I say I'll see her tomorrow. There is now forty-two cents in my checking account and one dollar in my savings account. I ask my aunt if I can borrow ten dollars.

"Do you have change for a twenty?" she asks me.

"No, I do not."

She gives me the twenty, and I stop at a gas station for ten dollars' worth of gas, then meet a Russian painter at a bar. When the bill comes, I offer my remaining ten dollars, and he pays the rest. We go back to his place. In the morning, when he is in the shower, I see his pants in a pile on the floor. My ten-dollar bill is sticking out of the pocket. Yes, of course, I take it. That's what I mean by poor.

AUGUST 2021

I arrive in Greece for the most lavish vacation I can imagine for myself, which is paid for by what is left over from a four-thousand-dollar check after a chunk of it goes to bills. I am thirty-seven. I am disabled and cannot backpack or survive on trail mix, even if I want to. It isn't that I can afford to pack extra kimonos and books—it is that I can afford a bag big enough to include them alongside my necessities of medications in two liter-sized Ziploc bags, a bottle of 150 Advil, a drum of magnesium powder. There will be no day on this trip where I'll need to ration anything. I have enough money to book a taxi to drive me to Gerolimenas, at the southernmost tip of the Mani Peninsula, rather than take a series of buses that would take nine hours, which I cannot manage alone anyway. I have enough money to tip well the drivers and porters who carry my bags. Feeling like a queen for a disabled person is often a feeling produced by much less aristocratic conditions—it's simply the feeling of having everything that we need. Of assuring that conditions won't impair our bodies more than they already are. Even though I know that, I still laugh at myself for being a diva.

I start in Athens, a couple days in a four-star hotel in the Plaka with a rooftop terrace. On the terrace at night I sit on a love seat aimed right at the Acropolis, like a box seat in a theater. I drink my cocktail and watch the red sun go behind the buildings and write in my notebook and look at the Acropolis glowing yellow above the city. I think of how this place was the most powerful empire in the world thousands of years ago, a centripetal force from the past that still pulls the city and its people toward this center. Every taxi driver I've ever had in Athens points out the Acropolis with pride.

A non-Greek teenager next to me scrolls through Instagram. There is an apocalyptic-feeling heat wave, over one hundred degrees Fahrenheit, which causes my joints to swell and ache. The pain in my ankles is like hot needles. I order a massage to my room and ask the man to touch only my feet and ankles for an hour. He strokes them over and over like I am a bed sheet he is smoothing out. Despite the heat wave and my joints, I still walk around the city in my big black sun hat, sending selfies to my family and friends, wearing red lipstick and sunglasses. I feel like a character in a Mavis Gallant or Ingeborg Bachmann story, expatriated, home nowhere, impudently glamorous, with a graceful risk of tragedy.

After Athens I go to a hotel I've read about in the novel *A Separation* by Katie Kitamura, which is a sort of existential murder mystery that takes place in Greece in an old stone hotel at the edge of the country right after fires have burned everything. Kitamura never names the hotel, but she describes it vividly as eerie, empty, with stone archways and a jetty slicing into the sea, amidst scorched hills and black trees, and it was so evocative I had to see it for myself. I sleuth on the internet and find what must be it and book three nights there, which cost more than one month's rent. It is neither empty nor murder mystery-y when I arrive but bustling with tanned middle-aged and upper-middle-class European tourists in little bathing suits swimming in the sea and lying flat on chaise lounges like seals. I am the only one not cooked brown by the sun. My skin almost looks blue in the sea water. The heat is too much, so I spend the day in bed reading with the AC on, then I go into the sea at sunset, with the locals, when the tourists go inside to get ready for dinner. The locals have the shapes and colors of manatees and walruses, large and round and slow and regal, bobbing in the water, wearing visors and hats. A group of three women float together in a circle, way out from the coast, cackling, a council of sea witches.

I watch the water change color with the sky and laugh out loud that I'd be in a place like this, that my own money has brought me here, and that I've made that money with my art. I think, of all things, of that scene in *Forrest Gump* where Lieutenant Dan makes his peace with god, swimming in the ocean at sunset. *It's easy to make one's peace with god in a place like this*, I think. I guess that's why god made places like this, so that we might forgive him. I hate the depictions of disability in *Forrest Gump*, but the sentimental ableism of movies like that are all Hollywood gives us. I ask the hostess at the restaurant for a reservation by the water, and she must like me, because she moves an entire table to the end of the jetty for only me. I eat my dinner there and again feel like a queen, a diva. Forgive me: I'm a romantic. Alone, dressed up, resting my swollen ankles on a chair, I always order dessert. I look at the stars with an app that identifies constellations, but I don't need an app to spot Cassiopeia, her throne that also looks like a wheelchair. I don't need or want fame or much money, and the little that I do want—for I do want a certain amount—even this is fleeting and untrustworthy, I know. It does not orient me nor the reasons I do my work. The main thing I want is to feel a kind of reward that belongs to me, that I can feel in my body. Floating in the Aegean Sea and thinking of the money I've received for the book that has taken me seven years to write and will take two more to get into the world, I think about how I wrote it for my mother, and that I accomplished it, I did it. And though she didn't get to read it, I think, *I am going to be capable of making a certain kind of peace with that, with her.*

When I told my somatic therapist in Berlin that I was going to Greece by myself and that I wanted to stay on the island of Hydra, he said, "Then you *must* meet Evangelia. Hydra is *her* island." He described her as a "voice shaman healer," a Greek woman who was raised partially in Germany, whom he'd met at some sort of new-age healing conference. He sent an email to both of us, saying we were some of his "favorite witches." She said I could stay at her house.

"It's my mother's house, a very beautiful house," she said to me over the phone. "You will have your own bathroom outside because I have health problems."

"Can you take a picture?" I'd asked, to know what I was in for—disabled friends had warned me that Hydra has no cars, only stairs, and parts of the island still have no running water or electricity. Hers did. My bathroom was a tiny stone outhouse painted pink inside, but like most of Greece, you could not put toilet paper in the toilet. At the Archaeological Museum in Athens, I'd heard a woman in the next stall muttering in anger to herself: "Paper in the toilet? Beasts!"

After the Gerolimenas hotel, I go to Hydra by ferry. Evangelia leaves me a voicemail that says she's hired a donkey taxi to pick me up at the port and that I will recognize the donkey "because it looks like a cow." My ferry arrives at nine p.m. Out of the throng of people at the port, a short, wiry man darts through and grabs my bags. He throws them onto the back of a donkey that looks like a donkey. I don't know how he knows it is me. We do not speak, but I follow him for twenty vertiginous minutes into the dark. The hooves clack on the stone. After a few minutes, there are no more tourists or lights, just houses shuttered against the heat. When the stairs get steep, the man hops atop his donkey, sidesaddle, and lights a cigarette. He smokes while I pant, and we climb into a quiet shredded by the cicadas of Greece.

We come to an old stone house painted yellow and white, high on a hill overlooking the sea. A girlish voice says my name as the gate cracks open. She is no larger than a child, standing at about five feet, with a little halo of fine blond curls. In November she will turn sixty-six, born the same year as my mother, but when she opens the door to her house, I jump because she has the same face as my grandmother: round blue eyes, tiny mouth and chin, a bird face. In a few days it will be the ninth anniversary of my grandmother's death, and I think of holding her hand as she breathed her last breaths in the hospital in Pasadena. Evangelia's nose is hooked above a shriveled mouth. She is bent, with rounded shoulders, and her toes are gnarled and frozen in wild curls. The joints on her hands are swollen to the size of walnuts in the shell. Then I see her right hand, which is flattened and stiff, fused into a sort of rigid flipper that can't be moved. Some of the fingertips have been cut off, the nails growing in shards out of the knuckles. She tells me she is going for a night swim. I ask if I can join, and she says sure but warns me that she swims for a long time. It is ten p.m. Looking at her, stooped and walking sideways like a crab, similar to the way I walk when the pain is bad, I think, *How long can it be?*

She leads me down narrow stairs that wind to a swimming beach. I slip a few times on the rocks and feel my center thrown. She asks if I am okay. I've told her I have health problems too. Her arthritis doesn't seem to bother her. She wears purple Crocs and carries a towel in a backpack whose proportions make her look like a turtle, a domed back, taking the stairs very slowly. She chatters on the whole walk down, explaining things about the island and this neighborhood and the sea, but I can't pay attention to anything except a queer but thrilling feeling that I do not know where I am and not just geographically.

When we get in the water she turns and asks if I know how to get home. I absolutely do not, so I say I'll wait for her. She warns me again that she'll be gone for a long time. "You just take the path up and go right, then left, then right, then left, then left again," she says. Her face is a small blot of light in the gentle waves. I go through the inventory of mythology's water-based spirits, their sprightly glee and hair that coils in the waves. She is a mermaid, a selkie. She swims into the darkness and disappears.

I stand on a rock with the water up to my neck, the sea lolling around me, pulling me toward the beach and then away. I push the water with my arms to stay on my rock and find a rhythm that keeps me upright. Sometimes I reach my foot up to the surface, pointing my toes at the stars. In the water, the pain in my joints stops screaming. The water is black with the sky, and glints of light skitter across the surface. I can't believe how warm it is. The sea makes the one-hundred-degree air feel cool. I laugh to myself out loud again. I feel the fact that my own money has brought me here and that I've made that money by sitting at a desk every day for seven years, reaching into a speculative space that no one, not even myself, could see, and trying to build something from what I found in that unknown. It spreads around and holds me. This is more than the spiritual or artistic satisfaction of looking at a finished manuscript after all those hours spent working at my desk, the rewards of being a servant to my craft. This is something legible as a material consequence to all the labor it took to get here, something that takes the edge off how it feels to relentlessly stare into the abyss—that shift from having what I need, to dreaming about what I might want. Dare I say, capitalist reward at its finest. Let me note again, this is not an opponent I will defeat. My thirties have felt survival as acute, a struggle, a drive, a constant pressure, so many days with only three dollars to my name, but in the water of the Aegean, I feel that move a little to the background and make space for something else that might not have to try so hard. At least now I can stare into the abyss while sitting in a comfortable chair.

Evangelia doesn't return for two hours. I start to freak out that something's happened to her out in the dark water. We are the only ones in the sea. I have no idea where I am, how to get back to her house. What will I do if something happened to her? There are not even addresses on the island. Sometimes a water taxi speeds past, but otherwise, it is dark and empty and I am alone. I get out and sit on a rock on the beach for over an hour. Far past midnight, her little glowing face comes through the black waves. "Oh, you waited for me!" she says. What was the other option? We climb the stairs home, and I feel exhausted but somehow not depleted. My room is upstairs in the house. There is a small piece of foam the size of a child for the bed. I fall on it and have no dreams that I remember except that there is good sex in them.

The next morning Evangelia informs me that she was very offended when our mutual friend introduced us as witches, because she is absolutely not a witch. She prefers the term "priestess" because she doesn't want there to be a "hierarchy" between her and her subjects, and, for reasons she does not explain, she thinks that the word "priestess" is somehow nonhierarchical. How exactly this is different from being a witch, I don't know—perhaps a combination of cultural context and old superstition. I find myself giving some Silvia Federici 101 lectures to no avail.

She tells me she went to art school to study painting and that she "used to want to be somebody," but she "couldn't survive conceptual art." She explains that she does that two-hour swim every night *and* every morning, and usually after her night swim she likes to walk into the mountains and have a conversation with a particular eucalyptus tree who is her friend. She offers to introduce me if I'd like to accompany her again.

She says swimming in the sea and walking in the mountains is the best treatment for the degenerative autoimmune disease she has, but she says the name of it in Greek, so I don't know what it is. She tells me she doesn't "believe in" doctors so doesn't take the meds that will stop the disease from progressing. She tells me she is dealing with her problems "in the way of the scholar"—which means not taking medicine of any kind. As a child, they'd cut off the tips of her fingers to try to cure her. I get it—what it's like to be a Sick Woman, a De-person, exposed to the mercilessness of the medical-industrial system. But her stance also means that her disease is getting worse, and when she broke her hand earlier this year, she didn't get it cared for. It's her painting hand, now stiff and unmovable. She asks me for advice on how to feel better about it because she hates it and finds it ugly. When I suggest that she put jewelry on it, she looks horrified. But then she spends the entire time I am with her telling me the secret to life is to love myself. Several times a day, she shouts at me: "Johanna! The secret to life is to love yourself! I love you!" Some of the most destabilizing encounters I've had with ableism have been seeing it in other disabled people. They hold on to a fantasy of healing and then hate themselves when it fails to arrive for them. I wonder what healing means to her, how she envisions it. Does she think her degenerative autoimmune disease, which she's had her entire life, will just vanish? That her broken hand will suddenly become lithe and beautiful? Does she think it is only a matter of loving herself enough?

She tells me she is terrified that I am a witch and interrogates me all afternoon, questions like, "So if a man hurt you, what would you do to him?" She says she can't sleep while I am in the house because her skin tingles all night. She can't wait to tell her friend who's a nun that she has a witch staying with her, as if this will evidence her daring. She keeps trying to give me one of her "shamanic voice healing sessions," and I keep begging off. There is a woman on YouTube who proclaims to be from the Pleiades, and Evangelia will not stop talking about how this woman saved her life, can cure anyone—"Come on, you must see it, let's watch her together"—and I change the subject.

She keeps trying to psychic me and failing, which is cute and a little annoying.

Her: "I had a vision you went to the village."

Me: "Actually, I went to the port."

Her: "I feel like your favorite color is purple."

Me: "Sorry, it's yellow."

Her healing powers extend to her spending the better part of an afternoon trying to convince me that my suitcase is a metaphor for my past trauma and that I need to let it go and be free. She looks rather crestfallen when I say that, actually, it is a big deal for me to finally be able to afford to bring a real bag on a trip.

When I tell her that my witchcraft is primarily astrology, her eyes quiver big and serious.

"Ah, so you are a strange woman," she says. (When English is a second or third language, I tend not to insist on they/them language. Also if I'm going to be called a woman, I definitely prefer to be a strange one.) "Do you read charts?"

"Yes," I say.

"Tell me," she says, "will I die when Pluto crosses my ascendant?"

I take a breath. In my years of reading charts, I have found that when a person asks a question like this, they already know the answer. "Are you really asking me? Because I can look. But you need to tell me that you want to know."

"Yes. I am really asking."

She pulls a book from a shelf, and in its pages is a crumpled, folded paper where someone drew her chart by hand decades ago. I look at it, bring up the twenty-first-century ephemeris on my phone, and find that Pluto will cross her ascendant in a few years. When looking for death in a chart, many things must be present at the same time. It's not one transit or one planet or one thing at all—it's usually closer to a dozen things that have been building for a while, which then all converge at the same time. There can be elements of an illness that is long and slow, of a relentless difficulty, whose intensity accumulates to the point of collapse. It can look like a leak on the forces of life, a vacuum that lines up and then squats on one's lights for months, more often years. There can be transits of accident, injury, and then planets that bungle the recovery process.

In the ancient world, a technique was developed to see death in the chart. It was primarily used to see if a newborn baby would live beyond ten hours, ten days, or ten years, and although it does not account for modern medicine and needs to be taken with a huge grain of salt, I still find it interesting and the insight it suggests useful. It involves a complicated calculation to determine three different forces in the chart: the giver of life, the giver of years, and the planet that has the power to affect both.

I stare at Evangelia's chart, the pen lines rickety on the paper. I tally up what I see. I look at her. "Do you already have a feeling? A feeling that you'll die then?"

"Yes," she says. "I have a feeling."

"Because there are certain things here that could indicate—if not death, then a long illness becoming worse."

"So, I will die from my disease?"

"Well, we don't need astrology to tell us that."

She looks away, crushed.

"How does that make you feel?" I ask.

"Upset!" she cries. "I'm very angry that I won't heal."

I don't press her on how exactly she thinks she's going to heal from the degenerative disease she's had her whole life. Instead, I say, "What are your plans?"

"There is so much! I *must* put my new self into the world before I die," she says.

I nod, of course. "What does that entail?"

"Well, I *really* need to make a new website."

SUMMER 2018

As soon as I learn how to do the astrological calculation for death, after I do my mother's, yeah, obviously, I calculate my own. According to the ancient technique, I'm to live to age 40.5. When I see that, my heart caves. *Fuck.* I've always had the feeling I wouldn't live long, but to see proof of it—I can't do anything for days but spiral. I wail and complain on the phone to a friend who's into astrology. My imminent demise! Just a few years out!

"Hang on, bitch," they say, "let me check your math." Twelve hours pass. (The calculation is complicated.) Then they call, cracking up. "Bitch, I have you living to be 93.8!"

William James said, "My first act of free will shall be to believe in free will." As someone who believes that fate and will are not mutually exclusive, I choose to believe that I will die, not at 40.5, but at 93.8 years old.

One of my favorite anecdotes about Clarice Lispector is the one where she's on a plane, with an assistant, and there's terrible turbulence. People start crying, clinging to each other, getting ready to die in the crash. The assistant is losing it, but Clarice is calm. "Don't worry," she says. "My astrologer told me I wouldn't die this way." And the astrologer was right.

AUGUST 2021

In the morning, when I come out of the outhouse, Evangelia calls to me from the terrace of her bedroom. She is naked in the doorway, waving her crooked hand. "*Kalimera*, Johanna," and, bleary with sleep and not wearing my glasses, I am briefly startled at the image of this Baba Yaga, the perfect picture of a happy little hag. When I had first seen her, I'd thought, apologetically, of a hag, and I've found myself trying to catalog un-hag-like features: the house has air conditioning and Wi-Fi, she has a laptop and watches YouTube, and her bathroom counter is strewn with expensive face creams.

I've been thinking a lot about hags, because I love them as a figure, and because a friend, the writer Tamara Antonijević, has
recently written "The Hag Theory," inspired in part by "Sick Woman
Theory," as a sort of proposal for what happens next to the Sick
Woman:

A Hag is not a Grandmother and she's not a Witch.

She doesn't have a set of loving grandchildren, or a comfortable rocking chair on her porch, or the gift of using magic.

The Grandmother is old and sick and then she dies.

The Witch is old and sick, but she can live forever or as long as
she wants to.

The Hag can be old and sick, but she lingers . . .

The Hag is prone to Sciatica and Migraines and has to remain
in a horizontal position for many days.

During those days she tosses around her bed and moans, she
cries, she pops pills, she breathes deeply, she masturbates,
she snores and curses. She knows the dull pain in her muscles, the
sharp pain in her tendons, the throbbing pain on the soft sides of
her head, the intense and burning pain in the lower left side
of her stomach, the sharp stabbing in her lower back. She understands the pain and she got to know her body through it. . . .

The Hag will not put a spell on anyone, she will not make any
man or woman fall madly in love with her. She will give no one
the best sex of their life or poison someone if she gets angry.
She's just a hag.

She's walking away, with her back bent forward, with her eyes
wandering, searching for a place to hold on to, to give it a

name, to claim it for herself, with painkillers in her pockets, mumbling sounds coming out of her chin, decorated with one spiky hair, because she's fucking nuts, she will rot, but she will not disappear.

When I first wondered, back in 2014, what would happen to the "Sad Girl" if and when she grows up, I'd arrived at the figure of the Sick Woman as a next phase of development. As the years passed and my Sick Woman made its odyssey through doctors' offices, waiting rooms, the lines of pharmacies, tearing at her hair in frustration, cackling at the Kafkaesque absurdity, she became a Psychotic Woman. There is a lineage from the Sad Girl to the Sick Woman to the Psycho and then to the Hag, as she lingers and malingers through life. It's not that the Hag has stopped fighting—her difficulties have been folded into her daily life, and perhaps the thing she now has at her disposal is some room, however small, to decide how she feels about them. Today she can be indifferent, tomorrow she can be enraged, and simply having the choice is a kind of freedom in where to go, who to be. The character arc of the story is also a path to move along. It is both history and prophecy, an ouroboros, a lemniscate, mirror and mattress.

For me, the Sick Woman as a place to start, chapter one of this story, was useful and good. But I am to live to be 93.8 years old, so I want to know about the next chapter, where this story can go, how this character can change, what are the possible endings. I love the word "hagiography" because it has the word "hag" in it.

Fate and will: As illness and disability solicit such figures—the Sad Girl, the Sick Woman, the De-person, the Freak, the Psychotic, the Hag—in turn, we sad, sick, psycho, freaky hags solicit language to account for ourselves. Sometimes that can be an act of reclaiming slurs, identifying with monsters, rollicking in a bestiary of all that stinks and sags; and sometimes that means refusing the language our conditions themselves solicit, though at times this is to our detriment. If Evangelia was taken out of Hydra and plopped into Manhattan, she would undeniably be seen as mad. *No, I am not a witch but a priestess; no, I will not take my medication, I will think and swim my way out of my disease; I come from the Pleiades, my best friend is a tree.*

When I was plucked out of Berlin and Los Angeles and set down on Hydra, in my big black hat and red lipstick, I was no longer psycho or sick. My hobbling became a considered gait, slow so I could take in the scenery, my staying in bed reading all day a charming eccentricity. I was now a sort of recalcitrant, solitary but captivating queen. Is this the figure I—we—can slouch toward as a sort of finale? The disabled diva? She is the stuff of myth because what she requires—money, support, recognition—is fantasy for most of us. She knows what she wants, where she wants to get to, she has big plans, she's reaching for the sun, she's limping, her back is bothering her, today is a high pain day, she's tired of having to explain ableism to people, she's had enough, that's it, she's going to bed. She's all the things Antonijević describes in the hag, but perhaps she's a touch more vain, longing to be bourgeois, devoted to keeping her skin creamy, and she wants to be fortified by expensively asymmetrical and well-tailored clothes, for they are a kind of iron-cladding. As a queen, no one questions why she is wearing armor; it is not seen as a sign of her weakness but a necessity of her station. She is armored, sitting in a comfortable chair, with an accomplished body of work she's had to fight for, that stretches back many decades to her name. Let's call her The Hag In Charge.

For disabled people to imagine ourselves growing old requires an almost delusional amount of belief, a trust of the future often in opposition to the prophecy of our current moment. How to tell when we will die when so much about the condition of our lives is not in our reach to tell? When I do allow myself to speculate into what kind of old age might collect me, I envision that I'll probably be old in the same way that Evangelia is. A kooky mystical what's-her-name who used to want to be somebody but then gives up to live on a small island away from the world. An old woman bent and hobbled by her illness, spouting quackery to explain her suffering, worried about making a website to advertise her voice shaman healing services. I won't survive in America, hence why I'll need to exile myself to somewhere, perhaps an island that's cheap (I won't be able to afford Hydra), somewhere warm so that my joints and lungs and spirit can survive the winter, and if I can't escape global warming, then somewhere near a body of water into which I can slip my burning feet.

Evangelia is also different from me in ways I envy, doing things I'm afraid to do, will likely always be afraid to do—swimming for hours in the dark, those long night walks in the mountains, always alone. Perhaps I am impressed by someone disabled and living solo, with no meds, on an island with no cars or hospital. One night, she takes me to a ruin of a narrow bridge in the mountains and stands at its apex, at least twenty feet off the ground. The bridge is terrifyingly narrow, with no guardrail. She lifts her face and arms toward the sky and says it is her favorite place. I lie that I like it too, but I am afraid of the height, feel dizzy and disoriented, and don't want to look down. All the stairs on the island are daunting to me. I can feel how tired I am at the end of the day, the pain in my joints spreading everywhere, but she moves slowly and seems unbothered by it. She takes her time.

Maybe this is what hags have learned—that there's time. And we're still in it.

Until there's not.

It strikes me that The Hag In Charge has fallen into the sea over and over and over again. She has gotten good at remaking her own wings after each fall.

JANUARY 10, 1929

At midnight, my grandmother, Kim Chung Boon-Yee, is born in Sangju, Korea. It is a dark moon, with both lights in Capricorn, Snake year. She grows up poor on a rural farm. Later she will tell stories of carrying her younger siblings on her back, how they piss on her clothes, which turns the fabric rotten. She will come to America at age twenty-eight, pregnant by an American soldier with a son, my uncle. My uncle, who will be retroactively diagnosed as having had Alzheimer's since his thirties, and who we all suspect is on the spectrum, will explain his strangeness, his discomfort in the world, by the fact that his mother carried him in her belly across the Pacific Ocean when fleeing a war for an unknown land. She will have another son, my father, by the American soldier two years later, and then be abandoned to raise her two young boys alone. She will have many boyfriends and a few more husbands, but by the time I am born, she is alone and so content at this solitude that she beams with it. It's how I understand her: in my earliest memories of her she makes the kind of sound of a tittering of magpies at the fact that her days belong only to herself.

My grandmother becomes Connie Park at some point in her life in America, but I don't know when. She will not respond to her Korean name anymore, and when I am a child and ask her about Korea, when she will take me there, when I can meet my cousins, aunts, uncles, she will practically spit that she never wants to go back. When she is old, befuddled by Alzheimer's, and I ask her to write her Korean name on a piece of paper so I can get it tattooed on myself, she will misspell it and have to try again. I will tattoo the mistake.

Aside from her independence and solitude, the primary thing that will define my grandmother is how hard she worked. Every time I see her throughout my life, she tells me, "I worked thirty-three years. I never took a day off." The one question she will always ask me, even when she doesn't remember who I am: "Working hard?"

I am vegetarian for ten years but break it on my annual visit to my grandmother's house when she cooks a mountain of bulgogi. She has a gold Buddha statue in her living room and grows her own vegetables. Her skin is porcelain, her smile is gorgeous, and she sounds like a girl when she laughs. When she retires, her days her own, she won't stop saying, "I am *happy*." She is tenacious, eccentric, and she keeps a tub of coconut oil by her bed and smears it on her creamy skin four or five times a day.

When I try to explain my Korean grandmother to people, the cultural specificity, I tell the story of how I once knit her a scarf, long and purple, for her birthday. I was a child; it took me weeks. She sent it back, saying she didn't like the color, the yarn wasn't soft enough.

A story my father tells becomes family myth, both about her and about me: Shortly after I am born, my parents want to take me to meet Halmeoni, Grandma. Every time they suggest this to her over the phone, she evades them. *Not now, come in the summer, come later.* This elusiveness troubles them, so eventually they get in the car with infant me and drive the four hours up the California coast to see what's going on. They arrive at night, and the house is dark and quiet. They ring the bell and knock on the door, then the windows, for a long time. Nothing. They start to get spooked. Finally, Grandma emerges from the bushes—she's been gardening. She's wearing a hat at night, which is weird, but she is glad to see them. Inside, one lightbulb works. She feeds them only rice. She takes off her hat, and her head is shaved bald. She'd always been so primped and coiffed, with a lustrous black updo. Now, she explains, she doesn't want to pay for hot water and shampoo and conditioner. Her last husband is making her buy out his half of the house, and she is determined to do it on her janitor's salary. They sit around the dinner table and eat together and start to relax. She is glad to meet me. At some point, everyone laughs loudly, and Grandma suddenly shushes them.

"Quiet! You'll wake up my roommate," she says.

"Roommate? Since when do you have a roommate?" my father asks, but no more information comes.

They go to bed. The next day, Grandma puts my father to work in her yard, which she always does. She is four foot ten but will pour her own concrete until age ninety-two. My dad is cutting rosebushes when my mother comes to get him, her eyes afraid and urgent.

"What's the matter?" he says.

"I—I—I think there's a dead man in the house," my mother says.

"WHAT?"

"The room at the end of the hallway, with the door closed—I went in."

"You went in?!"

"And there was a lump in the bed, and I pulled back the covers."

"You *what*?!"

"And it was a man with his eyes closed, and I think he's dead!"

"Shit!" my parents say. Is this why the house is dark? Did she shave her head so she can wear wigs as a disguise? Did he die in there and she hasn't noticed yet? Or did she murder him for some reason, to use his body for mulch in the garden?

My parents go for a drive, infant me in the car seat, to try to get their thoughts together. "What are we going to do?"

When they return, a small Korean man is sitting at the table with my grandmother, and she excitedly introduces them. "This is Mr. Lee! He's a businessman."

My parents exhale loudly and everyone smiles.

Mr. Lee is, in fact, a fortune teller (and, years later, we will learn he was one of Grandma's husbands and that his name was actually Mr. Park). He can tell your fortune based on your birthday and time, a practitioner of Saju, the Korean form of Chinese astrology. He tells my mother she will make her money with her hands. He tells my father he will not find happiness and security until later in life. When they offer my birthday and time, only a few months before, he frowns and shakes his head, grumbling angrily. Agitated, he gets up from the table, waving his hands in distaste and speaking in Korean.

My parents are afraid. "What's he saying? What's he saying?"

Finally, Grandma translates: "He say, too smart. She too smart."

OCTOBER 10, 2023

My grandma will die five days before I am to see her. She is in a care home in Sylmar, with advanced Alzheimer's. Although her mind has collapsed, she is physically as robust as ever. There are videos my father takes of her clanging steak knives together, threatening to murder him in his sleep. "You better not go to sleep tonight—you'll wake up *dead*." Dad calls this her "K-rage." She is ninety-four years old. She has stopped dying her hair black, and instead puts a black toupee on top of her head that only covers half of the straight silver hair that hangs to her shoulders.

Over the years, her Alzheimer's has meant that she spends her days in her house feeding her chickens dozens of a times a day because she forgets she already fed them. She goes in circles through her hard-won rooms, finding piles of old mail and reading them word for word. By the time she gets to the bottom of the page, she has forgotten why she's reading and so starts over again at the top. Old bills from 1998 or 2007, which have long been paid, alarm her when she gets to the part that says, *Amount owed*. When she reads her bank statements from ten years ago and sees the withdrawals her past self, now lost, made, she gets angry. "Somebody cheating me." When she cannot find the kitchen towel, she thinks someone has broken in and stolen it. My uncle, her oldest son, lives with her, and he, too, has Alzheimer's, and visiting them is one of the most heartbreaking farces I can think of, the lost leading the lost, and I will write about it all in detail one day, but not yet.

Some years before October 10, 2023, my Korean shaman tells me that once my grandmother dies, she will step into the role of the most authoritative of my ancestors, the one who will guide me the most. She'll start driving the bus, as it were, and the main thing she'll offer guidance and protection around is money and security. She'll never not want to know if I am working hard.

AUGUST 6, 2021, HYDRA

On the walk to the swimming beach, Deborah Levy passes us on the path. Holy shit! My face shocks with recognition, and I stumble. She does not look at me, and I say nothing. She is dressed in black, her hair wet and wavy from the seawater. She wears sandals and climbs the steps up as we walk down them. Later that night I Google her to make sure I've made the correct identification, and I learn that it is her birthday.

This moment feels preordained. She is one of my absolute favorite living writers. I've read all of her books, many more than once. I've listened to almost all her talks archived online, her appearances on podcasts. I've written out sentence after sentence of hers by hand in my notebook and sent them to friends in emails gushing about what she can do. She does her best writing in her forties, then tops it in her fifties, then gets better still in her sixties. After being a small-press weirdo for decades, her books are now available in airport bookstores, her back catalog bought and reissued by Penguin.

We are also connected in a specific way: the same small press bought our novels, ten years apart—and in fact, the press *started* in part all those years ago so that they could publish her. In this profound way, my career as a writer rests atop hers. I know the myth of that particular novel that began the press that would go on to publish me. After two decades of publishing novels and stories and plays, in her forties Levy went on submission with a new novel that was universally rejected. She writes about it in the great opening to the first volume of her living autobiography: "That spring when life was very hard and I was at war with my lot and simply couldn't see where there was to get to, I seemed to cry most on escalators at train stations." In a talk at the Lannan Foundation that's archived on YouTube (which I've watched several times), she reveals that she's crying on escalators because her new novel has been rejected. She's despairing that her writing will not see the light of day. "I felt like my voice had been shut down, like the lid of a piano," she says. Finally, the book, *Swimming Home*, inspires a group of literary-minded weirdos to start the nonprofit press, And Other Stories, and Levy's novel goes on to be short-listed for the Booker, launching her into the fame she enjoys today.

Now she is a kind of grand dame of intellectual fiction with page-turner plots, spiky, bright sentences of strange details, and characters that shimmer on the page with one or two perfect lines of dialogue. Her sentences are short, her vocabulary simple, and yet the distance and depth she engineers these to contain is stunning. She collapses time, fucks with structure, and the meaning that emerges in her taut lines never feels labored over, but as if she's simply reclining into profundity. The *New Yorker* said she has an "almost oracular pithiness," and I would agree. As someone who writes long, peregrinating sentences with four-dollar words, I don't know how she does it, getting all that meaning into something so small and plain. I have typed out her lines into my own manuscripts and then gone through word by word, changing each to a synonym or antonym, to try to understand how she conjures her syntax, how she can move so far in such a short space.

Then there is her lion's mane of hair, that patrician, feline face, the ample bosom carried high, the smartest clothes, even smarter shoes. She has a king-of-heaven vibe, holding court. When I've watched her talks on YouTube, I feel as if I am watching someone completely in command of her power, unhurried, almost luxuriating in it. She is proud, even arrogant, somehow without being pretentious yet also without feigned modesty. She seems to graciously accept the attention, the fact of her importance, her talent. She always says the full titles of her books, the full names of her characters, letting them take up space. As majestic as this is, there's something childlike too, a sort of playful wonder at the world and her own place in it. Of course, she's a Leo. I think about how, in astrology, the house of royalty is also the house of children—Leo's house. I think of how, by contrast, my sun is in the house of work and health. Lol. Her voice is deep and warm and she speaks slowly, and when asked to read aloud from her work for an hour, she seems to want to be nowhere else but here, on this stage, with an audience, sharing her genius with them, taking her time. I've often thought to myself that I want to be more like her, on the page, in interviews, in onstage conversations. The mantra is: "What would Deborah Levy do?"

She is the opposite of how I feel onstage, how I feel when asked to read my work aloud, because I have such a profound discomfort with being perceived at all. It's not only that I know I'll be not perceived on my own terms, the tropes my conditions will solicit, but also to be perceived as only one thing, that the audience, after an hour of me, will come away thinking that I am a discrete x, maybe if I'm lucky, also a specific y.

I have Uranus and the South Node smack on my rising in Sagittarius. For non-astrology people, this means the anus of the universe is squatting exactly on the place where I'm supposed to appear in the world. The boiling need to transgress and rebel is against my very self. It means "I" is multiplied, fractured, and grown through how it is expressed, but also intransigent in that none of these should be treated as the one authentic entity. It's what Mandelbrots my self.

It's why I've had so many names. They expand but they also remain tethered to the root from which they come. What's on the other side of my face is a stranger. The holy fire to me is about annihilation, surrendering to it. It means that I abandon my work into the world. It means that my persona, my public self, is already a ghost.

Levy seems to have the opposite—not only the assertion that she is alive, but that she deserves to exist in solid, grounded plenitude. It strikes me that she is one of the few writer role models I have who is not sick. This does not make me love her, or identify with her, any more or less. In fact, it functions even more like a compass. What would Deborah Levy do? She'd live, she'd struggle, she'd swim in the sea, she'd get her writing into the world and be happy when people read it.

The four-thousand-dollar check that I use to take me to Greece has, in the upper left corner, the name of the press that began because of her. Which god has arranged this?

On Hydra, I feel that the universe has set me on a sort of kairotic stage and furnished it with two of my most primary archetypes: the reclusive mystical priestess, disabled, deformed, rejecting the world, and the celebrity writer, finally famous in her sixties, after decades of insisting that her prickly, peculiar work is important, draped in her commitment to her ambition to get her talent into the world. These two women are set before me, as if Jung were in the director's chair.

One scuttles, and the other walks like a queen, and I am both.

2024 OR 2078

How do I get here, to my death?

Despite how many times I have tried to grab it, it has eluded me until now.

I am dying in a hospital bed in Pasadena, and someone I love is holding my hand, their body coiled around mine, and I am dying alone on the floor of my small room and won't be found for a few days, and I am dying hundreds of miles away from my house, thousands of miles from my homeland, in a care home where the staff call me a troublemaker, and I am dying because my insurance won't cover the treatment, or maybe I can't even afford insurance, and I fall from the sky in a plane crash, and I live alone on an island and refuse medical treatment, and one night I simply don't come back to shore after swimming in the black water, and I collapse on an escalator in the subway and am swarmed by strangers and taken to a bustling city hospital, and I am afraid, and I am trying to let go, and I do not want to leave, and the gratitude I feel at the stunning majesty of this fluke that I be thrown here, into this life, this body, this story, is an event horizon, and I hope to never return.

Is my death one that I will have authored?

I wonder what will become of my work after I'm gone. I can only hope that whatever myths helicopter around my name are fun, good stories. That all I ever worried about was my outfit. That I loved to punch men.

At birth we are given that DMV form to fill in, to start writing our own myth; the form is based on what we've been born into in terms of race, ethnicity, class, nation-state, family name, neighborhood, tribe, genes, epigenomes, intergenerational trauma, ghosts, family curses. Many of us, but not all, spend a lifetime trying to tear this form into little pieces, trying to reach for a new one. I've destroyed as best I could the form I've been born with (for it's never completely destroyed, is it?), trying to write my own story built from the stories of sick women, the psychos, the queerdos, the punks, freaks, and hags. I can only hope that the lines I've scratched into my pieces of paper can one day be used by someone else, become lines on the form that they—burning, aiming too far, longing for something they don't yet have—reach toward, to fill in with their own name in their attempt to write their own story and then all the other possible versions.

In the story I've been telling, the disabled person in the Aegean Sea with a suitcase of thirty books, who goes to Greece alone to stay in a hotel they read about in a novel, is the same broke student stealing back their only ten dollars from a one-night stand, is the same lone traveler with a backpack and blue cowboy hat on a train across America reading Sartre, is the same runaway homeless teenager who bought ice cream for dinner on a night that stretched out endlessly in front of them, scary and unknown and staggeringly free, and this person is both surrounded by darkness and keeps reaching into it; for this person, the darkness is their version of Icarus's sun. This is a person who woke up to themselves as a freak, a punk, an artist who preferred to buy books rather than meals, make art instead of money, be invisible rather than seen as what they were not, and who grandly set out on the romanticism of that path; who was then forced to understand themselves as a Sick Woman, crip, mad, stuck in bed, swimming in pain, crawling with ghosts, and who looked for who else was there, what friends they could make who spoke and understood this language, wondering what political power might be possible from this place, what worlds could be changed in the blast radius of disability; and then, after years of lying down, they have found some hours in which they can sit up every day, at least now in a somewhat comfortable chair, swollen ankles raised, red lipstick, suitcases of kimonos and books, stewarding a little more resources that can be shared, spread around, the ten-year goal achieved, four books by age forty, the Icarus-like aim instantiated when they turned thirty, with the hard little pearl of understanding that even if all the goals are achieved, all the ambitions accomplished, money, recognition, security, power, importance, all the gate-kept gates breached and left open for others, there will still be pain days that swallow everything, doctors who dismiss and disrespect, strangers who stare, weeks of flare, panic attacks, chronic pain, *fuck*, so much pain, walking with a cane, not being able to walk at all—so what is next that includes such knowledge? Where is there to reach knowing the weight of this body? What more can be known knowing that wisdom is the kind of knowledge that hurts? What is the new sun to fly toward that acknowledges the darkness that propels the aim, the fact of the waxen wings, how easily and often and inevitably they melt, what it takes to rebuild them each time, and with all of that, honest in its earthliness as much as it is buoyant in its skyward reach—who is it now, next, that they might be? Neither only brave nor only weak, neither between only darkness and light, but both a mess and an icon, a saint and a loon, a soothsayer and a person with a daily to-do list that they try to get through diligently but sometimes don't, a person who knows their talent, gives it all the space it needs and wants, loves and cares for and protects and laughs and dances with their friends, and who knows the prison of their body and mind, who can sometimes rewrite that prison to also be a room in which to live, who knows the work that needs to be done is never done, who sees that the road they are meant to be traveling on is already there, moving beneath feet which are clawed, hooved, clay, winged, throbbing, sometimes useless, and always sheathed in gorgeous shoes.

AUGUST 2021

Wildfires break out in Greece during my trip, turning the clear blue sky a sick, pinkish brown that feels leaden with doom. Evangelia is convinced my witch powers have brought the catastrophe with me. "You did this," she says, with a jumpy look of confusion on her face. "It's never looked like this before." Nevertheless, that evening she invites herself along to the dinner I am planning to have alone, and when the check comes, she pushes it in my direction without a word. (Iconic.) At dinner, she tells me that she never became a woman, that first she was a child, and now she is very old. She tells me she'd like to be with a man, but she likes them much younger. Young men are hard to come by, even when you are a priestess.

She says she wants to paint the portrait of everyone in the world, in watercolor, her chosen medium, and for the days I stay with her, she nags me to paint mine. Finally, on my second to last afternoon, she gets blunt: "So, are you going to let me paint your picture or what?" We sit on her terrace.

She becomes very cute, serious. She says she is in her "element." Sometimes the color is too strong, and she gasps and quickly tries to mop it up. She talks to herself while painting. Sometimes her eyes get wide and entranced at what she is looking at on the paper. She says it's hard to get all my hair in the frame, then asks how I feel about Medusa. I laugh and say I like her very much. She says I have an interesting face and wants to know where I got it. I tell her it is my mother's face, that she inherited it from her mother, but the shape of the eyes and cheeks is from my father, who got them from his mother. She doesn't finish that day; we'll need to do more tomorrow. "The hair still needs work."

OCTOBER 2022

I bring my partner, Johannes, to Hydra. For nearly ten years we've dreamed of taking a long Mediterranean summer holiday together, and in even more distant dreams, where we buy a ruin and rebuild it with our own hands, a place like this is where we want to retire. A relative of his has died and left a little money, and a few months ago I sold my fourth book (this book), so we decide to splurge. We rent a whole house for three weeks on the island. As excessive as it seems, we are still close to where we come from. The beds are small and hard, we have to turn on the water heater for thirty minutes to get five minutes of hot water, and because the Airbnb is so expensive, we mostly eat Greek salads we make ourselves. Every night, we sit on the rooftop terrace, and I show him my app identifying star constellations, and I tell the myths of them.

I plan to get in touch with Evangelia after we've been there for a while. Johannes has heard everything, I've told him the story over and over. She's become mythic in our house. One evening, we take a long walk down the coast to an outlook on a cliff. Evangelia had taken me there; it is the road to get to her eucalyptus tree. At the outlook, there are a few benches overlooking the sea. Johannes and I sit there, watching the sunset, at the sharp edge of the island. The oranges and yellows glow and then dim into cloudy blues and purples. We talk about getting old. We start walking back down the mountain on the deserted stone path. It is cold, and one of the Meltemi, the dry, seasonal winds, has picked up. Ahead of us, marching slowly uphill in the dusk, comes a tiny figure in a turquoise windbreaker. The hood is tied tightly around the little head. I know it is her immediately.

"Evangelia!" I call out. "It's Johanna! Johanna, from last year."

It takes her a moment to identify me, her swimmy eyes focusing and then alighting. "Ah, of course," she says. "So, you've returned."

"Yes, being here last year was very significant for me."

"For me too," she says.

Then, before I can answer, she abruptly turns to Johannes and declares, "When Johanna was here last year, she was always dressed to go to the opera. A big black hat." Her eyes quiver, large and excited, and she lifts her hands to start telling the story. "She was like a myth. The glamorous witch, all in black."

Acknowledgments

Much of this book was written on unceded Chumash, Tongva, Kizh, and Tataviam territories. I also want to acknowledge that a land acknowledgment is not the same as land.

A book that takes more than a decade must build its own world, laws of physics, equal parts momentum and support, and nothing about this can be done in a vacuum. I know I'm forgetting some of those who were with me along the way, and I'm going to resort to alphabetical order because I get too overwhelmed to think of any kind of hierarchy when I read each name, and then the next, and the next, and the next. There were so many over these years who gave me their hearts, homes, brains, critique, time, effort, skills, sweetness, budgets, advice, attention, and intention. Without them, this book would not have made it—I would not have made it.

Thank you to the editors, organizers, curators, copyeditors, fact-checkers, proofreaders, assistants, fans, helpers, volunteers, and sweet, cool people who spearheaded, aided, and participated in getting elements of this work and its politics into the world while it was in process. Thank you to the publications and projects that published earlier versions of these essays: *Mask* magazine; *GUTS*; *Triple Canopy*; *Topical Cream*; *Rockhaven: A History of Interiors* by Which Witch L.A.; *Asian American Literary Review*; *Public,*

Private, Secret by the International Center of Photography; *p5.js 1.0 Contributors Zine*; The Get Well Soon Project by Sam Lavigne and Tega Brain; New Alphabet School #5; Dundee Contemporary Arts; *The White Review*; LUX; Wellcome Collection; *C Magazine*; the Lily Cox-Richard exhibition catalog by MASS MoCA; *The Culture We Deserve*; and the anthologies *Intertitles: An anthology at the intersection of writing & visual art*, *Where Are the Tiny Revolts?*, and *Health* by Documents in Contemporary Art. Thank you to the universities and institutions who hosted me for talks, lectures, workshops, and residencies, and thank you especially to all the people working there who made these visits happen: Academy of Fine Arts, Nuremberg; Akademie Schloss Solitude; Amherst College; Armory Center for the Arts; ArtCenter College of Design; *Art in America*; *at land's edge*; "Away Message #2"; Bard College; Brown University; California Institute of the Arts; Carnegie Mellon; Chapter 510; company, Minneapolis; Corporeal Writing Center; FD13 Residency; The Future Minneapolis; the Goethe Institute; Goldsmiths, University of London; Gropius Bau; Haverford College; Hebbel am Ufer (HAU2); Human Resources Los Angeles; Hunter College; Ignota; Institute of Anxiety; Institute for Cultural Inquiry; JOAN Los Angeles; LACE; Los Angeles Municipal Art Gallery; Massachusetts College of Liberal Arts; Massachusetts Museum of Contemporary Art; MIT; National Autonomous University of Mexico, Mexico City; Migros Museum; MINT, Stockholm; Nottingham Contemporary; NYU; Otis College of Art and Design; Perdu; Pitzer College; Pomona College of Art; Pomona College Women's Union; Processing Foundation; Rehearsing Hospitalities; Rice University; Royal Academy of Art, The Hague; Royal College of Art, London; Royal Institute of Art, Stockholm; Sandberg Institute, Netherlands; Sector 2337, Chicago; Škuc Gallery; South of Sunset; University of Applied Arts, Vienna; University of Arts, Crafts, and Design, Stockholm; University of California, Los Angeles; University of California, Santa

Barbara; University of Cologne; University of Manitoba; University of Pennsylvania; University of Toronto; Virginia Commonwealth University; Wendy's Subway; Williams College; Wysing Centre for the Arts; and X Artists' Books. Thank you to everyone who made *I Wanna Be With You Everywhere* possible at Performance Space New York. Thank you to the following individuals for publishing, exhibiting, interviewing, translating, reviewing, critiquing, thinking of, and supporting this work: Addy Rabinovitch, Adriana Widdoes, Amanda Cachia, Amanda Yates Garcia, Amelia Groom, Amy Berkowitz, Barry Esson and Bryony McIntyre of Arika, Be Oakley, Bettina Korek, Brianna Albers, Cameron Gainer, Catherine X, Cecilia Tricker, Clem Macleod, Cynthia Spring, Denise Markonish, Emily Watlington, Emma Kemp, Eoin Dara, Erika Sprey, Francesca Wade, Gina Osterloh, Helena Chávez Mac Gregor; Iarlaith Ní Fheorais, Nadh Lingyun Cao, Femke Zwiep, Pelumi Adejumo, Asha Karami who made the Dutch translation release event so lovely; Ida Bencke, imogen xtian smith; everyone at the Institute of Anxiety: Ida Tausch, Eva Kot'átková, Barbora Kleinhamplová; Isa Hukka, Jaclyn Bruneau, Jeanne Gerrity, Jemina Lindholm, Jenni Tischer, Jeremy Wade, Jesse Miller, JinHwa Ahn, Joan Tronto, Joshua Wicke, Jussi Koitela, Kamila Metwaly, Katharina Heise, Kate Wong, Lara Plavčak, Levi Prombaum, Lily Cox-Richard, Liz Bowen, Liz Roberts, Leona Koldehoff, Lucy Blagg, Maddie Caldwell, Matilda Tjäder, Neha Choksi, Nora Brünger, Paul B. Preciado, Pavel Pyś, Pelin Uran, Philip Freeman, Philomena Epps, Rachel Kincaid; Ripley Soprano and Hanna Hurr, who accepted and edited the original version of "Sick Woman Theory" for *Mask* in 2016; Robert Maharajh, Ross Simonini, Sara Cluggish, Sarah Shin, Sarah Williams and everyone at the Feminist Center for Creative Work, Sonja Borstner, Stephanie Rosenthal, Thalia Ostendorf, Tony Wei Ling, Urska Aplinc, Victoria Papa, Will Rees, Yvonne Billimore; and everyone at Oz Björnsonova. Thank you to Abbey Williams and Roxie Carman of the Art Matters foundation; and to Jeff Rowlings and everyone at Shape Arts for the Adam Reynolds Bursary Award; the WCCW Health Grant; and the Disability Futures Fellowship funded by the Ford Foundation, Mellon Foundation, and United States Artists. Thank you to all the volunteers who've worked to translate and distribute the texts around the world: Aurora Birbilaj, Leah Whitman-Salkin; Dea Antonsen, Ida Bencke; Thalia Ostendorf, Asha Karami, Pelumi Adejumo; Chloé Peyronnet; Lane Peterson, Helene Bukowski; Stefania Arcara; Heo Ji-woo; Mohira Suyarkulova, Olesya Voitova, Nadya Sayapina; Zuzana Hrivňáková, Zuzana Miháliková, Olga Pek; zineditorial; Pelin çakır. Thank you to my students and clients for thinking and speaking with me over all these years. Thank you to the fans who've taken the time to tell me the work has mattered to you. Thank you to those who've trolled me online—I find having enemies so helpfully clarifying. Thank you to the shitty exes upon whose bones this book is built—how I got your bones at all, pulled from your proud houses, is a story I don't think needs any more of my sweat, I'm so grateful to be done telling it. Thank you to everyone who has shared the work, thought about it with, for, and because of me: you've made me into a better writer, thinker, and person because of your diligence, attention, jokes, critiques, ideas, brilliance.

Thank you to the friends, chosen family, colleagues, and mentors who have given me space, a place, have held me when I needed it, shown me where to go, and how to get there. Alexandra Grant, Alice Hattrick, AM Kanngieser, Amalle Dublon, Anaïs Duplan, Anna Scherk-Weber, Anne Boyer, Anselm Franke, Ariana Reines, Asher Hartman, Bárbara Rodríguez Muñoz, the Beck family, Benjamin Block, Bhanu Kapil, Brandon Shimoda, Brian Getnick, CAConrad, Candice Lin, Caren Beilin, Carolyn Lazard, Catherine Czacki, Chandler McWilliams, Charlotte Cotton, Christopher O'Leary, Christopher Weickenmeier, Cindy Chi, Constantina Zavitsanos, Dan Bustillo, David Naimon & Lucie Bonvalet, Dez'Mon Omega

Fair, Domingo Castillo, Emiliano Lemus, Evangelia Pitsou, Ezra Benus, Franz Kratochwil, Fred Moten, Gabie Strong, the Glover family, Hana Noorali, Harry Dodge, Heather Hannoura, Ian Byers-Gamber, iele paloumpis, Isabelle Albuquerque & Jon Beasley, Jamie Stewart, Janice Lee, Jasmine Albuquerque, Jason Hirata, Jessa Crispin, Jesse Darling, Jessika Khazrik, John Mandel, Jordan Lord, Josephine Sales, Julia Bonn, Julie Tolentino, Karen Lofgren, Ken Baumann & Aviva Baumann, Kerstin Stakemeier, Lara Mimosa Montes, Leah Clements, Leah Lakshmi Piepzna-Samarasinha, Legacy Russell, Leonie Ohlow, Ligia Lewis, Linda Hoag, Linda Owen, Lizzy Rose, Luke Fischbeck, Lynton Talbot, Maggie Nelson, Margeaux Feldman, Mark Allen, Matt Miller, Mattilda Bernstein Sycamore, Megan Daalder, Mel Shimkovitz, Michael Ned Holte, Michelle Dizon and everyone at *at land's edge*, Mudang Jenn, Neve Mazique-Bianco, Nick Duran, Nikki Wallschlaeger, Nora Khan, P. Staff, Pamila Payne, Park McArthur, Perel, Peter Hernandez, Philippa Snow, rafa esparza, Randall Dunn, Regina Gehrmann, Ron Athey, Sam Lavigne & Tega Brain, Samon Rajabnik, Sarah Godfrey, Sarah Petersen, Sarah Rara, Seren Sensei, Seth David Rodriguez, Seth Sher, Shoumik Bhattacharya, Sophia Al-Maria, Stefanie Rogoll, Suzy Halajian, Tamara Antonijević, Tosh Basco, Uma Breakdown, Vivian Ia, Vivian Sming & Three, Willem Henri Lucas, Wu Tsang, Yunuen Rhi, Z Layman, Zuzana Žabková.

Thank you to Joey Cannizzaro.

Thank you to Henry Glover.

Thank you to Emma Borges-Scott.

Thank you to Clare Mao.

Thank you to Caolinn Douglas.

Thank you to the spectacular team at Zando.

Thank you to Lena Waithe, Rishi Rajani, and Naomi Funabashi, and everyone at Hillman Grad. The world had better get ready!

Thank you, Rhi.

Thank you, Dad.

Thank you, Auntie.

Thank you to the ones who've joined the ancestors: Mom, Grandma Connie, Grandma Genny, and Grandpa Bud.

Thank you to my hair. Thank you to my death. The best motivators.

Thank you to Miss Penelope Puppy Pearl D'Abadie Schwarzweißer Flausch.

Thank you, thank you, thank you to Johannes.

Bibliography

Abdurraqib, Hanif. *A Fortune for Your Disaster: Poems*. Tin House Books, 2019.

Abdurraqib, Hanif. *They Can't Kill Us Until They Kill Us: Essays*. Two Dollar Radio, 2017.

Abdur-Rahman, Aliyyah I. *Against the Closet: Black Political Longing and the Erotics of Race*. Durham: Duke University Press, 2012.

Acker, Kathy. *Essential Acker: The Selected Writings of Kathy Acker*. Grove Press, 2002.

Acocella, Joan. *Twenty-Eight Artists and Two Saints: Essays*. Vintage Books, 2008.

Adler-Bolton, Beatrice, and Artie Vierkant. *Health Communism: A Surplus Manifesto*. Verso, 2022.

Ahmed, Sara. *The Cultural Politics of Emotion*. New York: Routledge, 2014.

Ahmed, Sara. "Melancholic Universalism." *Feministkilljoys* (blog), December 15, 2015.

Ahmed, Sara. "The Nonperformativity of Antiracism." *Meridians: Feminism, Race, Transnationalism* 7, no. 1 (2006): 104–26.

Ahmed, Sara. *The Promise of Happiness*. Durham: Duke University Press, 2010.

Ahmed, Sara. *Queer Phenomenology: Orientations, Objects, Others*. Duke University Press, 2006.

Ahmed, Sara. "Selfcare as Warfare." *Feministkilljoys* (blog), August 25, 2014. https://feministkilljoys.com/2014/08/25/selfcare-as-warfare/.

Akerman, Chantal, et al. *My Mother Laughs*. Translated by Daniella Shrier, Silver Press, 2019.

Allewaert, Monique. *Ariel's Ecology: Plantations, Personhood, and Colonialism in the American Tropics*. University of Minnesota Press, 2013.

Als, Hilton. *The Women*. New York: Noonday Press, 1998.

Als, Hilton. *White Girls*. San Francisco: McSweeney's, 2014.

Als, Hilton. "Enameled Lady." *The New Yorker*, April 20, 2009. https://www.newyorker.com/magazine/2009/04/20/enameled-lady.

Als, Hilton. "Gayl Jones's Novels of Oppression." *The New Yorker*, September 27, 2021. www.newyorker.com/magazine/2021/10/04/gayl-jones-novels-of -oppression.

Als, Hilton. "Ghosts in the House: How Toni Morrison Fostered a Generation of Black Writers." *The New Yorker*, October 27, 2003. www.newyorker.com /magazine/2003/10/27/ghosts-in-the-house.

Als, Hilton. "Ghosts in Sunlight." *The New York Review of Books*, July 10, 2014. https://www.nybooks.com/articles/2014/07/10/ghosts-in-sunlight/.

Alvarez, A. *The Savage God: A Study of Suicide*. Bloomsbury Publishing, 2002.

"An Overview of Dialectical Behavior Therapy." Psych Central. Last modified May 20, 2021. https://psychcentral.com/lib/an-overview-of-dialectical-behavior -therapy.

Antonijević, Tamara. "The Hag Theory." *Working Encounters*, 2020. workingencounters.qpress.tech/sljivar-antonijevic-the-hag-theory/.

Antrim, Donald. *One Friday in April*. Norton, 2022.

Arendt, Hannah. *The Human Condition*. Chicago: University of Chicago Press, 1958.

Arendt, Hannah, and Jerome Kohn. *Between Past and Future: Eight Exercises in Political Thought*. Penguin Books, 2006.

Arledge, Sara Kathryn. Unpublished autobiography manuscript. Courtesy Armory Centre of the Arts, Pasadena, CA.

Arnold, Lesley M. "Gender Differences in Bipolar Disorder." *Psychiatric Clinics of North America* 26, no. 3 (September 2003): 595–620. doi: 10.1016/s0193-953x (03)00036-4.

Badkhen, Anna. *Bright Unbearable Reality: Essays*. New York Review Books, 2022.

Baggs, Amanda. "In My Language." YouTube, January 14, 2007. Video, 8:36.

Baldwin, James. *Collected Essays*. Library of America, 1998.

Baldwin, James. *Early Novels and Stories*. Library of America, 2010.

Baldwin, James. *The Fire Next Time*. New York: Vintage International, 1993.

Bamford, Maria. "Maria Bamford – The Stigma Around Mental Illness." YouTube, August 12, 2014. Video, 1:10.

Barbarin, Imani. "Crutches and Spice." Crutches and Spice (Instagram, TikTok, Twitter), crutchesandspice.com

Barron, Benjamin. "Richard Prince, Audrey Wollen, and the Sad Girl Theory." *i-D*, November 12, 2014.

Bastién, Angelica Jade. "The Feminine Grotesque: A Unified Theory on Female Madness in Cinema and American Culture (Series Introduction)." Madwomen and Muses, Tumblr, September 17, 2015. madwomenandmuses.tumblr.com /post/129310217843/the-feminine-grotesque-a-unified-theory-on-female.

NEVE aka Lyric Seal. "Lyric Seal, Author at Crash Pad Series." Blog. Last accessed March 28, 2022.

NEVE aka Lyric Seal. "Incidentally, I Don't Just Write About Bodies, I Have a Body Too." Performance. Sick Fest. Oakland, CA, March 26, 2016.

Beilin, Caren. *Blackfishing the IUD*. Wolfman Books, 2019.

Belben, Rosalind. *The Limit*. New York Review Books, 2023.

Belcourt, Billy-Ray. *A History of My Brief Body*. Two Dollar Radio, 2020.

Bell, Quentin. *Virginia Woolf: A Biography*. Harcourt, 1972.

Bellamy, Dodie. *When the Sick Rule the World*. Cambridge: Semiotext(e)/Active Agents, 2015.

Berkowitz, Amy. *Tender Points*. Oakland: Timeless, Infinite Light, 2015.

Berlant, Lauren Gail. *Cruel Optimism*. Durham: Duke University Press, 2011.

Berne, Patty. "Disability Justice - A Working Draft by Patty Berne." *Sins Invalid*, September 24, 2021. www.sinsinvalid.org/blog/disability-justice-a-working-draft -by-patty-berne.

Bersani, Leo. *Is the Rectum a Grave?: And Other Essays*. University of Chicago Press, 2010.

Bingen, Hildegard von. *Hildegard von Bingen's Physica: The Complete English Translation of Her Classic Work on Health and Healing*. Healing Arts Press, 1998.

Bise, Michael. "Snake Oil: Taraneh Fazeli, Critical Writing Fellow, Core Program." *Glasstire*, May 9, 2016. https://glasstire.com/2016/05/09/snake-oil-taraneh -fazeli-critical-writing-fellow-core-program/.

Blagg, Lucy, and Johanna Hedva. "Lucy Blagg Talks to Johanna Hedva." *Graphite Interdisciplinary Journal of the Arts*, April 2, 2016.

Blackman, Marci. *Po Man's Child*. Manic D Press, 1999.

Blaque, Kat. "Kat Blaque." YouTube channel. Last accessed March 28, 2022.

Boggs, Grace Lee. *Living for Change: An Autobiography*. University of Minnesota Press, 2016.

Borkowski, Mary. "Interview with Kate Zambreno." *The New Inquiry*, November 12, 2012.

Bowles, Jane. *My Sister's Hand in Mine: The Collected Works of Jane Bowles*. New York: Farrar, Straus and Giroux, 2005.

Boyer, Anne. *Garments against Women*. Boise, ID: Ahsahta Press, 2015.

Boyer, Anne. "I Have Taken a Farm at This Hard Rent." *Poetry Foundation* (blog), January 11, 2016. https://www.poetryfoundation.org/harriet-books/2016/01 /i-have-taken-a-farm-at-this-hard-rent.

Boyer, Anne. "Tender Theory." *Poetry Foundation* (blog), January 28, 2016. https:// www.poetryfoundation.org/harriet-books/2016/01/tender-theory-.

Boyer, Anne. *The Undying Pain: Vulnerability, Mortality, Medicine, Art, Time, Dreams, Data, Exhaustion, Cancer, and Care*. Farrar, Straus and Giroux, 2019.

Brand, Dionne. "Between the Covers Dionne Brand: Nomenclature — New and Collected Poems." *Between the Covers*, Tin House, October 1, 2022.

Brand, Dionne, and Christina Elizabeth Sharpe. *Nomenclature: New and Collected Poems*. Duke University Press, 2022.

brown, adrienne maree. *Pleasure Activism: The Politics of Feeling Good*. AK Press, 2019.

Brown, Stephen Rex. "Woman Held in Psych Ward over Obama Twitter Claim." *New York Daily News*, March 23, 2015.

Butler, Judith. "Vulnerability and Resistance." Lecture. REDCAT. Los Angeles, California, December 19, 2014.

Butler, Judith. *Excitable Speech: A Politics of the Performative*. New York: Routledge, 1997.

Butler, Judith. *Gender Trouble: Feminism and the Subversion of Identity*. New York: Routledge, 2006.

Butler, Judith. *Precarious Life: The Powers of Mourning and Violence*. London: Verso, 2004.

Campbell, James. *Talking at the Gates: A Life of James Baldwin*. Polyon, 2021.

Campion, Jane, dir. *An Angel at My Table*. 1990. United States: Criterion Collection, 2005. DVD.

Carrington, Leonora, and Marina Warner. *Down Below*. New York Review Books, 2017.

Carrington, Leonora. *The Complete Stories of Leonora Carrington*. Dorothy, a Publishing Project, 2023.

Case, Sue-Ellen, ed. *Performing Feminisms: Feminist Critical Theory and Theatre*. Baltimore: Johns Hopkins University Press, 1990.

Carson, Anne. "Decreation: How Women Like Sappho, Marguerite Porete, and Simone Weil Tell God." In *Decreation: Poetry, Essays, Opera*, 155–83. New York: Vintage Contemporaries, 2005.

Carson, Anne. *Eros the Bittersweet: An Essay*. Princeton University Press, 2023.

Carson, Anne. *Men in the Off Hours*. Vintage Canada, 2014.

Carson, Anne. *Plainwater: Essays and Poetry*. Vintage Contemporaries, 2000.

Carson, Anne. "Semaine d'Artaud." In *Conjunctions:30*, Bard University, Annandale-on-Hudson, New York, 1998.

Césaire, Aimé, and Robin D. G. Kelley. *Discourse on Colonialism*. New York: Monthly Review Press, 2000.

Cha, Theresa Hak Kyung. *Dictee*. University of California Press, 2022.

Chakravartty, Paula, and Denise Ferreira da Silva. "Accumulation, Dispossession, and Debt: The Racial Logic of Global Capitalism—An Introduction." *American Quarterly* 64, no. 3 (2012): 361–85. doi:10.1353/aq.2012.0033.

Chee, Alexander. *How to Write an Autobiographical Novel*. Mariner Books, 2018.

Chiasson, Dan. "Sylvia Plath's Joy." *The New Yorker*, February 12, 2013.

Chu, Andrea Long. *Females*. Verso, 2019.

Chu, Andrea Long. "Hanya's Boys." Vulture, January 12, 2022. www.vulture.com /article/hanya-yanagihara-review.html.

Chu, Andrea Long. "On Liking Women." *N+1*, 2018. www.nplusonemag.com /issue-30/essays/on-liking-women/.

Chu, Andrea Long. "Ottessa Moshfegh Is Praying for Us." Vulture, June 16, 2022. www.vulture.com/article/ottessa-moshfegh-lapvona-review.html.

Chu, Andrea Long. "The Mixed Metaphor." Vulture, September 27, 2022, www .vulture.com/2022/09/the-mixed-asian-metaphor.html.

Chu, Andrea Long. "You've Heard This One Before." Vulture, September 7, 2021. www.vulture.com/article/maggie-nelson-on-freedom-review.html.

Clark, Heather L. Red Comet: The Short Life and Blazing Art of Sylvia Plath. Jonathan Cape, 2020.

Clark, Tiana. I Can't Talk about the Trees without the Blood. University of Pittsburgh Press, 2018.

Clements, Leah, Alice Hattrick, and Lizzy Rose. Access Docs for Artists, www .accessdocsforartists.com/homepage. Accessed January 20, 2024.

Cohen, Cathy J. "DEVIANCE AS RESISTANCE: A New Research Agenda for the Study of Black Politics." Du Bois Review: Social Science Research on Race 1, no. 1 (2004). doi:10.1017/s1742058x04040044.

Conrad, C. A. A Beautiful Marsupial Afternoon: New (soma)tics. Seattle: Wave Books, 2012.

Cowart, Leigh. Hurts So Good: The Science and Culture of Pain on Purpose. PublicAffairs, 2021.

Crashcourse. "Depressive and Bipolar Disorders: Crash Course Psychology #30." YouTube. September 8, 2014. Video, 9:59.

Crashcourse. "Psychology Playlist, 40 Videos – Crash Course Psychology #1." YouTube, February 3, 2014. Video, 10:53.

Crenshaw, Kimberle. "Mapping the Margins: Intersectionality, Identity Politics, and Violence against Women of Color." Stanford Law Review 43, no. 6 (1991): 1241–299.

Crenshaw, Kimberle. "Demarginalizing the Intersection of Race and Sex: A Black Feminist Critique of Antidiscrimination Doctrine, Feminist Theory and Antiracist Politics." The University of Chicago Legal Forum 140 (1989): 139–67.

Crispin, Jessa. The Dead Ladies Project. University of Chicago Press, 2015.

Crispin, Jessa. "Jessa Crispin: Why I Am Not Feminist." Lecture, YouTube, Wheeler Centre, May 29, 2017. https://www.youtube.com/watch?v=xy 44rZ87O-s.

Crispin, Jessa. My Three Dads: Patriarchy on the Great Plains. University of Chicago Press, 2022.

Crispin, Jessa. "Wounded Women." Boston Review, March 4, 2015.

Critchley, Simon. The Faith of the Faithless: Experiments in Political Theology. London: Verso, 2014.

Critchley, Simon. "Symposium: We, Ourselves & Us." Lecture presented at If We Can't Get It Together. The Power Plant Contemporary Art Gallery. Toronto, Canada, January 23, 2009.

Cvetkovich, Ann. *Depression: A Public Feeling*. Durham: Duke University Press, 2012.

Davis, Angela. *Angela Davis: An Autobiography*. International Publishers, 2008.

Davis, Davey. *X*. Counterpoint Press, 2022.

Debré, Constance. *Love Me Tender*. Semiotext(e) / Native Agents, 2022.

DeGruy, Joy. "Post Traumatic Slave Syndrome." Lecture. YouTube, September 12, 2016. https://www.youtube.com/watch?v=BGjSday7f_8.

De Veaux, Alexis. *Warrior Poet: A Biography of Audre Lorde*. W. W. Norton, 2006.

Diagnostic and Statistical Manual of Mental Disorders: DSM-5. 5th ed. Washington, DC: American Psychiatric Association, 2013.

DiAngelo, Robin J. *White Fragility: Why It's So Hard for White People to Talk about Racism*. Beacon Press, 2018.

Diaz, Natalie. *Postcolonial Love Poem*. Graywolf Press, 2020.

Diaz, Natalie. "Between the Covers Natalie Diaz Interview Part 1." *Between the Covers*, Tin House, October 22, 2020.

Diaz, Natalie. "Between the Covers Natalie Diaz Interview Part 2." *Between the Covers*, Tin House, December 9, 2020.

Didion, Joan. *Blue Nights*. Vintage Books, 2012.

Didion, Joan. *Joan Didion: The 1960s & 70s*. The Library of America, 2019.

Didion, Joan. *Let Me Tell You What I Mean*. Random House US, 2022.

Didion, Joan. *South and West: From a Notebook*. Alfred A. Knopf, 2017.

Didion, Joan. *The Year of Magical Thinking*. Alfred A. Knopf, 2005.

Dillon, Millicent. *A Little Original Sin: The Life and Work of Jane Bowles*. Berkeley: University of California Press, 1998.

Ditlevsen, Tove. *Dependency*. Farrar, Straus and Giroux, 2021.

Dodge, Harry. *My Meteorite, or, Without the Random There Can Be No New Thing*. Penguin Books, 2020.

Dolphin-Krute, Maia. "Daily Survivor #1." *Full Stop* (blog), November 25, 2015. https://www.full-stop.net/2015/11/25/features/essays/maiadolphinkrute/daily-survivor-1/.

"DSM-IV: Symptom, Syndrome, Disorder, Disease." DSM-IV: Symptom, Syndrome, Disorder, Disease. Last accessed March 28, 2022. https://www2.hawaii.edu/~heiby/overheads_classification.html.

Dublon, Amalle. "Lived Experience Autocorrecting to Loved Experience with Amalle Dublon and Johanna Hedva." ICI Berlin, July 8, 2020. https://www.ici-berlin.org/events/lived-experience-autocorrecting-to-loved-experience/.

Duplan, Anaïs. *Blackspace: On the Poetics of an Afrofuture*. Black Ocean, 2020.

Dunne, Griffin, dir. *Joan Didion: The Center Will Not Hold*. Netflix, 2017.

Edwards, Breanna. "Mentally Ill Cleveland Woman Was Killed by Police in Front of Her Family, Brother Says." *The Root*, November 17, 2014.

Ehrenreich, Barbara, and Deirdre English. *Complaints and Disorders: The Sexual Politics of Sickness*. Old Westbury, New York: Feminist Press, 1973.

Ehrenreich, Barbara, and Deirdre English. *Witches, Midwives, & Nurses: A History of Women Healers*. New York: Feminist Press at the City University of New York, 2010.

Ehrenstein, David. "Sinful Cinema: The Driver's Seat." *Slant Magazine*, March 25, 2013. www.slantmagazine.com/film/sinful-cinema-the-drivers-seat/.

Elainey, Annie. "Annie Elainey." YouTube channel. Last accessed March 28, 2022.

Elizabeth, Maranda. "Dreaming New Meanings Into Borderline Personality Disorder." *The Establishment*, August 11, 2016.

Elizabeth, Maranda. "How Magic Helps Me Live with Pain and Trauma." *The Establishment*, April 19, 2016.

Elliott, Paul. "Tony Iommi on Inventing Heavy Metal, Drinking with Gillan, and Not Being Evil." Louder, August 18, 2016. www.loudersound.com/features /tony-iommi-on-inventing-heavy-metal-drinking-with-gillan-and -not-being-evil.

Emezi, Akwaeke. *Dear Senthuran: A Black Spirit Memoir*. Riverhead Books, 2022.

Emezi, Akwaeke. *Freshwater*. Grove Press, 2018.

"Emotional Health." APA.org. Last accessed December 31, 2015. https://www.apa .org/topics/emotions.

Ernaux, Annie. *Happening*. Translated by Tanya Leslie, Fitzcarraldo Editions, 2022.

Euripides. *Grief Lessons: Four Plays*. Translated by Anne Carson, New York Review Books, 2008.

Fain, Jean. "Eve Ensler on Cancer, Her Body and 'The Body of the World'." *The Huffington Post*, April 26, 2013.

Faludi, Susan. "Shulamith Firestone's Radical Feminism." *The New Yorker*, April 8, 2013. www.newyorker.com/magazine/2013/04/15/death-of-a-revolutionary.

Fanon, Frantz. *Black Skin, White Masks*. New York: Grove Press, 2008.

Farah, Safy Hallan. "All Alone in Their White Girl Pain." Hip to Waste, August 1, 2020, hiptowaste.substack.com/p/all-alone-in-their-white-girl-pain.

Fassler, Joe. "How Doctors Take Women's Pain Less Seriously." *The Atlantic*, October 15, 2015.

Fazeli, Taraneh. "Notes for 'Sick Time, Sleepy Time, Crip Time: Against Capitalism's Temporal Bullying' in Conversation with the Canaries." *Temporary Art Review*, May 26, 2016. https://temporaryartreview.com/notes -for-sick-time-sleepy-time-crip-time-against-capitalisms-temporal-bullying -in-conversation-with-the-canaries/.

Febos, Melissa. *Girlhood: Essays*. Bloomsbury Publishing, 2022.

Federici, Silvia. *Beyond the Periphery of The Skin: Rethinking, Remaking, and Reclaiming the Body in Contemporary Capitalism*. Between the Lines, 2020.

Federici, Silvia. *Caliban and the Witch: Women, the Body and Primitive Accumulation*. New York: Autonomedia, 2003.

Federici, Silvia. *Witch-Hunting, Past and Present, and the Fear of the Power of Women = Hexenjagd, Vergangenheit Und Gegenwart, Und Die Angst Vor Der Macht Der Frauen*. Ostfildern, Germany: Hatje Cantz, 2012.

Felker-Martin, Gretchen. *Manhunt*. Nightfire, 2022.

Ferguson, Anni. "'The Lowest of the Stack': Why Black Women Are Struggling with Mental Health." *The Guardian*, February 8, 2016.

Fisher, Carrie. *Wishful Drinking*. New York: Simon & Schuster, 2008.

Fisher, Mark. *Ghosts of My Life: Writings on Depression, Hauntology and Lost Futures*. Zero Books, 2022.

Fisher, Mark. *The Weird and the Eerie*. Random House, 2017.

Fitzgerald, Helen. *The Mourning Handbook: The Most Comprehensive Resource Offering Practical and Compassionate Advice on Coping with All Aspects of Death and Dying*. Simon & Schuster, 1995.

Flanagan, Bob. *Pain Journal*. Autonomedia, 2001.

Foucault, Michel. *Madness and Civilization: A History of Insanity in the Age of Reason*. New York: Vintage Books, 1988.

Frame, Janet. *Faces in the Water*. Braziller, 2007.

Fraser, Kennedy. *Ornament and Silence: Essays on Women's Lives from Edith Wharton to Germaine Greer*. Vintage, 1998.

Furlong, Monica. *Visions and Longings: Medieval Women Mystics*. Boston: Shambhala, 1996.

Fuss, Diana. *Essentially Speaking: Feminism, Nature & Difference*. New York: Routledge, 1989.

Ghansah, Rachel Kaadzi. "The Weight of James Arthur Baldwin." BuzzFeed, February 29, 2016. www.buzzfeed.com/rachelkaadzighansah/the-weight-of-james-arthur-baldwin-203.

Goldhill, Olivia. "Palestine's Head of Mental Health Services Says PTSD Is a Western Concept." Quartz, January 13, 2019. qz.com/1521806/palestines-head-of-mental-health-services-says-ptsd-is-a-western-concept.

Gordon, Avery. *Ghostly Matters: Haunting and the Sociological Imagination*. University of Minnesota Press, 2011.

Greenfield-Sanders, Timothy, dir. *Toni Morrison: The Pieces I Am*. 2019.

Guibert, Hervé. *My Parents*. Serpent's Tail, 1993.

Guibert, Hervé. *To the Friend Who Did Not Save My Life*. Semiotext(e), 2020.

Haidrani, Salma. "The Wellness Movement Has A Race Problem." Originally published at *The Establishment*, July 14, 2016. Republished at *RoleReboot* with permission.

Halberstam, Jack. "Jack Halberstam: Zombie Humanism at the End of the World." Paper presented at *Weak Resistance: Everyday Struggles and the Politics of Failure*. Berlin, Germany, May 27, 2015.

Hamilton, Ian. *Robert Lowell: A Biography*. Random House, 1982.

Hamilton, Michael, dir. *Bisping*. 2021.

Hamilton, Saskia. *As for Dream*. Graywolf Press, 2001.

Haraway, Donna J. *Cyborg Manifesto*. Camas Books, 2018.

Haraway, Donna J. *Staying with the Trouble: Making Kin in the Chthulucene*. Duke University Press, 2016.

Hardwick, Elizabeth. *Collected Essays of Elizabeth Hardwick*. Edited by Darryl Pinckney. New York Review Books, 2017.

Hardwick, Elizabeth. "On Sylvia Plath." *The New York Review of Books*, August 12, 1971.

Hardwick, Elizabeth. *Seduction and Betrayal: Women and Literature*. New York Review Books, 2001.

Hardwick, Elizabeth. *The Uncollected Essays of Elizabeth Hardwick*. Edited by Alex Andriesse. New York Review Books, 2022.

Harman, Claire. *Charlotte Brontë, A Life*. New York: Penguin Books, 2016.

Harney, Stefano, and Fred Moten. *The Undercommons: Fugitive Planning & Black Study*. New York: Minor Compositions, 2013.

Harney, Stefano, and Fred Moten. Zun Lee (photographs); Denise Ferreira da Silva (preface). *All Incomplete*. Minor Compositions, 2022.

Hartman, Saidiya V. *Scenes of Subjection: Terror, Slavery, and Self-Making in Nineteenth-Century America*. Oxford: Oxford University Press, 2010.

Hartman, Saidiya V. *Wayward Lives, Beautiful Experiments: Intimate Histories of Social Upheaval*. W. W. Norton & Company, 2019.

Hattrick, Alice. *Ill Feelings*. The Feminist Press at the City University of New York, 2022.

Headley, Maria Dahvana. *Magonia*. HarperCollins, 2016.

Hedva, Johanna. "My Body Is a Prison of Pain so I Want to Leave It Like a Mystic But I Also Love It & Want It to Matter Politically." Lecture. Human Resources. Los Angeles, California, October 7, 2015.

Heidegger, Martin. *Being and Time*. Harper Perennial Modern Thought, 2008.

Herrera, Hayden. *Frida, a Biography of Frida Kahlo*. Perennial, 2002.

Hoffmann, Yoel. *Japanese Death Poems: Written by Zen Monks and Haiku Poets on the Verge of Death*. Tuttle Publishing, 2018.

Holladay, Hilary. *The Power of Adrienne Rich: A Biography*. Knopf, 2021.

Hollywood, Amy. "On the Materiality of Air: Janet Kauffman's Bodyfictions." *New Literary History* 27, no. 3 (1996): 503–25. doi:10.1353/nlh.1996.0036.

Hollywood, Amy. "The Mystery of Trauma, and the Mystery of Joy." Erasmus Society Lecture. Westmont College. Montecito, California. January 27, 2014.

Hollywood, Amy. *Sensible Ecstasy: Mysticism, Sexual Difference, and the Demands of History*. Chicago: University of Chicago Press, 2002.

Hong, Cathy Park. *Minor Feelings: An Asian American Reckoning*. One World, 2020.

hooks, bell. *All about Love: New Visions*. William Morrow, an imprint of HarperCollins Publishers, 2022.

hooks, bell. "Bell Hooks at The New School." Residency Lectures. The New School for Social Research. New York, NY, 2015.

Howland, Bette. *W-3*. Public Space Books, 2021.

Hughes, Ted. *Birthday Letters*. Farrar, Straus and Giroux, 1998.

Hurston, Zora Neale. *Dust Tracks on a Road*. New York: Harper Perennial Modern Classics, 2006.

Ikpi, Bassey. *I'm Telling the Truth, but I'm Lying: Essays*. Harper Perennial, 2019.

Jabr, Samah. "Isip Palestine Focus: Dr. Samah Jabr on Reconceptualizing Mental Health in the Context of Palestine." YouTube, ISIP International Students of Islamic Psychology, November 13, 2023. www.youtube.com/watch?v=Csy4TeqoldY.

Jackson, Zakiyyah Iman. *Becoming Human: Matter and Meaning in an Antiblack World*. New York University Press, 2020.

Jamison, Kay R. *Touched with Fire: Manic-Depressive Illness and the Artistic Temperament*. New York: Free Press, 1993.

Jamison, Kay R. *An Unquiet Mind: A Memoir of Moods and Madness*. New York: Vintage Books, 1996.

Jamison, Leslie. *The Empathy Exams: Essays*. Graywolf Press, 2014.

Jamison, Leslie. *The Recovering: Intoxication and Its Aftermath*. Little, Brown and Company, 2018.

Janisse, Kier-La. *House of Psychotic Women: An Autobiographical Topography of Female Neurosis in Horror and Exploitation Films*. Fab Press, 2014.

Jefferson, Margo. *Constructing a Nervous System: A Memoir*. Vintage, 2022.

Johnson, Cyrée Jarelle. *Slingshot*. Nightboat Books, 2019.

Jones, Gayl. *Corregidora*. Virago Press, 2019.

Jordan, June. *The Essential June Jordan*. Copper Canyon Press, 2021.

Kafer, Alison. *Feminist, Queer, Crip*. Bloomington: Indiana University Press, 2013.

Kahlo, Frida, Carlos Fuentes, and Sarah M. Lowe. *The Diary of Frida Kahlo: An Intimate Self-Portrait*. New York: Harry N. Abrams, 2005.

Kapil, Bhanu. *Ban En Banlieue*. New York: Nightboat, 2015.

Kauffman, Janet. *The Body in Four Parts*. St. Paul, MN: Graywolf Press, 1993.

Kavan, Anna, and Victoria Walker. *Machines in the Head: Selected Stories*. New York Review Books, 2019.

Kavan, Anna. *Sleep Has His House*. London: Peter Owen, 2002.

Kavan, Anna, and Virginia Ironside. *Julia and the Bazooka*. London: Peter Owen, 2009.

Kim, Eunjung. *Curative Violence: Rehabilitating Disability, Gender, and Sexuality in Modern Korea*. Durham: Duke University Press, 2017.

Kim, Hyesoon. *Autobiography of Death*. Translated by Don Mee Choi, New Directions, 2018.

Kim, Hyesoon. *Phantom Pain Wings*. Translated by Don Mee Choi, New Directions, 2023.

Kitamura, Katie. *A Separation*. Clerkenwell, 2018.

Knapp, Andrew, and Dave Munday. "Filing: Jailed Woman Left to Die; Ailing Inmate Untended, Deprived of Water as She Vomited All Night, Attorneys Say." *Post and Courier*, November 2, 2016. https://www.postandcourier.com/archives/filing-jailed-woman-left-to-die-ailing-inmate-untended-deprived-of-water-as-she-vomited/article_a23d27f7-abdd-52ae-8753-119aa0802413.html.

Kraus, Chris. *After Kathy Acker: A Literary Biography*. Semiotext(e), 2017.

Kraus, Chris. *Aliens & Anorexia*. Semiotext(e), 2000.

Kristeva, Julia. *Black Sun: Depression and Melancholia*. Translated by Leon S. Roudiez, Columbia University Press, 1989.

Kristeva, Julia. *Powers of Horror: An Essay of Abjection*. Columbia University Press, 1984.

Laing, R. D. *The Divided Self*. Pantheon Books, 2010.

Lam, Alice. "Bipolar Disorder in Men and Women: What's the Difference?" International Bipolar Foundation, June 14, 2022, ibpf.org/articles/bipolar-disorder-in-men-and-women-whats-the-difference/.

Laymon, Kiese. *Heavy: An American Memoir*. Bloomsbury Publishing, 2018.

Lazard, Carolyn. "How to Be a Person in the Age of Autoimmunity." Originally published in *The Cluster Mag*, January 16, 2013. Currently linked through *Triple Canopy*.

Lazard, Carolyn. "Accessibility in the Arts: A Promise and a Practice." promiseandpractice.art/. Accessed January 20, 2024.

Lee, Hermione. *Virginia Woolf*. Vintage, 1999.

Lee, Janice. "Books Are Not Products, They Are Bridges: Challenging Linear Ideas of Success in Literary Publishing." Vol. 1 Brooklyn, December 5, 2019, vol1brooklyn.com/2019/12/04/books-are-not-products-they-are-bridges-challenging-linear-ideas-of-success-in-literary-publishing/.

Lee, Janice. *Imagine a Death*. Texas A&M University Press, 2021.

Lee, Janice. "On Memory & Why I Can't Remember My Mother's Face." *Berfrois*, September 17, 2015.

Lee, Janice. *Reconsolidation: Or, It's the Ghosts Who Will Answer You*. Los Angeles: Penny-Ante, 2015.

Leibowitz, Tovah. "Crip Lit: Toward an Intersectional Crip Syllabus." *Autostraddle*, May 23, 2016.

Levitsky, Steven, and Daniel Ziblatt. *How Democracies Die*. Broadway Books, 2019.

Levy, Deborah, and Andrew Durbin. "Deborah Levy - Real Estate." YouTube, Politics and Prose, August 30, 2021. www.youtube.com/watch?v=6c1PHJVGbkw.

Levy, Deborah, and Jakuta Alikavazovic. "Deborah Levy | A Living Autobiography | Edinburgh International Book Festival." YouTube, Edinburgh International Book Festival, March 30, 2022. www.youtube.com/watch?v=DG8FKr9aTN0.

Levy, Deborah, and Julia Bell. "In Conversation: Deborah Levy with Julia Bell (Arts Weeks 2020: Online)." YouTube, Birkbeck, University of London, May 19, 2020. www.youtube.com/watch?v=OtcWVDJ1mLI.

Levy, Deborah, and Merve Emre. "Merve Emre and Deborah Levy: On Mrs Dalloway." YouTube, The Royal Society of Literature, November 10, 2021. www.youtube.com/watch?v=gjk79LJ4mGk.

Levy, Deborah, and Rosie Goldsmith. "Fashion and Fiction: Divas, Delusions and Desire. From Bowie to Freud with Deborah Levy." YouTube, Sounds Right, May 11, 2018. www.youtube.com/watch?v=UZY0XkGnvPA.

Levy, Deborah, and Tash Aw. "A Conversation between Deborah Levy and Tash Aw | Library Chat." YouTube, Columbia Institute for Ideas and Imagination, May 29, 2021. www.youtube.com/watch?v=YX3pZxIU32c.

Levy, Deborah, and Tash Aw. "Deborah Levy on Real Estate with Tash Aw." YouTube, The Center for Fiction, September 29, 2021. www.youtube.com /watch?v=vq7072vJY7Q.

Levy, Deborah. "Deborah Levy in Conversation at #britlitberlin 2015." YouTube, British Council Literature Seminar, February 19, 2015. www.youtube.com /watch?v=904G1YT2W6A.

Levy, Deborah. "Deborah Levy in Her Writing Shed, on Her Book an Amorous Discourse in the Suburbs of Hell." YouTube, And Other Stories, May 15, 2018. www.youtube.com/watch?v=awYHxyrEbm8.

Levy, Deborah. "Deborah Levy, Conversation, 30 October 2019." YouTube, Lannan Foundation, November 3, 2019. www.youtube.com/watch?v=eZ1ZgLigItU.

Levy, Deborah. "Deborah Levy, Reading, 30 October 2019." YouTube, Lannan Foundation, November 3, 2019. www.youtube.com/watch?v=-j5_404EyVg.

Levy, Deborah. "Deborah Levy: The Psychopathology of the Doppelgänger (February 6, 2019) | Mercredis de l'institut." YouTube, Columbia Institute for Ideas and Imagination, June 3, 2019. www.youtube.com/watch?v=y ID4W1dGREQ.

Levy, Deborah. *Hot Milk*. Penguin, 2017.

Levy, Deborah. *Real Estate: A Living Autobiography*. Bloomsbury Publishing, 2021.

Levy, Deborah. "Story/Teller: Deborah Levy Presents the Man Who Saw Everything." YouTube, The Center for Fiction, December 13, 2019. www .youtube.com/watch?v=ZB2i4W4_JQ0.

Levy, Deborah. *Swimming Home*. And Other Stories, 2017.

Levy, Deborah. *The Cost of Living: A Working Autobiography*. Bloomsbury Publishing, 2018.

Levy, Deborah. *Things I Don't Want to Know: A Response to George Orwell's 1946 Essay "Why I Write."* Notting Hill Editions, 2013.

Levy, Deborah. "'In Fiction, You Have Characters Who Are Your Avatars.' | Writer
    Deborah Levy | Louisiana Channel." YouTube, Louisiana Channel,
    December 29, 2022, www.youtube.com/watch?v=uTxkwexPgNc.
Lewis, Talila. "January 2021 Working Definition of Ableism." *TALILA A. LEWIS*,
    January 1, 2022: https://www.talilalewis.com/blog/working-definition-of-ableism
    -january-2022-update.
Linton, Simi. *Claiming Disability: Knowledge and Identity*. New York: New York
    University Press, 1998.
"Looking for Language in the Ruins: JJJJJerome Ellis, Saidiya Hartman, and Erica
    Hunt." YouTube, The Center for African American Poetry and Poetics,
    September 30, 2020. https://www.youtube.com/watch?v=2bSu_ysGzVQ.
Lomax, Tamura. "Rethinking Forgiveness in the Face of Unceasing Black
    Trauma." *The Feminist Wire*, July 15, 2016.
Lord, Catherine. *The Summer of Her Baldness: A Cancer Improvisation*.
    University of Texas Press, 2004.
Lorde, Audre. *The Black Unicorn: Poems*. Norton, 1978.
Lorde, Audre. *A Burst of Light: Essays*. Ithaca: Firebrand Books, 1988.
Lorde, Audre. *The Cancer Journals. Special ed*. San Francisco: Aunt Lute Books,
    1997.
Lyons, Gila. "Creativity and Madness: On Writing through the Drugs." *The
    Millions*, February 27, 2014.
Machado, Carmen Maria. *In the Dream House: A Memoir*. Graywolf, 2019.
Mailhot, Terese Marie. *Heart Berries: A Memoir*. Counterpoint, 2019.
Malcolm, Janet. *Psychoanalysis, the Impossible Profession*. New York: Vintage
    Books, 1982.
Malcolm, Janet. "Susan Sontag and the Unholy Practice of Biography." *The New
    Yorker*, September 16, 2019. www.newyorker.com/magazine/2019/09/23/susan
    -sontag-and-the-unholy-practice-of-biography.
Malcolm, Janet. *The Silent Woman: Sylvia Plath and Ted Hughes*. New York: A.A.
    Knopf, 1994.
Manguso, Sarah. *The Guardians: An Elegy for a Friend*. New York: Farrar, Straus
    and Giroux, 2012.
Manguso, Sarah. *The Two Kinds of Decay*. New York: Farrar, Straus and Giroux,
    2008.
Manguso, Sarah. "You'll Love Her! She's Crazy!" *The New Yorker*, February 11,
    2013.
Mantel, Hilary. "Every Part of My Body Hurt." *The Guardian*, June 7, 2004.
Marya, Rupa, and Raj Patel. *Inflamed: Deep Medicine and the Anatomy of
    Injustice*. Picador, 2022.
Maté, Gabor. *In the Realm of Hungry Ghosts: Close Encounters with Addiction*.
    North Atlantic Books, 2020.

Max, D. T. *Every Love Story Is a Ghost Story: A Life of David Foster Wallace.*
Penguin Books, 2013.

May, Katherine. *Wintering: The Power of Rest and Retreat in Difficult Times.*
Rider & Co, 2021.

Mbembe, Achille. "Necropolitics." Translated by Libby Meintjes. *Public Culture*
15, no. 1 (2003): 11–40. doi:10.1215/08992363-15-1-11.

McArthur, Park, and Constantina Zavitsanos, "The Guild of the Brave Poor
Things." In *Trap Door: Trans Cultural Politics and the Politics of Visibility.*
Edited by Reina Gossett, Eric A. Stanley, and Johanna Burton. Cambridge:
MIT Press, 2017, 238.

McArthur, Park, and Constantina Zavitsanos. "Other Forms of Conviviality: The
Best and Least of Which Is Our Daily Care and the Host of Which Is Our
Collaborative Work." *Women & Performance: A Journal of Feminist Theory*
23, no. 1 (2013): 126–32. doi:10.1080/0740770x.2013.827376.

McCarthy, Jesse. *Who Will Pay Reparations on My Soul?* W. W. Norton, 2022.

McRuer, Robert. *Crip Theory: Cultural Signs of Queerness and Disability.* New
York: New York University Press, 2006.

Meinhof, Ulrike Marie. *Everybody Talks about the Weather . . . We Don't: The
Writings of Ulrike Meinhof.* Seven Stories Press, 2008.

Middlebrook, Diane Wood. *Anne Sexton: A Biography.* Vintage Books, 1992.

Miklowitz, David J. *The Bipolar Disorder Survival Guide: What You and Your
Family Need to Know.* New York: Guilford Press, 2011.

Mingus, Mia. *Leaving Evidence* (blog). March 28, 2022.

Mingus, Mia. "Access Intimacy: The Missing Link." *Leaving Evidence*, August 15,
2017, leavingevidence.wordpress.com/2011/05/05/access-intimacy-the-missing
-link/.

Mingus, Mia. "Moving Toward the Ugly: A Politic Beyond Desirability." *Leaving
Evidence* (blog), August 22, 2011. http://leavingevidence.wordpress.com/2011
/08/22/moving-toward-the-ugly-a-politic-beyond-desirability/.

Mingus, Mia. "Wherever You Are Is Where I Want to Be: Crip Solidarity." Leaving
Evidence, July 14, 2010, leavingevidence.wordpress.com/2010/05/03/where
-ever-you-are-is-where-i-want-to-be-crip-solidarity/.

Miserandino, Christine. "The Spoon Theory Written by Christine Miserandino."
*But You Don't Look Sick: Support for Those with Invisible Illness or Chronic
Illness.* Last modified April 25, 2013. https://butyoudontlooksick.com/articles
/written-by-christine/the-spoon-theory/.

Montes, Lara Mimosa. *Thresholes.* Coffee House Press, 2020.

Moore, Anne Elizabeth, and Johanna Hedva. "Afterparty: A Community Guide for
the Future." Kickstarter. Last modified December 2, 2015.

Moorhead, Joanna. *The Surreal Life of Leonora Carrington.* Virago, 2019.

Morrison, Toni. *Beloved.* Vintage, 2019.

Morrison, Toni. *Playing in the Dark: Whiteness and the Literary Imagination.*
Cambridge, MA: Harvard University Press, 1992.

Morrison, Toni. *The Source of Self-Regard: Selected Essays, Speeches, and Meditations.* Alfred A. Knopf, 2021.

Morrison, Toni, and Junot Díaz. "Toni Morrison and Junot Díaz | LIVE from the NYPL." Lecture. The New York Public Library. New York, NY, December 12, 2013.

Moser, Benjamin. *Sontag: Her Life and Work.* Ecco, 2019.

Moser, Benjamin. *Why This World—A Biography of Clarice Lispector.* Penguin Books, 2014.

Moten, Fred. *Black and Blur (consent not to be a single being).* Duke University Press, 2017.

Moten, Fred. "Blackness and Nothingness (Mysticism in the Flesh)." *South Atlantic Quarterly* 112, no. 4 (Fall 2013): 737–80. doi:10.1215/00382876 -2345261.

Moten, Fred. *The Little Edges.* Middletown, CT: Wesleyan University Press, 2014.

Moten, Fred. *In the Break: The Aesthetics of the Black Radical Tradition.* University of Minnesota Press, 2003.

Moynihan, Thomas. *Spinal Catastrophism: A Secret History.* Urbanomic Media, 2020.

Mukherjee, Siddhartha. *The Gene: An Intimate History.* Scribner, 2017.

Muñoz, Bárbara Rodríguez. *Health.* Whitechapel Gallery, 2020.

Ndikung, Bonaventure Soh Bejeng. *The Delusions of Care.* Archive Books, 2021.

Nelson, Maggie. *The Argonauts.* Graywolf Press, 2016.

Nelson, Maggie. *The Art of Cruelty: A Reckoning.* W. W. Norton & Company, 2012.

Nelson, Maggie. *Like Love: Essays and Conversations.* Graywolf Press, 2024.

Nelson, Maggie. *On Freedom: Four Songs of Care and Constraint.* Graywolf Press, 2022.

Nelson, Maggie. *The Red Parts: A Memoir.* Free Press, 2007.

Niedecker, Lorine. *Lorine Niedecker: Collected Works.* University of California Press, 2004.

Nightingale, Florence, and Myra Stark. *Cassandra: An Essay.* Old Westbury, NY: Feminist Press, 1979.

Nguyen, Mimi Thi. "Riot Grrrl, Race, and Revival." *Women & Performance: A Journal of Feminist Theory,* 2012: 173-96.

Nunez, Sigrid. *Sempre Susan: A Memoir of Susan Sontag.* Riverhead Books, 2014.

Padel, Ruth. *In and Out of the Mind: Greek Images of the Tragic Self.* Princeton University Press, 1995.

Parker, Morgan. "Between the Covers Morgan Parker: Magical Negro." *Between the Covers,* Tin House, May 14, 2019.

Parker, Morgan. *Magical Negro.* Corsair, 2019.

Parker, Morgan. *There Are More Beautiful Things than Beyoncé.* Little, Brown, 2017.

Patel, Raj, and Jason W. Moore. *A History of the World in Seven Cheap Things: A Guide to Capitalism, Nature, and the Future of the Planet.* University of California Press, 2018.

Peck, Raoul, dir. *I Am Not Your Negro.* 2017.

Perry, Jade T. "For Colored Gurls Who Consider Blogging & Glitter When Chronic Illness Gets Too Real, and Waiting Rooms Get Too Stuffy, and Folk Don't Have No Act-Right." *Jade T Perry* (blog), January 2016.

Phillips, Rasheedah. *Black Quantum Futurism: Theory and Practice.* Afrofuturist Affair/House of Future Sciences Books, 2015.

Phillips, Rasheedah. *Space-Time Collapse. Black Quantum Futurism.* Afrofuturist Affair/House of Future Sciences Books, 2020.

Piepzna-Samarasinha, Leah Lakshmi. "Fragrance Free Femme of Colour Genius." October 2, 2018. brownstargirl.org/fragrance-free-femme-of-colour-genius/.

Piepzna-Samarasinha, Leah Lakshmi. *Care Work: Dreaming Disability Justice.* Vancouver: Arsenal Pulp Press, 2018.

Piepzna-Samarasinha, Leah Lakshmi. *Dirty River: A Queer Femme of Color Dreaming Her Way Home.* Arsenal Pulp Press, 2022.

Piepzna-Samarasinha, Leah Lakshmi. *The Future Is Disabled: Prophecies, Love Notes, and Mourning Songs.* Arsenal Pulp Press, 2023.

Piepzna-Samarasinha, Leah Lakshmi, and Cyree Jarelle Johnson. "AAWWTV: Dreaming Disability Justice with Leah Lakshmi Piepzna-Samarasinha and Cyree Jarelle Johnson." YouTube, October 28, 2018. www.youtube.com /watch?v=8UpQVlT2wCQ.

Pinckney, Darryl. *Come Back in September: A Literary Education on West Sixty-Seventh Street, Manhattan.* Farrar, Straus and Giroux, 2022.

Pitcher, Ben, and Henriette Gunkel. "Q&A with Jasbir Puar." *Dark Matter Journal*, May 2, 2008.

Plath, Sylvia. *The Bell Jar.* London: Faber and Faber, 1966.

Plath, Sylvia, and Ted Hughes. *The Collected Poems.* New York: Harper Perennial, 1992.

Plath, Sylvia, and Karen V. Kukil. *The Unabridged Journals of Sylvia Plath, 1950-1962.* New York: Anchor Books, 2000.

Plath, Sylvia. *The Letters of Sylvia Plath*, Volume 1: 1940-1956. Edited by Karen V. Kukil and Peter K. Steinberg, HarperCollins Publishers, 2017.

Plath, Sylvia. *The Letters of Sylvia Plath*, Volume 2: 1956-1963. Edited by Peter K. Steinberg and Karen V. Kukil, HarperCollins Publishers, 2018.

Plath, Sylvia. *Ariel: The Restored Edition: A Facsimile of Plath's Manuscript, Reinstating Her Original Selection and Arrangement.* London: Faber, 2007.

Plath, Sylvia. "Sylvia Plath Reads Her Poems: Daddy; Fever 103; Lady Lazarus and Ariel." YouTube, April 11, 2013. Video, 10:44.

Plessix, Gray Francine Du. *Simone Weil.* Viking, 2001.

Poitras, Laura, dir. *All the Beauty and the Bloodshed.* Neon, 2023.

Pollan, Michael. "The Trip Treatment." *The New Yorker*, February 9, 2015.

Porete, Marguerite. *The Mirror of Simple Souls*. Translated by Ellen L. Babinsky, New York: Paulist Press, 1993.

Prescod-Weinstein, Chanda. *The Disordered Cosmos: A Journey into Dark Matter, Spacetime, & Dreams Deferred*. Bold Type Books, 2022.

Price, Devon. *Unmasking Autism: Discovering the New Faces of Neurodiversity*. Harmony Books, 2022.

Puar, Jasbir K. *The Right to Maim: Debility, Capacity, Disability*. Duke University Press, 2017.

Puar, Jasbir K. *Terrorist Assemblages: Homonationalism in Queer times*. Durham: Duke University Press, 2007.

Reed, Justin Phillip. *With Bloom upon Them and Also with Blood: A Horror Miscellany*. Coffee House Press, 2023.

Reines, Ariana. "An Hourglass Figure: On Photographer Francesca Woodman." *Los Angeles Review of Books*, April 4, 2013.

Reinoos, Dana. "House of Psychotic Women - Movie List." MUBI, mubi.com/en /lists/house-of-psychotic-women.

Rich, Adrienne. *Of Woman Born: Motherhood as Experience & Institution*. W. W. Norton, 1996.

Rich, Adrienne, and Barbara Charlesworth Gelpi. "The Burning of Paper Instead of Children." In *Adrienne Rich's Poetry and Prose: Poems, Prose, Reviews, and Criticism*. New York: Norton, 1993.

Rieff, David. *Swimming in a Sea of Death: A Son's Memoir*. New York: Simon & Schuster, 2008.

Robinson, Roxana. "Joan Didion's Priceless Sunglasses." *The New Yorker*, November 16, 2022. www.newyorker.com/culture/culture-desk/joan-didions -priceless-sunglasses.

Rose, Jacqueline. *The Haunting of Sylvia Plath*. Virago Press, 2013.

Rose, Jacqueline. *On Not Being Able to Sleep: Psychoanalysis and the Modern World*. Princeton, NJ: Princeton University Press, 2003.

Rhys, Jean. *Wide Sargasso Sea*. New York: Norton, 1992.

Russ, Joanna, and Jessa Crispin. *How to Suppress Women's Writing*. University of Texas Press, 2018.

Russell, Legacy. *Glitch Feminism: A Manifesto*. Verso, 2020.

Sa'dāwī, Nawāl. *Woman at Point Zero*. Zed Books, Limited, 2015.

"Saidiya Hartman & Arthur Jafa." YouTube, Hammer Museum, June 10, 2019. https://www.youtube.com/watch?v=YGxZQ3Py4-A.

Salek, Yasi. "[CULT TALK] Audrey Wollen on Sad Girl Theory." *CULTIST ZINE*, June 19, 2014.

Scarry, Elaine. *The Body in Pain: The Making and Unmaking of the World*. Oxford University Press, 1988.

Schaber, Amythest. "Neurowonderful: Ask An Autistic." YouTube.

Schacter, Cara. "Worn out: Shrugging towards Bethlehem." *Spike Art Magazine*, November 30, 2022. www.spikeartmagazine.com/articles/worn-out-shrugging -towards-bethlehem.

Schmitt, Carl. *The Concept of the Political*. University of Chicago Press, 2008.

Schopenhauer, Arthur. *Schopenhauer: Parerga and Paralipomena: Short Philosophical Essays*. Cambridge University Press, 2015.

Schulman, Sarah. *Conflict Is Not Abuse: Overstating Harm, Community Responsibility, and the Duty of Repair*. Arsenal Pulp Press, 2021.

Schwartz, Alexandra. "In Coming-of-Middle-Age Stories, Adults Grow up, Too." *The New Yorker*, August 9, 2021. www.newyorker.com/magazine/2021/08/16 /in-coming-of-middle-age-stories-adults-grow-up-too.

Sedgwick, Eve Kosofsky, and Adam Frank. *Touching Feeling: Affect, Pedagogy, Performativity*. Durham: Duke University Press, 2003.

Sedgwick, Eve Kosofsky, Andrew Parker, and Andrew Ford. "Katharsis: The Ancient Problem." In *Performativity and Performance*. Edited by Andrew Parker and Eve Kosofsky Sedgwick. New York: Routledge, 1995, 109–32.

Sehgal, Parul. "The Case against the Trauma Plot." *The New Yorker*, December 27, 2021. www.newyorker.com/magazine/2022/01/03/the-case-against-the -trauma-plot.

Sellars, Peter, dir. "The Tristan Project." Gustavo Dudamel leads Wagner's Tristan und Isolde. Los Angeles, Walt Disney Concert Hall, December 15, 2022.

Sensei, Seren. *So, About That . . . A Year Of Contemporary Essays on Race and Pop Culture*. CreateSpace Independent Publishing Platform, August 13, 2015.

Sensei, Seren. Sensei Aishitemasu. YouTube channel. Last accessed April 1, 2022.

Seresin, Asa. "Might Trick Me Once." Asa Seresin, August 13, 2020. asaseresin .com/2020/08/10/might-trick-me-once/.

Seresin, Asa. "On Heteropessimism." *The New Inquiry*, October 9, 2019. thenewinquiry.com/on-heteropessimism/.

Seymour, Miranda. *I Used to Live Here Once: The Haunted Life of Jean Rhys*. W. W. Norton 2022.

Shackelford, Ashleigh. "Why I'm Nonbinary But Don't Use 'They/Them'." *Wear Your Voice*, July 7, 2016.

Sharpe, Christina Elizabeth. *In the Wake: On Blackness and Being*. Durham: Duke University Press, 2016.

Shimoda, Brandon. *Evening Oracle*. Seattle: Letter Machine Editions, 2015.

Shimoda, Brandon. *The Grave on the Wall*. San Francisco: City Lights Books, 2019.

Shire, Warsan. *Teaching My Mother How to Give Birth*. London: Flipped Eye Publishing Limited, 2011.

Showalter, Elaine. *The Female Malady: Women, Madness, and English Culture, 1830-1980*. New York: Pantheon Books, 1985.

Silva, Denise Ferreira da. "No-Bodies: Law, Raciality and Violence." *Griffith Law Review* 18, no. 2 (2009): 212–36.

Silva, Denise Ferreira da. "To Be Announced: Radical Praxis or Knowing (at) the Limits of Justice." *Social Text* 31, no. 1 (114) (2013): 43–62. doi:10.1215 /01642472-1958890.

Silva, Denise Ferreira da. *Toward a Global Idea of Race*. Minneapolis: University of Minnesota Press, 2007.

Silva, Denise Ferreira da. *Unpayable Debt*. Sternberg Press, 2022.

Singh, Julietta. *No Archive Will Restore You*. Punctum Books, 2018.

Singh, Julietta. *Unthinking Mastery: Dehumanism and Decolonial Entanglements*. Duke University Press, 2018.

Siobhan, Scherezade. "The End of Separateness." *Berfrois*, June 21, 2016.

Smilges, J. Logan. *Crip Negativity*. University of Minnesota Press, 2023.

Smith, Andrea. "Indigeneity, Settler Colonialism, White Supremacy." *GLOBAL DIALOGUE* 12, no. 2 (Summer 2010).

Smith, Linda Tuhiwai. *Decolonizing Methodologies: Research and Indigenous Peoples*. London: Zed Books, 2012.

Smith, Richard Curson, dir. "Ted Hughes: Stronger than Death." Produced by Richard Curson Smith and Lucy Evans. Aired October 10, 2015, BBC Two.

Smith, William. "NEMESIS." A Dictionary of Greek and Roman Biography and Mythology, Public domain, 1849.

Snow, Philippa. *Which as You Know Means Violence: On Self-Injury as Art and Entertainment*. Repeater, 2022.

Solnit, Rebecca. "The Most Radical Thing You Can Do." *Orion Magazine*, October 1, 2008.

Solomon, Rivers, and Daveed Diggs, William Hutson, and Jonathan Snipes. *The Deep*. Saga Press, 2020.

Sontag, Susan. *Against Interpretation, and Other Essays*. Farrar, Straus and Giroux, 2007.

Sontag, Susan. *As Consciousness Is Harnessed to Flesh: Journals and Notebooks, 1964-1980*. Picador, 2013.

Sontag, Susan. *Illness as Metaphor*. New York: Farrar, Straus and Giroux, 1978.

Sontag, Susan. "Pilgrimage." *The New Yorker*, December 14, 1987. www .newyorker.com/magazine/1987/12/21/pilgrimage-susan-sontag.

Sontag, Susan. *On Photography*. Picador, trademark used by Farrar, Straus and Giroux, 2014.

Sontag, Susan. *Reborn: Journals and Notebooks, 1947-1963*. Picador, 2009.

Sontag, Susan. *Regarding the Pain of Others*. New York: Farrar, Straus and Giroux, 2003.

Sontag, Susan. *The Volcano Lover: A Romance*. Picador, 2004.

Staff, P., dir. *Bathing*. 2018.

Staff, P., dir. *Weed Killer*. 2017.

Stanley, Jason. *How Fascism Works: The Politics of Us and Them*. Random House Publishing Group, 2018.

Starhawk. *Dreaming the Dark: Magic, Sex, and Politics*. 2nd ed. Boston: Beacon Press, 1988.

Steinberg, Marlene, and Maxine Schnall. *The Stranger in the Mirror: Dissociation: The Hidden Epidemic*. New York: Harper, 2001.

Stevens, Mark, and Annalyn Swan. *De Kooning: An American Master*. Knopf, 2011.

Stovall, Natasha. "Whiteness on the Couch: Clinical Psychologist Natasha Stovall Looks at the Vast Spectrum of White People Problems, and Why We Never Talk about Them in Therapy." *Longreads*, August 2019.

Stevens, Wallace. "Bouquet of Roses in Sunlight." *Poetry Magazine*, October 1947.

Suzuki, Daisetz Teitaro. *Mysticism: Christian and Buddhist*. Routledge, 2018.

Sycamore, Mattilda Bernstein. "Between the Covers Mattilda Bernstein Sycamore: Touching the Art." *Between the Covers*, Tin House, November 9, 2023.

Sycamore, Mattilda Bernstein. *The Freezer Door*. Semiotext(e), 2020.

Sycamore, Mattilda Bernstein. *Touching the Art*. Soft Skull, 2023.

"Sylvia Plath Ted Hughes Interview 1961." YouTube, April 30, 2015. Video, 20:11.

Tagaq, Tanya. *Split Tooth*. And Other Stories, 2023.

Taylor, Leila. *Darkly: Black History and America's Gothic Soul*. Repeater Books, 2019.

Taylor, Sunaura. *Beasts of Burden: Animal and Disability Liberation*. New Press, 2017.

Thacker, Eugene. *Cosmic Pessimism*. Univocal Publishing, 2015.

Thacker, Eugene. *In the Dust of This Planet: Horror of Philosophy (Volume 1)*. Zero Books, 2011.

Thacker, Eugene. *Infinite Resignation*. Repeater Books, 2018.

Thacker, Eugene. "Mysticism and Darkness." Lecture presented at *Dark Materialism*. Natural History Museum, London, United Kingdom, January 16, 2011.

Thacker, Eugene. *Starry Speculative Corpse: Horror of Philosophy (Volume 2)*. Zero Books, 2015.

Thacker, Eugene. *Tentacles Longer Than Night: Horror of Philosophy (Volume 3)*. Zero Books, 2015.

Theroux, Alexander. *The Secondary Colors: Three Essays*. New York: Henry Holt & Co., 1996.

Thiong'o, Ngũgĩ Wa. *Decolonising the Mind: The Politics of Language in African Literature*. London: J. Currey, 1986.

Thom, Kai Cheng, "Why Are Queer People so Mean to Each Other? How Brain Science Explains Queer Trauma, Conflict and Call-Out Culture." *Xtra*, August 16, 2019.

Thurman, Judith. "A Loss for Words: Can a Dying Language Be Saved?" *The New Yorker*, March 30, 2015.

Thurman, Judith. *A Left-Handed Woman: Essays.* Farrar, Straus and Giroux, 2022.

Thurman, Judith. *Cleopatra's Nose: 39 Varieties of Desire.* Farrar, Straus and Giroux, 2007.

Tuttle, Lisa. *My Death.* New York Review Books, 2023.

UdosTelevision. "Sylvia Plath Documentary [complete]." YouTube, June 26, 2012. Video.

Van der Kolk, Bessel. *The Body Keeps the Score: Brain, Mind, and Body in the Healing of Trauma.* New York: Penguin Books, 2014.

Vankin, Jonathan. "Kam Brock: The Reason They Threw Her In A Mental Ward Was Crazy — What Happened Next Was Even Crazier." *The Inquisitr News*, March 24, 2015.

Wade, Francesca. *Square Haunting: Five Writers in London between the Wars.* Tim Duggan Books, 2020.

Wallenhorst, Maxi. "Like a Real Veil, like a Bad Analogy: Dissociative Style and Trans Aesthetics." *e-flux journal* #117, Apr. 2021, www.e-flux.com/journal/117/385637 /like-a-real-veil-like-a-bad-analogy-dissociative-style-and-trans-aesthetics/.

Wang, Esmé Weijun. "Journal: On Rewriting Your Narrative and Telling a Different Story." Blog. March 2016.

Wang, Esmé Weijun. "Toward a Pathology of the Possessed." *The Believer*, Fall 2015.

Weigel, Moira, and Mal Ahern. "Further Materials Toward a Theory of the Man-Child." *The New Inquiry*, July 9, 2013.

Weil, Simone. *Gravity and Grace.* Routledge, 2004.

Weil, Simone. *Waiting for God.* Harper Perennial Modern Classics, 2009.

Wendell, Susan. "Unhealthy Disabled: Treating Chronic Illnesses as Disabilities." *Hypatia* 16, no. 4 (2001): 17–33. doi:10.1111/j.1527-2001.2001.tb00751.x.

Wheeler, Lauren. "Actually, I Don't Have Time: Breaking up with Orange Is the New Black." *Black Nerd Problems*, August 14, 2016. https://blacknerdproblems .com/actually-i-dont-have-time-breaking-up-with-orange-is-the-new-black/.

Whitehead, Colson. "A Psychotronic Childhood." *The New Yorker*, May 28, 2012, www.newyorker.com/magazine/2012/06/04/a-psychotronic-childhood.

Whitney, Emerson. *Daddy Boy.* McSweeney's, 2023.

Whitney, Emerson. *Heaven.* McSweeney's, 2020.

Wilby, Emma. *The Visions of Isobel Gowdie: Magic, Witchcraft and Dark Shamanism in Seventeenth-Century Scotland.* Sussex Academic Press, 2013.

Wilderson, Frank B., III. "We're Trying to Destroy the World: Anti-Blackness and Police Violence after Ferguson." Interview by Dr. Hate, Todd Steven Burroughs, and Jared Ball. IMIXWHATILIKE, October 1, 2014. https://imixwhatilike .org/2014/10/01/frankwildersonandantiblackness-2/.

Wittgenstein, Ludwig. *Tractatus Logico-Philosophicus.* Routledge, 1998.

Wojnarowicz, David. *Close to the Knives: A Memoir of Disintegration.* Vintage Books, 1991.

Wong, Alice. *Disability Visibility: First-Person Stories from the Twenty-First Century*. Vintage Books, 2022.

Wong, Alice. *Year of the Tiger: An Activist's Life*. Vintage Books, 2022.

Woolf, Virginia. *On Being Ill*. Ashfield: Paris Press, 2012.

Woolf, Virginia, and Leonard Woolf. *A Writer's Diary: Being Extracts from the Diary of Virginia Woolf*. San Diego: Harcourt, 1982.

Wynter, Sylvia. *Sylvia Wynter: On Being Human as Praxis*. Edited by Katherine McKittrick. Durham: Duke University Press, 2015.

Yanagihara, Hanya. *A Little Life*. Anchor Books, 2016.

Zambreno, Kate. "Anna Kavan: Context N°18." *Dalkey Archive Press* (blog), September 13, 2013. https://www.dalkeyarchive.com/2013/09/13/anna-kavan/.

Zambreno, Kate. *Heroines*. Cambridge, MA: Semiotext(e), 2012.

Zavitsanos, Constantina, Denise Ferreira da Silva, Rizvana Bradley, and Che Gossett. "Speculative Planning Session with Denise Ferreira da Silva, Rizvana Bradley, and Che Gossett." Lecture presented as part of *THIS COULD BE US*. New Museum. New York, NY, May 7, 2015.

Zavitsanos, Constantina, Fred Moten, and Stefano Harney. "Constantina Zavitsanos: Speculative Planning Session with Fred Moten and Stefano Harney." Lecture presented as part of *THIS COULD BE US*. New Museum. New York, NY, March 25, 2015.

Zürn, Unica. *The House of Illnesses*. Atlas Press, 2019.

About the Author

JOHANNA HEDVA is a Korean American writer, artist, and musician who was raised in Los Angeles by a family of witches and now lives in LA and Berlin. Hedva is the author of the novel *Your Love Is Not Good*, which *Kirkus* called a "hellraising, resplendent must-read," and the novel *On Hell*, which was named one of Dennis Cooper's favorites of 2018. They are also the author of *Minerva the Miscarriage of the Brain*, which collects a decade of work in poetry, plays, performances, and essays. Their artwork has been shown internationally, and their albums are *Black Moon Lilith in Pisces in the 4th House* and *The Sun and the Moon*.